MORTGAGE FRAUD

MORTGAGE FRAUD

by

Caroline Osborn
LLB, LLM, Solicitor

CLT PROFESSIONAL PUBLISHING
A DIVISION OF CENTRAL LAW TRAINING LTD

Published by
CLT Professional Publishing
A Division of Central Law Training Ltd
Wrens Court
52–54 Victoria Road
Sutton Coldfield
Birmingham B72 1SX

ISBN 1 85811 025 4

Typeset by Bookworm Typesetting, Manchester
Printed in Great Britain by The Lavenham Press Ltd

Contents

Foreword vii
Table of Cases ix
Table of Statutes xiii

1. Introduction 1

2. Why Solicitors Should be Concerned about Mortgage Fraud 13

3. How to Avoid Becoming involved in Fraud 23

4. How to Do a Mortgage Fraud – the Fraudster's Point of View 27

5. The Practitioner's Viewpoint 39

6. The Law Society 51

7. The Lender 55

8. Mortgage Fraud – Civil Litigation Fall-out 59

9. Fraud Prosecution 77

10. Evidential Matters in Mortgage Fraud Trials 91

11. Prosecuting Bodies 123

12. A Checklist for the Prevention and Recognition of Mortgage Fraud 135

Bibliography 141
Case Studies 143
Sample Documents 169
Tables and Bar Chart 286
Index 293

Foreword

"There is always a solicitor involved"

Our profession picks up most of the bill for mortgage fraud. The honest members of the profession pay for the activities of the guilty. This unwanted financial burden alone should provide ample incentive for solicitors to be on guard against dishonest practitioners in particular, and mortgage fraudsters in general.

Of course, nothing that I can say will prevent would-be mortgage fraudsters who are not solicitors from attempting to make this sort of fraud profitable. Nor will it prevent the criminally inclined practitioner from joining the ranks of those solicitors who are convicted of crimes and who are separated from their practising certificates and fined by the Solicitors' Disciplinary Tribunal.

What I hope that the contents of this book will do is to persuade the profession to be proactive in the prevention, not only of mortgage fraud, but of all sorts of fraud, because it is in our own interests to do so. Exhortations to better behaviour are not usually, in fact, effective without both financial and personal incentives.

This book contains a number of case studies and examples, drawn from cases where the fraudsters were convicted. Solicitors who are involved in mortgage fraud are that much easier to catch, as all their transactions are recorded in their books of account and their conveyancing files.

The last ten years have seen substantial inroads into the solicitor's duty of confidentiality and into professional privilege. Solicitors now have an obligation to report money-laundering and fraudulent clients, unless they are genuine criminal specialists advising a potential defendant.

Solicitors have, however, a greater duty to themselves and to the profession to create a climate in which fraud is not so easy to undertake. The problem of unknown introducers should be stressed. The legal profession has a part to play, not only in regulating itself, but in ensuring that all professions that provide financial services are prevented as far as possible from using their profession as a vehicle for fraud, or through sloppy practices being used by criminals. We can no longer ignore the activities of our partners, branch offices and staff, admitted and/or unadmitted. We have a responsibility to ourselves and to our honest clients, to whom we pass on the cost of increased insurance and any other financial contribution we may have to make. We must listen to staff who think they have discovered a fraud and must take steps to encourage vigilance. In the meantime, mortgage fraud by solicitors continues.

The *Daily Telegraph* of 20 January 1995 carried a report on two solicitors who had been jailed for their parts in a multi-million pound mortgage fraud. At the time of writing, police had not yet recovered most of the £8 million which had passed through one of the solicitors' client account after it had been obtained from various building societies in what Judge David Martineau called "a sophisticated swindle" in which the guilty solicitor had "salted away" some £7.5 million. There was evidence that some of the money had been sent to numbered accounts in Switzerland. The solicitor involved was sentenced to six years' imprisonment and has been struck off the Roll for what was described as a very serious fraud and breach of trust. He had told his bank to return more than 1,500 cheques. The other solicitor involved in the fraud, who carried out some of the conveyancing, was jailed for two years for his part in the conspiracy.

A solicitor fraudster is likely to receive a greater punishment than a non-professional. The matters to be considered in sentencing defendants who are convicted of mortgage fraud were set out in the case of *R* v *Stevens* by the Court of Appeal (*The Times*, 5 November 1992), where it was indicated that the part played by the accused in the fraud should be considered in the context of the fraud as a whole. It was an aggravating factor if the accused recruited others to the fraud. Also relevant was the length of time the accused was involved in the fraud or frauds, as well as the extent of any personal benefit, and it was relevant if there was a genuine intent to repay loans, thereby avoiding loss to the institutions involved. The amount lent should be taken into account, as well as losses sustained. The court also stressed the importance of considering whether any person involved was a professional or quasi-professional, for the special reason that if a professional played a part in such a fraud there was necessarily a breach of trust.

Delay either between the end of the defendant's involvement and his arrest, or between his arrest and plea of guilty or conviction, or between his plea of guilty and conviction and sentence together with what might have befallen the defendant during any such period of delay, would be relevant. The nature and timing of any plea of guilty and any help given to the prosecution should be considered.

Solicitors in private practice are the profession's front line in the fight against fraud. Unless mortgage fraud is to become an ever-growing burden to the profession as a whole, individual solicitors must take a proactive role in preventing it.

Table of Cases

AGIP (Africa) Ltd v Axon [1991] 3 WLR 116....68
AT & T Istel Ltd and another v Tully [1992] 2 All ER 28....62
Abandon (1983) 76 Cr App R 48....108
Anderson [1972] 1 QB 304....107
Anderson v Bank of British Columbia (1876) 2 Ch 644....84
Anglia Hastings & Thanet Building Society v House & Son [1981] 260 EG 1128....72
Anton Piller v Manufacturing Process Ltd [1976] Ch 55, [1976] 2 WLR 162 [1976] 1 All ER 776....64
Ayres [1984] AC 447, HL....120, 128

Bailey (1977) 66 Cr App R 31....107
Barclays Bank v Taylor [1989] 3 All ER 563, [1989] 1 WLR 1066, CA....82
Barker [1941] KB 381, [1941] 3 All ER 33....130
Birley and others, unreported, 13 February 1993....20
Boyle and Mears (1992) 94 Cr App R 158....119, 120
Bradshaw (1985) 82 Cr App R 79....107
Bristol Corporation v Cox (1884) 26 Ch D 678....84

Cate Access Floors Inc v Boswell [1990] 3 All ER 303....84
Central Criminal Court, ex p Adegbesan [1986] 3 All ER 113, [1986] 1 WLR 1292....82
Central Criminal Court ex p AJD Holdings Ltd (1992) The Times, 24 February 1992....81
Central Criminal Court ex p Francis & Francis [1989] AC 346, [1988] 1 All ER 677....82, 85
Chief Constable of Lancashire ex p Parker and McGrath, Independent 1 April 1993....82
Cole (1990) 90 Cr App R 478....99, 100
County Nat West and others....124

Dadson, unreported....80
Dawson v Lunn [1986] RTR 234....108
Dhillon [1992] Crim LR 889....118, 120
Doyle v Olbey (Ironmongers) Ltd [1969] 2 QB 158....70
Dubai Bank v Galadari (1991)....66

English Exporters (London) Ltd v Eldonwall (1973) Ch 415....107

Firm of Solicitors re [1992] 1 All ER 353.....86
Folkes v Chad (1782) 3 Doug KB 157.....106

Ghosh [1982] QB 1053.....121
Gomez [1992] 3 WLR 1067.....119
Goody v Baring [1956] 1 WLR 50.....67
Gran Gelato Ltd v Richcliff (Group) Ltd [1992] 1 All ER 865.....74
Guildhall Magistrates' Court ex p Primlaks Holding Co (Panama) Inc [1990] 1 QB 261, [1989] 2 WLR 841.....82

Halai [1983] Crim LR 624.....117, 118

IRC ex p Goldberg [1988] 3 All ER 248.....84
IRC ex p Mead and Cook [1993] 1 All ER 772.....134
IRC v Rossminster [1980] AC 952, [1980] 1 All ER 80.....131
Inner London Sessions Crown Court ex p Baines [1988] QB 579, [1987] 3 All ER 1025.....82

J (a Minor) re (1990) TLR 568.....105

Kellard and others, unreported.....124
Kenally [1994] Crim LR (Jan), CA.....100
King [1991] 2 WLR 246.....119

Lanfear [1968] 2 QB 77.....107
Lyell v Kennedy (1984) 27 Ch 1.....84

Maidstone Crown Court ex p Waitt [1988] Crim LR 384.....83
Manchester Crown Court ex p Taylor [1988] 2 All ER 769, [1988] 1 WLR 705.....82
Manjadria [1991] Crim LR 73.....119, 120
Marcel v Metropolitan Police Commissioner [1992] Ch 225, [1992] 1 All ER 72, [1992] 2 WLR 58.....83
Mareva Compania Naviera SA v International Bulk Carriers SA [1980] 1 All ER 213.....60
Marlborough Street Magistrates' Court, Metropolitan Stipendiary Magistrate ex p Simpson (1980) 70 Cr App R 291, [1980] Crim LR 305, DC.....80
Midland Bank v Stubbs & Kemp [1979] Ch 384.....71
Minors v Harper [1989] 1 WLR 44, CA.....101
Moody v Cox [1917] 2 Ch 71.....67
Mount Banking Corporation Ltd v Brian Cooper & Co [1952] 35 EG 123.....72

National Justice Compania Naviera SA v Prudential Assurance Company Ltd (The Ikarian Reefer) [1993] 2 Lloyd's Rep 68....105
Neill v North Antrim Magistrates' Court [1992] 1 WLR 1221, HL for Northern Ireland....100

Panel on Takeovers and Mergers ex p Al Fayed, The Times, 15 April 1992....134
Parry Jones v the Law Society [1969] 1 Ch 1....84
Patel [1993] Crim LR 29, CA....99, 100
Pilkington v Wood [1953] Ch 770....74

Scholes v Brooks [1891] 63 LT 837....71
Shepherd [1993] 1 All ER 225, HL....101, 102
Silverlock [1894] 2 QB 766....107
Spiby (1990) 91 Cr App R 186, CA....101
Stevens, The Times, 5 November 1992....vii, 121
Swingcastle v Gibson [1991] 2 WLR 1091....73

Teong Sun Chuah and another, unreported, 19 February 1991....118
Trustee Savings Bank of Wales and Border Counties v Taylor [1989] 3 All ER 563, [1989] 1 WLR 1066, CA....82
Turner [1975] QB 834....106

University of Warwick v Sir Robert McAlpine (1988) 42 BLR 1....105

Whitehouse v Jordan [1981] 1 WLR 246....103
Widdowson (1985) 82 Cr App R 314....117
Williams and Crick, 29 July 1993, Transcript Nos 91/3265/W3 and 91/3266/W2....118

Table of Statutes

Bankers' Book Evidence Act 1879 ....80, 81
ss 3-10....80
Banking Act 1987....133
Building Societies Act 1986....125

Civil Evidence Acts 1968 and 1972....92
Civil Evidence Act 1968
s10....96
Companies Act 1948
s 165....123
Companies Act 1967
s 109....123
Companies Act 1985....133
s 151....106
s 432....125
ss 446-447....123
Computer Misuse Act 1990....106
Criminal Evidence Act 1965....93
Criminal Evidence Act 1988
s 23....96, 97, 98, 99
s 24....97, 98, 99
s 25....98, 99
s 26....98, 99, 100
Criminal Justice Act 1987....132
s 1....132, 134
s 2....77, 80, 133, 134
s 4....126, 133
s 12....128
Sched 1....132
Criminal Justice Act 1988
s 7....87
s 23....96, 97, 98, 99
s 24....97, 98, 99, 101
s 25....98, 99
s 26....98, 99, 100
s 30....109
s 93A-D....87, 88, 89
Sched 4....87
Criminal Justice Act 1992....128
Criminal Justice Act 1993
s 49....87
Criminal Justice and Public Order Act 1994
s 4....134
s 44....134

Drug Trafficking Act 1994....85
ss 50, 52....86
Drug Trafficking Offences Act 1986 ....86, 87
s 24....87

Evidence (Proceedings in Other Jurisdictions) Act 1975....94

Financial Services Act 1986....27, 106, 125, 133
Finance Act 1990
s125....130

Income and Corporation Taxes Act 1988
ss 745, 788....130
Insolvency Act 1986 125
s 218....125
Insurance Companies Act 1982..125

Local Government Act 1972....125
Lotteries and Amusements Act 1976....125

Police and Criminal Evidence Act 1984....21
s 8....83

s 9....81, 83
s 10....82, 84, 85
s 14....81
ss 15-16....82
ss 17-23....83
s 66....79
s 68....94
s 69....94, 101, 102
s 76....96, 97
s81....108
s 114....127
Sched 1....81, 83
Sched 3....94
Prevention of Terrorism (Temporary Provisions) Act 1989....86, 87
s 11....86
s 12....87
Prosecution of Offences Act 1985....128
s 10....127

Solicitors Act 1941
s 2....13
Solicitors Act 1965....13
Solicitors Act 1974
s 35....14
s 36....14, 15
s 37....17, 18
ss 41-44....25
s 68....67
Scheds 1-2....14
Supreme Court Act 1981
s 72....62

Taxes Management Act 1970
s 20....129, 130
s 20A....130
s 20B....130, 131
s 20C....130, 131
s 98....130
s 105....130
Theft Act 1968
s 4....118
s 15....119
s 20....119
s 31....62
Theft Act 1978
s 1....117, 120

CHAPTER 1

Introduction

Solicitors and the mortgage fraudster

Solicitors are an easy target for the mortgage fraudster. We provide connections and facilities which would otherwise take a would-be confidence trickster years to build up. As well as providing conveyancing services, we can advise on and provide contacts with sources of finance and local businesses, to whom the fraudster would not normally have access. Most local high street practices have a unique knowledge of their own area, and local contacts to match.

Despite recent headlines about dishonest solicitors, the majority of the profession are perceived as trustworthy by the general public; or at least as comprehensively insured. Unfortunately we also provide a convenient defence for the fraudster, especially if we are lazy about attendance notes. "My solicitor said it was OK" has all the familiarity of a music hall chorus in the Crown Court.

Because of the emphasis on a consumer-led market, which has coincided with a fall in the housing market, high street firms who specialise in residential conveyancing, and property practitioners everywhere, have had to become much more cost effective to stay in business. Consequently a busy solicitor is more likely to feel relief at the thought of potential fee income when he meets a new client, than to consider whether that client is a fraudster.

Policemen and prosecutors tend to sneer at solicitors who are involved, however innocently, in a mortgage fraud. The sad truth is that it is much easier to spot a mortgage fraud once you have already experienced one. However, this is an expensive way to learn. But learn we must. Solicitors are ideally placed to stop such fraud. Because the innocent pay for the guilty, through increased insurance premiums and contributions to the Compensation Fund, there is already ample incentive to make mortgage fraud less attractive. The purpose of this book is to help to stop the annual waste of money and human resources caused to the profession by this type of fraud.

Mortgage fraud occurs when a borrower obtains a loan in circumstances where, if the lender had known the true facts about either the borrower himself or the property upon which the loan was secured, or both, the loan would not have been made. From the fraudster's point of view, mortgage fraud is attractive since it involves a low investment of capital and resources in return for a relatively high yield over a period of time. Moreover, the lending institutions which are the victims of mortgage fraud are not politically attractive victims in the same way as the little old lady who loses her pension to an accomplished fraudster. The principal disadvantage to mortgage fraud so far as the fraudster is involved is that it involves a great deal of paperwork. One of the ways in which mortgage fraud is detected is that the names of borrowers whether they are fictitious or real, and the addresses of properties used for reference addresses, residences and as security, are often recycled in such a way as to form a pattern. There are examples of this in Case Study 4 and the sample documents.

The scale of mortgage fraud

Estimates of the scale of mortgage fraud vary. Mortgage fraud has been very much in the news recently because of a number of high-profile cases. Reporting seems to have moved on from the one-off borrower and residential mortgage fraud, to large-scale scams where commercial loans are obtained through organised fraud rings, involving valuers, solicitors, brokers and lenders' own staff. Estimates vary as to the amount of money at risk. In 1991 a report carried in the *Law Society Gazette* suggested that as many as one in twenty loans were fraudulent. Understandably, the Council of Mortgage Lenders, amongst others, considered this to be a considerable overstatement, although the head of investigations for the Nationwide Anglia Building Society said in his presentation at the Council of Mortgage Lenders' Annual Mortgage Fraud Conference in October 1992 that fraud could account, on a conservative estimate, for £500 million per year. Reports are still coming in of a very high level of mortgage fraud claims, despite the fall in the property market. The Metropolitan Police Fraud Squad alone is said to be handling claims worth more than a billion pounds.

As the economic climate changes, so does the fraudsters' technique. When the property market was buoyant and property prices rose by a substantial percentage each year, simple mortgage fraud was profitable and "rollover fraud" was particularly attractive, as each time a property was sold the fraudster could pocket the profit made on the deal. As the property market began to fall it became necessary to provide more complicated reasons for the rise in value of a property. With business properties this was not difficult to do, so long as it was possible to convince the lender that there had been a substantial rise in the value of a business and of its assets. Residential properties could be made to yield an improvement in value either by way of building works, where the property was, for example, converted into two flats, or by using the property to bring in rental income by letting them out, particularly to local authority tenants. Mortgage fraud does not carry the same risks as bank robbery, nor are mortgage fraudsters readily identifiable as potential criminals in the same way as football hooligans are. A check-list appears in Chapter 12 indicating those matters which should give rise for further enquiry as being tell-tale signs that fraud may be occurring, or may have already occurred.

Mortgage fraud involves two basic deceptions. The fraudulent borrower lies about himself, his identity and his ability to make the repayments due under the mortgage deed. He also lies about the property which is the security for the mortgage advance by misrepresenting its value as a security. These two basic deceptions give rise to a number of well-recognised categories of mortgage fraud. (See for example Clarke's *Mortgage Fraud* (Chapman and Hall, 1991) for a detailed academic study of the criminology of mortgage fraud.)

Simple fraud

Applicants for building society mortgages may misrepresent their circumstances in a variety of ways in order to obtain a loan, or one that is larger than they would otherwise have been granted. The majority of these applicants are basically honest, and the fraud consists of manipulating earnings from overtime or the black economy in order to meet the gap between what the applicant can afford to pay as a deposit from his own resources and what he can expect to borrow from the lender. The borrower may seek to overcome restrictions on certain categories of potential borrower. For example, a newly self-employed borrower may not have the necessary accounts to produce to the building society manager, and may therefore arrange for these to be prepared by a less than reputable accountant. Income may depend on overtime, a wife's earnings, or gratuities which the applicant regards as a reliable source of income, but which the lender will regard in a less sanguine fashion. Optimum earnings will be shown as average. A reference may be "improved" (see Case Study 1 for the consequences of this deception).

Perhaps the hardest fraud to detect is that by fraudsters who misrepresent their financial circumstances in order to obtain a loan to which they are not entitled, with the sole intention of becoming owner/occupiers themselves and repaying the loan. All of the major lenders agree that this is a substantial group, but also that it is the least expensive group for lenders. Some of these borrowers may become part of the various fraud statistics if their circumstances alter substantially, for example if a wife becomes pregnant and her income can no longer be counted on, or if the market turns against the borrower and interest rates rise with a corresponding fall in the property value, as has happened in recent years. The majority of these borrowers survive and do not form a recognisable class of potential defendants in fraud prosecutions or repossession proceedings. The interest portion of the mortgage repayments may be met by benefit or insurance during sickness or unemployment. In these circumstances many lenders will agree to a temporary moratorium on the capital element of repayment. Alternatively the term of the mortgage may be extended. The essence of this type of fraud is the desire to become an owner occupier.

The second group of simple fraudsters are those whose intentions are fundamentally dishonest. These frauds vary in complexity. The basic version involves a borrower applying for loans in different names (these may be genuine or fraudulent) on separate properties with a view to either rapid resale at a profit, if the market allows, or to letting out the property to tenants and using the rent to repay the loans. The false documentation required for this fraud is more complex. A fictitious identity will require false employment references with a fictitious income or false accounts at least, if not false banking records and payslips. There will of course be allied frauds against the Inland Revenue through the MIRAS scheme and in respect of any capital gain made on the resale of the property stock. A copy of standard mortgage conditions which are common to all the main lenders appears at pages 202 *et seq* from which it may be seen that loans are made in respect of domestic properties on the condition, *inter alia*, that the prospective borrower has no other mortgages. Most non-criminal borrowers would not be able to support more than one mortgage out of earned income, in any event!

Thanks to increased awareness among the major lending institutions, particularly the building societies, these frauds are often detected at application stage by building society staff. Such a loan application would invariably be refused and the applicant would probably be rejected for all further business. If the case is not detected until arrears have accrued, the revenue frauds would be referred to the Inland Revenue and at the least the borrower would be required to convert the loan on the property to a commercial loan, which would carry higher rates of interest. An alternative would be for the building society to seek repossession. Repossession in these cases often causes hardship to innocent tenants who may not know that their landlord has obtained his mortgage by fraud, or that the property that they occupy is subject to a mortgage. It is for this reason that many lenders will commercially manage the situation by converting the loan to a commercial loan. It goes without saying that lenders do not generally lend for commercial purposes at the same rates of interest as for residential properties which are to be occupied by a single private occupier.

A variation of the simple mortgage fraud occurs where a dishonest broker or other professional arranges mortgages for applicants who either would not otherwise obtain a mortgage or where the applicants speak poor English and may not therefore be able or may not feel able to arrange finance for themselves. An example of this sort of mortgage fraud appears as Case Study 2. The broker will undertake to arrange and process the loan for a fee, usually between £250 and £2000. This may well involve a package deal whereby the applicant is supplied with a false address, references and/or accounts to support the application and it is often the case that the applicant will be sold an endowment policy or other insurance. The insurance tends to be chosen with an eye to the need to earn commission. A dishonest broker can manipulate the applicant to keep silent either by threatening to expose breaches of immigration rules or simply playing on the knowledge that the application forms were clearly untruthful when signed. Again the purpose of the fraudulent application is for such applicants to become an owner/occupier. They may be regarded as victims of the more skilled conman because they are made to pay "commission" or a fee to achieve a mortgage at all.

It should be recognised that, although there have been a number of cases of this type of fraud in the Asian community, it is not confined to any particular ethnic minority. Income for confidence tricksters, in the form of brokerage fees and commission from obtaining mortgages on the basis of falsifying applicants' status, is not confined to schemes in which groups are exploited in the process. It is a sad aspect of this sub-group of fraud that many of the applicants still do not achieve a financially beneficial outcome. They may be persuaded, for example, to take a mortgage on which they cannot realistically hope to keep up the repayments. Mortgage brokers and other commission-dependent professionals play a large part in the systematic status abuse which lies behind the substantial mortgage frauds described below and in Case Studies 2 and 3.

Systematic status abuse

This type of fraud may be said to differ only in degree from that described above. However, it represents a separate category, because the fraudsters who systematically falsify applications in these cases are involved in what might be called "factory" mortgage fraud. The basic fraud is repeated systematically and on a substantial scale.

It is common knowledge among conveyancing solicitors and building society staff that building societies do not lend money for property development or the purchase of houses for rent at the same preferential rate as for house purchase by owner/occupiers. Nevertheless, each year, the newspapers carry reports of mortgage frauds involving very large sums of money and which are based upon one or two main players exploiting a stable of addresses, false identities and false references as a means of running a property empire. It is not unusual for the fraudster to own a large number of properties in this way, and to meet the mortgage payments, where a quick resale is not possible, from rental income. It is also not unknown for fraudsters to tenant properties intensively, particularly with tenants who are introduced by the local authority housing department. Housing benefit can be paid directly to the landlord, and this provides a secure income. Again, of course, the Revenue is defrauded under the MIRAS scheme and in respect of capital gains. The object of the exercise is to exploit tax and mortgage concessions available to owner/occupiers by dealing with a number of properties whilst being assured of a high income with relatively little effort and ultimately a high profit on the resale on the properties. Case Studies 3 and 4 are examples of this sort of fraud. Some of these frauds have been exposed either because the fraudsters have applied for improvement grants or because properties have been deemed unfit for human habitation and the local authority has started enforcement proceedings. The principal fraudster will have a pool of source names and/or nominees, who may be employees or business associates of the principal fraudster and either parties to the main fraud or paid to lend their names in use for application stock. Sometimes the identities of innocent strangers will be used. The principal fraudster will continue to make the payments on the mortgage loan. It is not unusual for local authority improvement grants to be obtained by the nominee, who will then arrange for the work to be carried out by the principal fraudster or his associates. One type of fraud which occurs in these circumstances is that of splitting a property into maisonettes or flats, creating several units which can be resold at a substantial profit. While it is not necessary for the fraudster to have the active assistance of a professional, either a solicitor or an estate agent, in this scam, it is often helpful. There have been many cases where the fraudsters have maintained a number of professional advisors so that no single solicitor has seen enough of the fraud to spot what is going on easily. An example appears as Case Study 3. Factory mortgage frauds are undertaken with a view to the main perpetrators achieving a portfolio of properties for rental, property development or even as builders who "improve" and then resell. A side effect of such intense activity is that the perpetrators, always assuming that they are not caught, develop a stable of contacts with solicitors, estate agents and in local authority departments, as well as a knowledge of local property markets. As the business expands they may move beyond fraudulent activity to legitimate property development. They may also, of course, move on to other sorts of fraud.

Detection

Mortgage fraud cases are detected in two main ways. It should of course be said that many fraudsters do not confine their activities solely to mortgage fraud. It is not unusual for a practised fraudster to combine one financial fraud with another. The practice of providing finance for business by means of stand-by letters of credit and other dubious investments is commonly combined with mortgage fraud. Amateur fraudsters tend to overstretch themselves and thus be unable to keep pace with their repayments or other financial obligations. A minor player may turn informer. The decline in residential property prices and consequent decline in capital value of investments has led to the discovery of many mortgage frauds. Those fraudsters who based their business plan on rising property prices have had to adapt or go under. The second and more satisfactory way of detecting mortgage fraud is through the vigilance of professionals who deal with property transactions and who are not parties to the fraud. It is particularly important for solicitors who are solely involved in the conveyancing process to be taught to recognise mortgage fraud in all its varieties because their profession carries the major financial burden of this sort of crime. This is dealt with in greater detail in Chapter 3. Even if an investigation by the police fails to turn up enough evidence to charge and prosecute the main perpetrators, it may still be the case that their activities are limited by civil proceedings either by the building societies who are the main losers, or indirectly, for example through professional negligence claims by the lenders against those professionals involved in the transaction who failed to spot what was going on.

Rollover frauds

In a rising property market the most productive fraud is where properties are purchased and then sold off, sometimes many times. On each sale and resale the perpetrators achieve a profit. This is a fraud which depends on either a rising market, or inflated valuations of properties. The fraudster begins by selling a property at an increased price to a conspirator who obtains the highest possible mortgage, which may exceed the true market value of the property. The process is repeated, each time with a further mortgage based on this valuation. Occasionally the property will be let out on a shorthold tenancy to enhance its income in the intervals between sales. This fraud may be very successful, particularly if there are solicitors and valuers involved.

An example of this sort of fraud may be seen in Case Study 3. A feature of this case study is that the main fraudsters make use of a number of solicitors, both in and outside of the area of the fraud, to deliberately conceal what is happening. Their defence will then consist of a twofold argument:

1. that they had been advised that there was nothing legally wrong with a sub-sale; and
2. that the building societies and other lending institutions from which they borrowed were the authors of their own misfortune because of their lax lending practices.

The fraud may be assisted by the use of the services of a corrupt broker who has access to a large number of lending sources and whose principal interest in the latter is the commission he achieves on each new insurance policy. A major factor in preventing this type of fraud has been the institution of lenders panels of valuers in an effort to restrict abuse, and to the employment in-house of valuation staff where this is appropriate to the area. Financial service provider regulation since the Financial Services Act 1986 has been an important preventative factor.

Commercial mortgage fraud

It should be remembered that mortgage fraud is not always confined to domestic properties. Commercial mortgage fraud also happens. Those societies which have recently become involved in financial mortgage lending have, it seems, become an easy target for this type of fraud. The risks are more substantial because the loans are larger and because the range of legitimate variation in valuation is greater as commercial properties vary and the factors that have to be considered, such as goodwill, depend to a great extent on the individual valuer's opinion. Needless to say, the valuation depends on the profitability both of the business and of the site on which it stands. At its simplest the fraudster may produce a set of tenancy documents showing intensive occupation, which can increase the valuation of the property. If these are not checked, or if a corrupt valuer is used, then the lender is at risk because the valuation upon which the loan is based will be falsely inflated. A further source of risk is that the borrower will not necessarily be an individual but may be a limited liability company. The lender has little chance of recovering moneys against such a borrower if faced with corporate insolvency (see Case Study 5).

Solicitors' fraud

Lenders depend upon solicitors who act for them to ensure that they secure a good title for the borrower, and that the property which the borrower purchases with a building society's money is charged with the lender's interest. It follows that any factor which affects the property as security, either in respect of its value or its marketability in the event that the borrower defaults, is a matter which should be reported to the lender.

Solicitors are not the only professionals involved in the conveyancing process. However, while a valuer who provides a valuation which turns out to be wrong may defend that value, especially if it is less than the purchase price, on the basis that his opinion was justified at the time, a solicitor who fails to secure a good title or to complete the registration process and register the lender's interest properly will leave himself open for a claim in professional negligence, and possibly even to criminal charges as well. Even those cases where criminal proceedings are not clearly merited may still result in disciplinary proceedings before the Solicitors' Disciplinary Tribunal.

How solicitors become involved

Solicitors may become involved in mortgage frauds in a number of ways. It is possible for a naive or inept solicitor to inadvertently assist in mortgage fraud by failing to observe the use of fraudulent devices such as nominee purchases (see Case Study 4).

As described in Chapter 6 below, the Law Society has published guidance to its members in the form of a green card which aims to show steps to minimise the risk of being involved in a mortgage fraud. It is to be hoped that professional education will reduce the risk of this sort of involvement.

Solicitors may be involved marginally by assisting the dealers in systematic status abuse. It is not unusual for these solicitors to deny any knowledge of the crime, while at the same time assisting the fraudster to acquire a portfolio of properties. "Guilty knowledge" has to be proved on the criminal standard. The main object in cases such as these is for the solicitor to increase his profit costs, whilst the risk to his professional status and earning capacity is minimal. Some solicitors do decide to become involved in mortgage fraud either by assisting the fraudsters actively or by setting up their own portfolio of properties. Sometimes both these courses are pursued at the same time. As may be expected, the lending institutions then have a claim against the solicitor which will in fact be paid by either the Solicitors' Indemnity Fund, or in the case of a fraudulent sole practitioner, by the Compensation Fund. Whenever a solicitor becomes involved in mortgage fraud, he or she is bound to be caught eventually because of the very nature of a solicitor's conveyancing practice. All financial transactions will be recorded in the practice books of account, and the steps in the conveyancing process will appear in the conveyancing files. Experienced investigators will confirm that it is often the absence from a conveyancing file of documents or letters requesting instructions which gives the game away. Sometimes these documents can be quite simple. In the example of Case Study 4 it may be seen that although there is a transfer of the property from the names of husband and wife into the names of husband and co-habitee, there was no correspondence with the file relating to divorce or separation, no court order disposing of matrimonial property, no documentation splitting the proceeds of sale, although the property was held as joint tenants and no attempts were made at tax, stamp duty or land registry saving which can be appropriate where a conveyance is made "in consideration of natural love and affection" or in consideration of a matrimonial property settlement.

There is quite extensive media interest in mortgage frauds by solicitors. Nevertheless, most lenders continue to instruct the borrowers' solicitors to act for them. This has recently been the subject of discussion and correspondence, as can be seen from articles and the letters column in the *Law Society Gazette*. It used to be the case that institutional lenders would retain their own solicitors. With the pressure on solicitors to provide a value-for-money service, following the abolition of scale fees, dual instructions became more common. A solicitor's duty to both parties is discussed in Chapter 6 (see also specimen documents at pp 249 *et seq*).

Scope and organisation of this book

This is not a conventional legal textbook. It contains several items which are not found in the many admirable volumes already published on professional negligence, crime and conveyancing. Apart from the narrative chapters, there is a section containing five case studies. These are not intended to be law reports. They cover factors which are common in mortgage fraud cases, and are not based on any particular decided case or investigation. The characters were invented – if they bear any relation to real life this is an accident and no more significant than the identities of characters in solicitors finals and law degree examination problem questions. The case studies are intended as maps of the areas where fraud occurs, or guides to common pitfalls.

The letters and documents in the documents section are illustrative of matters which should give the prudent practitioner cause for concern. Because mundane examples are far more effective than theory, they are presented as examples from wholly fictitious solicitors' files. Most conveyancing letters are stereotyped and without literary originality. The reader will no doubt recognise those matters which are usually raised at each stage in a sale or purchase. For those who are less familiar with the conveyancing process, there is a guide to the steps in a routine transaction at pages 169–171. The italicised steps in this chart are those which mortgage fraudsters routinely take. It is hoped that these dummy documents will serve as a reminder to experienced, honest practitioners, and that they will bring to life the Law Society's green card for the trainees who read this book.

Throughout the text there are cross-references to case studies or documents if it is felt that they will make a point clearer. In addition, because pictures are far more powerful than words, there are bar charts, tables and dummy ledger cards throughout the text.

Lastly, in Chapter 12 there is a simple check-list and at page 34 two exercises which it is hoped will be of some use to the lawyer who is trying to investigate a mortgage fraud. It is intended to help identify the sort of pattern which indicates that fraud is occurring. These are tools - no more. The final chapter also includes sources of help which all practitioners should be aware of.

CHAPTER 2

Why Solicitors Should be Concerned About Mortgage Fraud

There are four reasons why solicitors should be concerned about mortgage fraud. The first is the cost to the Compensation Fund, and therefore to the profession as a whole through Compensation Fund contributions and through any professional levy. Secondly there is the cost of negligence claims which have to be met by the Solicitors' Indemnity Fund as the profession's insurers. Thirdly, every reported case leads to a loss of respect from the public and therefore reduced overall confidence in the profession and its honesty and professional competence. Lastly solicitors pay individually not just in lost insurance excesses but in terms of unremunerated professional time assisting in the investigation of the fraud, as well as stress and damage to professional prospects.

The Compensation Fund

By section 2 of the Solicitors Act 1941, which came into force on November 16, 1942, a fund was established to compensate those who sustained loss through the dishonesty of a solicitor in connection with practice as such. For many years dishonesty was the only ground which gave rise to a grant from the fund, but experience showed that hardship could and did arise in other cases, particularly where the solicitor had failed to account to his client but there was no evidence of dishonesty as such.

In practice, it is a simple matter for an applicant to prove dishonesty where the solicitor concerned has been convicted in the criminal courts of an offence relating to the applicant's money or where the applicant has a judgment based on fraud which the adjudicator is unable to satisfy or where there has been a finding of dishonesty in a report by the Law Society's investigation accountants. This will occur following an inspection of the solicitor's books for account, where the investigation accountants' report refers specifically to the money of the applicant and states that this has been misappropriated.

The Law Society were aware, however, that in cases where the applicant was unable to prove dishonesty on the criminal standard, hardship was occurring. Compensation in cases of hardship caused by failure to account was therefore introduced in the Solicitors Act 1965.

Funding

The Compensation Fund is funded by contributions made by practising solicitors. Solicitors are required by Schedule 2 of the Solicitors Act 1974 to pay annual contributions to the fund at the same time as paying their annual practising certificate fee. Solicitors who have held clients' money during the previous year can also be required to pay a special levy. This is a source of particular irritation to honest members of the profession. Those solicitors applying for their first three certificates after admission are exempted from paying the contribution or any levy, and those applying for their fourth, fifth and sixth certificates need only pay half. There are provisions for reduced contributions in certain cases, such as solicitors on a very low income.

Operation of the Fund

The fund is operated as a discretionary trust of which the Law Society is trustee. The Law Society regards itself as having responsibility for the good name for the profession. The Law Society Council has delegated the day-to-day operation of the fund first to its Professional Purposes Committee and subsequently to that committee's successor, the Adjudication and Appeals Committee. The procedure relating to applications is set out in the Compensation Fund Rules 1975, which are made pursuant to conditions of section 36 (8) of the Solicitors Act 1974. In order to ensure that the fund is operated on a consistent basis, guidelines have been established to assist the committee in the exercise of its discretion.

The fund is a fund of last resort. It is there to relieve loss, not necessarily to make it good in every single case. If the Society receives an application for a grant from an individual or an institution which is insured, the applicant will be advised that a claim under the insurance policy should be pursued and that no grant will be forthcoming. One of the major consequences is that grants are rarely made for the solicitor who is dishonest whilst in partnership, since the dishonesty of a solicitor's partners or employees is effectively covered by the Solicitors' Indemnity Fund and perhaps also by top-up insurance. An applicant for a grant from the fund will be informed that he should pursue a claim against the Indemnity Fund on the basis that the surviving partners (assuming that the dishonest partner will have been expelled) will make a claim under the firm's indemnity insurance. It follows that a grant will not normally be authorised when a solicitor whose alleged acts have given rise to the application is capable of being sued to judgment and execution of that judgment.

The majority of applications arise where the Committee knows, following an inspection of a solicitor's books of account, that there is a shortfall in client account and indeed the Committee may have resolved to intervene in that solicitor's practice pursuant to the provisions of section 35 and of Schedule 1 of the Solicitors Act. The Compensation Fund staff take every possible step to make recoveries, as may be seen from the Compensation Fund's Annual Report. Applications are received in a variety of circumstances including those which may arise during the course of mortgage fraud.

A number of applications are pursued following an alleged breach of an undertaking by a solicitor. The purpose of the Compensation Fund is to replace money stolen by a solicitor or for which he has failed to account and accordingly the Council of the Law Society does not consider it the function of the Fund to underwrite generally the performance of solicitors' undertakings. The one exception to this is where an undertaking is fraudulently given *ab initio* and the applicant has decided to part with the money as a result of that fraudulent undertaking.

Lending institutions and the fund

Institutional undertakings such as banks and building societies have hitherto been treated in the same way as any other applicant for a grant, and provided that the application is properly made of the fund, the grant will be authorised. It has long been established, however, that corporate applicants cannot, by their very nature, suffer hardship, thus their applications must be made under section 36(2)(a) of the Act which means that they must satisfy the Council that their loss arises as a result of the dishonesty of the solicitor(s).

A lending institution may make an application where a solicitor has misappropriated the proceeds of the sale of the property, including the funds required to redeem the seller's mortgage. In such instances the mortgage will not have been effectively discharged and both the seller and the buyer are at risk if the mortgage is not repaid—the seller is at risk since he is still liable, and the buyer since he has not acquired a clear title. In such circumstances, although the institution is often the nominal applicant for the grant, the committee will authorise a grant for the purpose of relieving the loss, whether or not proof of dishonesty is available, since an application could alternatively have been made by the buyer or the seller.

Some applications arise not because the solicitor concerned simply stole the money which was already in his hands, but because the solicitor fraudulently induced the applicant to part with his money in the first place. Before making a grant in such cases the committee will consider what enquiries were made by the applicant before agreeing to the advance and whether the applicant has contributed to his own misfortune, perhaps by contributing to negligence during the course of the transaction. Some institutions insure against the possibility that money is stolen by the dishonest actions of their own staff or other agents. In recent years, however, such institutions have discovered that insurers are less and less willing to underwrite such insurance, or have imposed a substantial excess. As long as such institutions have access to the Compensation Fund in cases of such loss, there is little incentive for them to take out insurance cover. By relying on the Compensation and Indemnity Funds, institutions have been able to relax their business practices in controlling funds paid to solicitors. Lenders are now rarely separately represented and postal completions are the norm rather than the exception. The rise in grants from the Compensation Fund in the 1980s can be said to have coincided with the trend to such relaxation in conveyancing procedures. Changes in those procedures among more prudent practices may delay transactions and increase expense to the public, which is unlikely to be popular.

Conspiracy cases

There is a further problem in mortgage fraud cases which very often involves conspiracy charges. The conspiracy may involve not only solicitors but, for example, estate agents, property developers, valuers, bank managers and others. It is clearly not right that the fund should pay where the loss arises wholly or mainly from the dishonesty from players other than solicitors. One possibility would be to make a value judgement on the part played by the solicitor and to make a grant proportionally. However, there is a practical difficulty in that fraud trials tend to be complicated and lengthy and do not necessarily result in verdicts which would allow the apportionment of loss to be established clearly.

Reducing the financial burden on solicitors

In 1992 the Law Society published "The Cost of Default: A Consultative Paper", which set out the history of the Compensation Fund and the Solicitors' Indemnity Fund. The appendix to this paper set out a table of defaulting practices whose misdeeds had resulted in claims on the Compensation Fund of £1million and above, and the cost of the Compensation Fund related to the growth of the number of solicitors. The report was prepared in the face of what the Law Society called "a rising tide of dishonesty". A number of methods of reducing the financial burden on the profession, which the Council regarded as intolerable, were canvassed in the report and a list of questions for the profession was included. The views of all members of the profession, whether or not members of the Law Society, were canvassed, with a closing date for replies of 30 September 1992. The then President of the Law Society, M H Shealden, wrote to members of the profession enclosing a copy of the Council's reports on the cost of default together with the green mortgage fraud warning card, a note about financial/investment scams and the pink "SMART" undertakings checklist card.

As far as the Compensation Fund and the Indemnity Fund were concerned, claims and payments were to be reduced by the following measures.

Anti-mortgage fraud procedures were to be prepared after consultation with the lending institutions. Compensation Fund payments to lending institutions were to be reduced where there had been contributory fault. A "SMART" pink card was to be circulated pointing out how claims could be avoided by making undertakings "Specific, Measurable, Agreed, Realistic and Timed". The Solicitors' Indemnity Fund was to undertake claims prevention work.

It was decided that "capping" should not be introduced for the Compensation Fund because, first, there would be no immediate saving, given the number of claims in the pipeline. Secondly, there would be no significant saving unless payment was set at a very low level, as the majority of claims are for small amounts. Thirdly, the house-buying public would suffer if lending institutions restricted their choice of solicitors. Fourthly, the root cause of claims would not be dealt with if the cap were instituted. Lastly, and perhaps most importantly, a cap on the Compensation Fund would adversely affect the reputation of solicitors, by penalising the innocent victims of a solicitor's dishonesty. On the effect of mortgage fraud, the report had this to say:

> "It is not thought that claims arising from mortgage fraud will continue to increase in 1993 because lenders are now taking greater precautions. They have stopped granting unsecured loans and take greater care in checking the credentials of borrowers. This has led to a fall in the value and number of claims."

Part of the reduction in mortgage fraud claims, it was acknowledged, was because there had been a general downturn in the business done in conveyancing because of the recession. The use of the green card and specific precautions, both in general and those recommended in the profession, are considered in Chapter 12.

Professional indemnity insurance and the role of the SIF

Section 37 of the Solicitors Act 1974 gave the Law Society three options by which it could provide professional indemnity cover for solicitors. Option one (which has never been implemented) was a system of "authorised insurances" under which solicitors would negotiate their own cover. The second option was that of a "master policy" under which the society would negotiate a master policy covering the entire profession and issue certificates of insurance to individual firms. Such a scheme existed from 1975 until 31 August 1987. The third option, which is the basis of the current system, provides for the profession to become "its own insurer", *i.e.* whereby the society runs its own indemnity fund.

The role of the fund

The purpose of the Indemnity Fund is primarily to protect clients, and secondly to protect solicitors and their own staff. Lord Brightman in *Swain* v *The Law Society* said:

"The scheme is not only for the protection of the premium-paying solicitor against the financial consequences and mistakes... but also, and far more importantly, to secure that a solicitor is financially able to compensate his clients. Indeed, I think it is clear that the principal purpose of section 37 was to confer on the Law Society powers to safe guard the lay public and not professional practitioners since the latter can look after themselves. So, there is no doubt at all in my mind that the power given to the Law Society by section 37 is applied to be exercised not only in the interests of solicitors' profession but also, and more importantly, in the interests of those members of the public who resort to solicitors for legal advice".

The fund provides indemnities for solicitors and former solicitors and employees, or former employees in respect of losses arising from claims in respect of civil liability incurred in private practice. The level of cover is limited to £1 million for each and every claim (including claimants' costs). For further details of the scheme the reader is referred to *The Guide to Professional Conduct of Solicitors 1993*, Chapter 28.

Policy exclusions

For reasons of public policy, the fund cannot provide indemnity for losses for claims in respect of a person's own dishonest or fraudulent act or admission. However, this exclusion does not prevent any partner of a firm who is not involved in dishonesty or fraud from being indemnified. It follows that the fund provides cover to an innocent partner irrespective of the dishonesty of his partners or employees, and also provides cover to an innocent sole practitioner in respect of the dishonesty of his employees, provided that in each case clients' money is involved. Solicitors still need fidelity insurance in respect of defalcations from their office account. Where the client suffers loss and it is a result of a sole practitioner's own dishonesty (or in the case where all the partners of a firm have been dishonest), such losses can only be met by the Compensation Fund.

The Indemnity Fund is a fund of legal liability. It has no discretion but is obliged to pay all proven claims up to the £1 million limit. The Indemnity Fund does not pay claims below the minimum deductible excess. In the event that an individual claim exceeds £1 million, the partners may have to look for any excess from top-up cover or their own resources, or alternatively those who have suffered loss may have to do so. The main difference in the degree of protection offered to claimants by the funds is that the Compensation Fund does not in general pay claims for damages for consequential loss. It follows, therefore, that there is a difference in treatment of clients of partnerships and the clients of sole practitioners.

Reorganisation of the funds

Consideration has been given to transferring all claims for dishonesty out of the Indemnity Fund and into the Compensation Fund. The Compensation Fund would then deal with all the dishonesty cases, and not just those from sole practitioners. In addition there would be a distinction between the cost of negligence, which would fall on the SIF, and the cost of dishonesty, which would fall on the Compensation Fund.

Predicting the likely extent of dishonesty in the future is difficult, in addition to which claims on the SIF are often tainted with dishonesty and it would be difficult to know to which fund some claims should go. The SIF would also have to distinguish between dishonesty and negligence in claims handling. At present, every partnership and every sole practitioner has virtually complete cover up to £1million per claim in respect of both dishonesty and negligence by an employee. Were the system to be changed, most partnerships would find it necessary to carry yet further insurance against the risk of claims arising from the dishonesty of a partner or an employee to the extent that it was not covered by the Compensation Fund. This would of course affect top-up insurers who at present cover against dishonesty.

Consideration has also been given to merging the two funds. There would be the following disadvantages.

1. If the single fund were adopted the SIF approach to consequential loss would increase the total payments and thus the burden on the profession.
2. All claims would be subject to the Indemnity Fund's £1 million limit.
3. There would be two categories of additional costs:
   - **(a)** the payment of grants to claimants who are at present unable to claim from the Compensation Fund because they have their own insurance;
   - **(b)** higher interest payments (at present the Compensation Fund pays interest at 7%, whereas the Indemnity Fund pays at commercial rates).

Any change in the existing system would require an amendment to the Solicitors Act and this of course requires legislative time.

Loss of public respect and confidence

Mortgage frauds by solicitors have been reported in the national newspapers, in local papers, and in the professional press and law reports. It is such reports in the media which most damage the profession's reputation. Two examples follow.

"A developer operated a £1.5 million mortgage fraud on building societies as he tried to build up 'a small property empire on the Yorkshire coast'. Leeds Crown Court heard yesterday that builder Stephen Birley bought a large amount of properties in Scarborough and Bridlington often at knock down prices and quickly sold them on to his own nominees who got higher mortgages as a result of inflated values on the premises concerned.

Jailing Birley for three and half years, Judge Herrod QC said that he had been at the hub of huge ring of fraud during the eighties and the principal beneficiary of it all.

The fraud had extended over a period of three years. Just under £1.5 million had been obtained in mortgage advances and the total lost to the building societies or insurance companies was just over £400,000.

Birley, 38, of Prospect Road, Scarborough had admitted conspiracy to obtain by deception and 23 offences of obtaining properties by deception.

Birley's solicitor, Neil Dunbar, 38, of Holt Pound, Hampshire, was jailed for 12 months after he also admitted conspiracy to obtain by deception.

Judge Herrod told him 'This is a sad day for you because you allowed Stephen Birley to use your professional skills as a solicitor in the web of fraud he had woven'."

Yorkshire Post, 13 February 1993

Those with an interest in mortgage fraud cannot have failed to have noticed the reports in the national press on the fraud involving the firm of R. L. Lucas & Sons, involving Guy Lucas. The case has been referred to in "Private Eye". Guy Lucas and others have been committed for trial to the Crown Court and at the time of writing the case was likely to be heard early in 1995.

It goes without saying that locally reported cases can damage the business of a local firm for those partners who were not involved in the fraud at all. The guilty partner will presumably have been dismissed or allowed to resign, assuming that he or she has not just disappeared.

Personal cost

To the extent that their insurance excesses are at risk, or that they are not covered by insurance, solicitors are personally liable for losses caused by mortgage fraud. There is an additional cost for solicitors who, however innocently, are involved in such a fraud. Solicitors are obliged to assist their insurers by providing information to facilitate the official processing of claims. Time spent preparing this information, looking for files and interviewing staff is unremunerated. Other unremunerated hours can be spent assisting the police with their enquiries as a result of an order under the Police and Criminal Evidence Act 1984 (as amended) or as result of a search warrant. An insurance or a police investigation may split a partnership and may certainly cause stress not only to solicitors but to their unadmitted and secretarial staff. The legal employment agency, Chambers & Co. was sufficiently concerned about how solicitors survive financial scandal to include reference to the matter in a recruiting advertisement in the summer of 1994. It does not take a great deal of imagination to appreciate the difficulties of job-hunting whilst previous employers are the subject of an investigation. It can be much more difficult to prove non-involvement than is generally supposed.

So solicitors have much to lose from mortgage fraud. The innocent members of the profession often suffer real financial and professional hardship to protect the profession's good name.

CHAPTER 3

How to Avoid Becoming Involved in Fraud

Solicitors are bombarded with advice from every side, from the Law Society and lending institutions, on how to avoid mortgage fraud. There is also a wealth of courses on fraud. (These usually include a "module" which attempts to deal with mortgage fraud in the same way as it deals with other sorts of fraud which do not so intimately involve solicitors.) But for the solicitor seeking to avoid becoming involved in a mortgage fraud, life could hardly be more difficult. The solicitor in private practice has to fit in fraud prevention education, with other aspects of continuing education, such as courses on how to make litigation pay, how to get more out of your bank, European law, law and computers, computerised conveyancing, stress management, staff management, money management, and courses on bookkeeping systems so sophisticated that only a Martian would still be awake at lunchtime. Reported mortgage fraud cases are not much help in crime prevention, either. Although they typically contain a wealth of detail, it will relate to the criminal law or negligence issues, in which case they do little towards helping the solicitor to prevent a fraud occurring in his own office.

In reality the people who learn most about mortgage fraud are those who least need to know about it, namely those members of the profession and the Law Society panel who regularly prosecute or defend solicitor mortgage fraudsters in front of the Solicitors' Disciplinary Tribunal. The case studies and advice which follow are therefore based on observation of recurring factors and patterns in these cases.

Where fraud is most likely

One of the reasons why law reports tend to not deal with the facts of mortgage fraud cases in any great depth is that even in simple mortgage fraud the detail can be overwhelming. Much of this detail may, however, be relevant to the solicitor who seeks to avoid becoming embroiled in one of these very time-consuming investigations.

The reader should consider first those scenarios where mortgage fraud is most likely to happen. Whilst it is true that there have been a number of cases involving sole practitioners who have been involved or recruited into mortgage fraud in a desperate effort to keep an unprofitable practice afloat, mortgage fraud is by no manner of means a risk only to small, high street practices. It can occur in any firm where conveyancing, whether domestic or commercial, forms a substantial part of the firm's business, or of a department of a larger firm's business.

It is certainly true that financial pressure is one of the factors which plays a part in mortgage fraud. With the recession and the consumer-led market for services in which we all have to work, domestic conveyancing in particular has become less and less profitable. Commercial customers are slower and slower at paying their bills for business conveyancing. The conveyancing solicitor has to work ever harder and, these days, he will very likely have to be a specialist rather than a GP to achieve his share of the firm's profit costs. Case Study 4 is a typical example of a solicitor in financial difficulties who was initially involved in the mortgage fraud probably innocently, but who later played an active part.

As we shall see from the in-depth study of the specimen documents at pages 169 *et seq*, any solicitor who stops to think about the factors which recur, such as transactions where members of a family are alleged to be purchasing from one another, and the payment of direct deposits, will spot a pattern and will then have to make a number of difficult decisions. For sources of advice see Chapter 12.

Case Study 3 is an example of an extensive scam where two brothers, who were the driving force, went to great efforts to conceal what was going on by using a number of firms of solicitors. To make efficient use of offshore companies requires professional skills which are not normally found in high street firms; accordingly the two brothers consult a number of West End firms and at least one City firm. The assistant concerned will simply be asked whether sub-sales were illegal. This is a relatively unusual question to ask in the context of domestic conveyancing and it often seems to be answered *in vacuo*, rather than after an investigation as to why the client requires this information. Naivety and lack of detailed education as to those factors which should trigger an investigation of any aspect of the transaction seem to have played a major part in cases like this.

Those lawyers who investigate mortgage fraud on a regular basis find over and over again that, however large the firm, it is still possible for one partner or one assistant solicitor or unadmitted member of staff to play an active part in mortgage fraud apparently without anyone else in the firm realising what is going on. It is important that solicitors not only realise their responsibilities towards their staff, but also take practical steps to ensure their staff will recognise fraudulent activity, by providing proper examples rather than just general advice, and putting in place a reporting system.

Staff supervision

Chapter 3 of the *Guide to the Professional Conduct of Solicitors* deals with unadmitted staff. "A solicitor is responsible for exercising proper supervision over both admitted and unadmitted staff". It is made clear in the commentary to this principle that "staff" covers not only employees but also independent contractors like consultants, locums and unadmitted solicitor's clerks. The result, particularly in a small firm, of employing a dishonest solicitor's clerk who is engaged in wholesale commercial mortgage fraud of the type described in Case Study 5 is that not only will the clerk be prosecuted and probably convicted, but the partners - even if they are without any degree of criminal guilt - will find themselves the subject of professional negligence claims and of disciplinary proceedings before the Disciplinary Tribunal. The solicitor's clerk will be unlikely ever to be employed in a solicitors' office again.

No solicitor can avoid responsibility in the legal and moral sense for work carried out by members of his firm by leaving it entirely to his or her staff, however well qualified they may be. The Law Society gives practice guidelines on the recruitment and supervision of employees who undertake investment business in Annex 261 of the *Guide to Professional Conduct*.

As a result of sections 41–44 of the Solicitors Act 1974, solicitors are restricted in the employment of any person who, to the solicitor's knowledge, is disqualified from practising as a solicitor by reason of having been struck off the Roll, suspended from practice or by reason of being an undischarged bankrupt.

Under section 43 of the Act, the Solicitors' Disciplinary Tribunal have power to order that no solicitor shall employ a named clerk without permission from the Law Society. It is prudent when employing staff to check with the Law Society Records Office to see whether an order restricting the employment of a particular clerk is in existence, or whether a certain solicitor has been struck off.

Rule 13 of the Solicitors' Practice Rules 1990 sets out the minimum standards for supervision. Every office has to be attended on each day that it is open to the public or open to telephone calls from the public by a solicitor who holds a practising certificate and has been admitted for at least three years. In the case an office from which no right of audience or right to conduct litigation is exercised, and from which no exercise of any such right is supervised, a registered lawyer who is a principal of the firm and who has similar qualifications in his own jurisdiction must attend. The lawyer concerned must spend sufficient time at the office to ensure adequate control of the staff employed there and to provide facilities for consultations with clients. The solicitor must be a principal, employee or consultant of the firm.

The person with the requisite qualifications under this rule must normally be in attendance at the office during all the hours it is open to the public or when it is open to telephone calls from the public. There is an exception in the case of an office dealing solely with conveyancing, in that a licensed conveyancer may be in attendance. The Council are reluctant to grant waivers to sole practitioners who wish to practise from more than two offices and a sole principal, who wishes to practise from more than one office including a consulting room and who does not propose to employee a person qualified to manage each office in accordance with Rule 13, must consult the Professional Ethics Department of the Law Society with regard to a waiver. Supervision becomes more difficult where the supervising partner is not working in the same building as the people he is supposed to supervise, as may be seen in Case Study 5.

As a result of the Money Laundering Regulations 1993 many firms of solicitors will have in place a compliance officer and a system for making reports that junior staff can use in the event that they are suspicious with regard to a transaction that may involve money laundering. It would also be prudent for staff to ensure that their junior staff can recognise other fraudulent transactions which may involve a solicitors' firm, such as standby letter of credit frauds and mortgage frauds, and ensure that junior staff know where to go for advice and further information should they believe such a fraud is occurring. If no such system is in existence, and it is undoubtedly "best practice" to have such a system, then the partners risk their firm being involved in a mortgage fraud, and with it the consequences of unremunerated time spent assisting in the investigation, and professional censure or at worst a criminal trial, a professional indemnity insurance claim and proceedings in front of the Solicitors' Disciplinary Tribunal.

CHAPTER 4

How to Do a Mortgage Fraud – The Fraudster's Point of View

From a fraudster's point of view a solicitor is a very useful, indeed essential part of mortgage fraud. In reality there are not many licensed conveyancers (though they too have had problems with mortgage fraud) and therefore the solicitors' profession is the most essential element. What every enterprising fraudster needs is a solicitor who is either naive, or so grossly overworked as to be unlikely to notice what is going on, or possibly better yet, criminally inclined.

Like all fraud, the motivation behind the mortgage fraud is that of making as much money as possible with as little work as possible. One way of spotting mortgage fraud is the recycling of names and addresses for different purposes, as we shall see from both the case studies which provide specimen scenarios and the specimen documents. Solicitors are a soft target for mortgage fraud because as a whole, the profession is perceived as trustworthy (or at least as comprehensively insured). Solicitors' practices do not do the equivalent of a moonlight flit because this would jeopardise their practice which is dependent usually upon some degree of local connection. According to the nature of their practice, solicitors may have access to financial advice and sources of finance which are not available to ordinary members of the public. They may be licensed to give investment advice in accordance with the Financial Services Act 1986. Many solicitors, particularly those in suburban practices, are under considerable financial pressure as a result of the decline in the property market: while mortgage finance is still available, fewer and fewer houses are being sold. It therefore follows that when the overworked solicitor's secretary announces a new client in the waiting room the solicitor will be welcoming, rather than on his guard. There is still a substantial element of "it couldn't happen here" in the profession. Solicitors are also convenient cover for the confidence trickster who would not normally be an acceptable customer to a bank or building society. We shall see how this operates in Case Study 5.

Case studies

Case Study 1 – Grape and Quince

This is a very simple fraud which is most likely to be detected only when Grape fails to meet the repayments on the mortgage. Although there may be minimal criminal consequences, Chapter 18 of the *Guide to the Professional Conduct of Solicitors* sets out the following principle:

> "Solicitors must not act, whether in their professional capacity or otherwise towards anyone in a way fraudulent, deceitful or otherwise contrary to their position as solicitors. Nor must solicitors use their position as solicitors to take unfair advantage either for themselves or another person."

The commentary to this principle deals at paragraph 4 with the question of giving a reference. When giving a reference as to character and financial standing a solicitor is obliged to give one which is true. A solicitor who gives a false reference may be guilty of unbecoming conduct, which is a matter for the Disciplinary Tribunal and which may also incur a potential civil liability, if a misleading reference is given and a member of staff actually turns out to be dishonest. Giving a bogus reference for a member of staff is hardly likely to enhance the solicitor's reputation with the local financial institutions, either. The clerk concerned also lays himself open to criminal charges and a Disciplinary Tribunal hearing by using a false reference.

Case Study 2 Drum

The case of Drum represents a phenomenon which is referred to in Clarke's, *Mortgage Fraud* (Chapman and Hall, 1991). Drum has had no connection with any financial service regulator. He makes a substantial income out of the interest on the premiums paid by applicants, which he does not pay over promptly to the insurers, and a further income out of the commission paid on insurance policies. In simple terms, his business depends upon preying on vulnerable members of his own community and their insecurities about obtaining mortgages legitimately. Perhaps the saddest aspect of this case is that many of the applicants involved would have been able to obtain mortgages perfectly legitimately from the local authority without having to pay a premium or risk the repossession of their premises and the possible attentions of any unofficial protection racket run by Drum.

Case Study 3 Trumpeter and Trombone

This case study is unusual in that it shows the way fraudsters sometimes use legitimate sources of finance to set up a business which had the appearance of being legitimate. The attraction of becoming property developers seems to have been that it promised quick money and a luxurious lifestyle for relatively little investment of effort or capital. Among the documents which one might expect to be found by the police in this case are the unofficial business plans, showing how each transaction was to be rolled over into the next to maximise the available profit. Because the fraudsters are careful to keep up a stable of financial advisors and solicitors, no one sees the full picture, though there were particular transactions where the solicitors concerned, if they pause for thought, should have spotted that something sinister was happening. There was one relatively simple question which several of the suburban firms failed to ask, which is why so many members of the borrowers' entourage kept repeatedly moving house!

This case study also illustrates a phenomenon common in those mortgage frauds where the fraudsters have set out to set up a property portfolio, rather than to make profits on quick resales, using mortgaged properties for rental income and splitting them into separate residential units using their friends to undertake refurbishing work in order to qualify for improvement grants. It is worth speculating about how many residential units can actually be achieved in an ordinary terraced house.

Case study 4 Wagner, Bach and Deadlocks

This case study concerns a fraud by a solicitor who actually succumbed to the temptation to assist in the fraud and acquire his own portfolio of properties. This case study has been written to illustrate most of the common symptoms of mortgage fraud which are dealt with in the green card. Peter Deadlock is a composite and fictional character composed of elements in a number of mortgage frauds involving solicitors. The documents which appear in the next chapter are those which are commonly found in mortgage frauds. They are unexceptional and contain nothing very unusual in terms of literary merit or content. Their principal use is to illustrate, practically, the kind of matters which should trigger caution in a vigilant solicitor in accordance with the Law Society's green card.

Case Study 5 Salt, Peach and Kumquat

Case Study 5 illustrates the pitfalls in employing a solicitor's clerk without checking with their previous employers as to their competence and honesty. The solicitor's clerk concerned in this example may have been dismissed from his previous employment. Salt works in a different office from his supervising partner and it seems that the partner concerned did not attribute the unusual profits which Salt made to anything other than exceptional diligence, not even when attention had been given to the day-to-day supervision of Salt, who was an unadmitted clerk. The partners concerned should have spotted an unusual use of offshore companies and also the unusual profits Salt was making for the firm. A more experienced, and less criminally inclined, lawyer might also have questioned the stories told by Peach and Kumquat, referred to in section 2 of the case study. It may be easier for a solicitor's clerk to constantly lie to lending institutions than it is for one of the partners to do so—see in particular section 5 of this case study. This case study also illustrates the very substantial profits available for mortgage fraudsters who act in a concerted and business-like fashion.

Much of the evidence of the cost of mortgage fraud which appears in the media is based on anecdote. Lenders will quote figures based on the valuations of the property. Insurers will quote figures based on losses sustained. There is a kind of "agony olympics" between those who prosecute mortgage fraud and those who defend it, as to who can achieve the largest sum at risk. It should be borne in mind that the properties involved in the fraud are generally eventually repossessed by the building society, which will thereby recover at least some of their perceived loss on the repossession sale. Perhaps this is just as well for the legal profession.

The green card

The green card is now incorporated in the *Guide to Professional Conduct*. It lists the following signs of mortgage fraud:

1. Solicitors are warned against fictitious buyers, particularly if they are introduced to the practice by an unfamiliar third party such as a broker or an estate agent. It is hoped that the specimen documents section will enable solicitors to spot invented clients.

2. Solicitors are cautioned against unusual instructions, examples of which appear at pages 237 *et seq* of the documents supplied. The example given on the green card is of a solicitor being instructed to remit the net proceeds of sale to the estate agent.

3&4. "Misrepresentation of the purchase price" should be read together with item 4 "directly paid deposits", since the purchase price is often adjusted, according to the funds available, by the use of a deposit which is alleged to have been paid directly to the vendor. A particularly clear example of this malpractice can be seen at pages 206 *et seq*. A recent case concerned a solicitor who was reluctant, once the Law Society restricted those circumstances in which a firm might act for both vendor and purchaser, to give up what he regarded as a legitimate portion of his income. Accordingly, as well as having a practice in the centre of town, he opened his own kitchen table practice to deal with those matters on which the firm could not act. It can be seen from the specimen letters that substantial adjustments can be made to the price to be paid by the use of non-existent deposits.

5. "Incomplete contract documentation" is illustrated by the documents at pages 251 *et seq*. It is a feature of domestic mortgage fraud, as opposed to commercial mortgage fraud, that the solicitors involved are often particularly sloppy in keeping their records up to date. This is very often the result of using unadmitted staff, particularly secretaries, as part of the conveyancing transaction. The files in the specimen documents at page 249 particularly illustrate this point. Here a secretary is being used as a clerk and she becomes so overwhelmed by the fraudulent transaction that she actually tells the solicitor to sort it out himself. This is not what the Law Society had in mind when it set out those limited occasions when a solicitor may act for both vendor and purchaser. It will be clear to the reader that this particular example is simply a fund-raising transaction where the property is transferred from the husband and wife's name into the name of the husband and the wife using her maiden name. The whole transaction is fraudulent from start to finish. The contract documentation remains incomplete because the poor secretary who deals with one side of the transaction cannot believe what she has been told to do.

6. The changes in the purchase price are designed to prevent the use of actual cash, and needless to say this is an unusual transaction within item 7. Of course the unusual transaction in Case Study 5 also comes within this caveat.

The rest of the green card deals with the steps which a solicitor should take to minimise the risk of fraud. These are as follows:

1. Verify the identity and bona fides of your client. Clients should be personally introduced and interviewed wherever possible.
2. Question unusual instructions. See again Case Study 5.
3. "Discuss any aspects of the transaction which worry you with your client" is perhaps more difficult to deal with. The reader is referred to Chapter 12 of this book for sources of help, should this appear to be a current problem. It is not usually the case that a solicitor would see a fraudulent application, but fraudulent applications and references are included in the sample documents with this text since they complete the picture and may enable a solicitor to make suitable enquiries of a lender/client or to assist lender/clients.
4. Many building societies insist that the true price should be shown in all documentation, for obvious reasons. It is good practice to explain to a vendor or purchaser/client that a solicitor also has duties to the lender, and to make it clear that all allowances and incentives should be reported to the mortgagee before exchange of contract. Solicitors should also be wary of the situation where there is a last-minute adjustment in price to cover negotiations in respect of fixtures and fittings. It may well be that there are items which suddenly prove to be too costly to move but the price which is allocated should be realistic. It is sometimes safer to deal with the matter by way of separate agreement.

5&6. Items 5 and 6 are self-evident.

7. A company search is particularly important to lenders because their chances of recovering any part of the value of their security may be vanishingly small with a limited liability company which is insolvent.

The green form ends as follows: "Remember, that even when investigations result in a solicitor ceasing to act for a client the solicitor will still owe a duty of confidentiality which would prevent the solicitor passing on information to the lenders. It is only when the solicitor is satisfied that there is a strong prima facie case that the client was using him to further a criminal purpose or fraud that the duty of confidentiality would not apply."

Solicitors who find themselves in this position are recommended to refer to Chapter 12 and to make use of the sources of help shown there. This is perhaps the moment to remind the reader that in conveyancing, files may be read not only by supervising partners but also by the police, the prosecuting authorities, the Solicitors Complaints Bureau, those who defend solicitors who are accused of criminal activity, negligence or professional misconduct, insurers and their panels of solicitors, not to mention Court officials and Judges. It is hoped that this will provide an incentive to produce proper attendance notes.

Sample documents

The first section of the sample documents included with this book includes a number of documents which would normally only be seen by the lending institutions. There are a variety of false references from former landladies and accountants, a set of business accounts, and a genuine reference which should give rise to enquiry. These items are likely to be of assistance to building society staff and to those who prosecute and defend mortgage fraud cases. When investigating potential mortgage frauds it is sensible to look for repeating items which form a pattern where no pattern should exist. Addresses will be recycled, a property which has been mortgaged as a private dwelling house will reappear as a business address. Businesses are reused. The basic stationery may be the same but only the heading is changed. Today the fraudsters will have the use of a desk top publishing package with a variety of fonts. It is important to check that the business exists, by using quite simple things like the telephone book or *The Thomson Directory*. For instance, the restaurant at page 188 was not in the telephone directory. The company at page 187 does not contain the registered particulars and a company search may reveal that it does not exist. The property at 116 Gray Road may already be mortgaged to the same society, who appear not to be aware that it is part of their portfolio. Forged references are often very clumsy and may be written on lined paper or cash book pages. Pages 185 and 186 show two attempts at a reference for the same person. The landlord's reference at pages 173 and 174 shows Miss Bach as a landlady in one version and as a tenant in the second.

Accounts

When dealing with sets of accounts (see p 175 *et seq* which include a set of accounts and the references based on those accounts) it is elementary to check whether the business concerned will support all the staff that are supposed to work for it. Again the registered office is a residential property charged to the same building society. The business is not in the telephone book. Accounts should be checked to see what period they cover and how up to date they are. Building society lenders have their own systems of checks.

References

Bank references can be equally revealing. Consider the bank reference at page 172: by damning the customer with faint praise the bank is in fact indicating that this particular customer is already overstretched.

Common sources of false references are community centres, self-employed trades such as window cleaners and minicab drivers, restaurants where many casual staff are employed, hairdressers and the financial services industry. The reference at page 172 is genuine but reveals that the employee has not been with the local borough for very long. The position can hardly be described as permanent. It is not unusual for mortgage fraudsters to take temporary employment with respectable bodies to achieve a genuine reference in a portfolio of forgeries. Some of the specimen documents contain instructions to solicitors. With the green card advice in mind, a vigilant solicitor should check for the following:

- That there is no substitute when meeting the client. It does no harm when meeting the client for the first time to record in the attendance note as many distinguishing features as possible. Try to imagine you have to identify the client some years later to enable the police to arrest him!
- The letter of instruction at page 192 should be treated with a very considerable caution: it is typed, the signature is illegible and at that stage the solicitor has not met the client.

- The instruction forms which appear on pages 198–199 are a feature of mortgage fraud cases occurring in small suburban firms. Most prosecutors can recollect cases where there have been letters on the solicitor's files sending out the pro forma instructions in batches. As these batches were all sent to the same person at the same address, even the learned leader for the defence can be hard put to find an honest explanation.

It may be difficult to spot a mortgage fraud the first time the fraudster uses a firm, but if the partners make an invariable practice of meeting their clients and obtaining individual instructions whilst at the same time keeping a careful check on names used, as well as addresses, it should not prove too difficult to observe when a pattern develops.

There are two simple exercises which can be undertaken to see if a pattern exists where there should not be one. The first is to list the addresses to which a particular fee earner writes - see page 286 *et seq*. The second is to list the following salient points for each transaction:

(a) Address
(b) Name of vendor
(c) Name of purchaser
(d) Building society
(e) Vendor's solicitors
(f) Solicitors for the purchaser and for the lender
(g) The date of instruction
(h) The date of completion or last letter on file.

The resulting pattern, indicative of mortgage fraud, form Case Study 4, and the specimen documents appear at pages289–290.

Correspondence

The letter to the bank manager at page 196 of which the solicitor was sent a copy, should have put the solicitor on enquiry at once. If you receive a similar letter, you should refer to the green card and also to the Law Society's SMART undertaking card. There is no way in which paragraphs 2 and 3 can be consistent with an ordinary residential purchase. Many fraudsters slip up and may make a mistake as to which name a property should have been conveyed into. An example of this occurs at page 200. Inter-office memos can be interesting; see page 201. These instructions were important for the information which they did not include, which one would have expected, were it a legitimate transfer from husband to wife or from joint names into the single name of either spouse. The transaction is treated as an arm's-length one, and the possibility of tax, land registry and stamp duty savings is not covered. One would have expected such matters to be discussed were the transaction genuinely in consideration of natural love and affection, or as a result of a court order in divorce proceedings. The next section contains extracts from a standard set of instructions to solicitors and licensed conveyancers; see page 202.

The section which relates to exchange and reduced deposits contains a variety of letters which should inspire the vigilant solicitor or mortgage fraud investigator to ask questions, particularly in view of the contents of the Law Society green card.

The next section headed Report on Title, contains typical clauses which are included in all the major lenders report forms.

Financial documents

The first of these entries shows transfers to and from a ledger card which does not relate to the named client. The last item is a refund of Land Registry fees, which again does not relate either to the named client or to the property concerned. The financial statement at page 213 shows a number of items which one would not expect to find in a straightforward sale and purchase for a first-time buyer. As with all the matters included as examples in these documents, of themselves these items simply indicate a need for vigilance, they are not necessarily overwhelming evidence of fraud.

Lies to building societies

The letter on page 214 carries a scribbled note asking for the solicitor to verify something for the fraudster. Needless to say, such verification should not be given unless it is genuine.

A common excuse to building societies where mortgage fraud is occurring is that the deeds have been delayed at the Land Registry, or that there is a first registration. In fact the matter is simply one of dealing with an existing registered title. It should be borne in mind that building society deeds departments regularly ring the Land Registry to check that these time limits are in fact genuine.

Page 216 indicates that this is not an arm's-length transaction and that the firm is acting for both vendor and purchaser. The deposit alone is above the financial limit permitted by the Law Society, and there is no indication that the parties are within any of the categories permitted in the *Guide to Professional Conduct*.

The documents at pages 217 *et seq* reveal that this is another in-house transaction where the building society's interest is not properly protected. The letter of 13 August 1992 contains a lie. A review of preliminary enquiries and requisitions on title would have revealed that there is a mortgage fraud. It will be hardly surprising if the response to this letter resembles the one dated 16 August 1992. The prompt response by Deadlocks on 21 August 1992 is the only way in which they can meet the dilemma. It is even less surprising that by 4 October 1992 their client has apparently left the country with no intention of returning! A successful mortgage fraudster may well decamp.

Tenancy arrangements

Because of the fall in property prices it is now no longer possible for the mortgage fraudster to make a guaranteed profit on the resale of property. Accordingly many fraudsters have acquired portfolios of properties which are let, particularly to local authority tenants, since this provides a guaranteed rental income. Some building societies are happy to allow their borrowers to let mortgaged premises, provided that this is done very short-term and on a shorthold tenancy. Obviously the building society is anxious to ensure that they can realise their security.

The usual reason given for letting property is the classic "working abroad". So frequently does this happen that, as can be seen by document number 265, the building society response is often to seek an undertaking from the borrowers that they will not let properties without permission from the building society. Lettings can be discovered either from estate agents, management accounts and shorthold tenancy documents, or from DIY efforts by the fraudster using forms sold by law stationers. These understandably present problems for the building society, since the necessary notices under the Housing Act to create a shorthold tenancy will not necessarily have been given and the building society may have difficulty in obtaining possession when the fraudster defaults on the mortgage payments.

A copy of the standard building society conditions relating to letting appears as document number 264, as does the fraudster's response to enquiries in the example on page 226. It is a pity that the building society did not check the address given, which in the originals from which this example is taken was the property which was charged to the society as security. This elementary check would have revealed that the fraudster had two transactions on stream at once.

Standard local authority tenancy documents appear at 267–268. Many fraudsters are not even prepared to pay the cost of managing property to a managing estate agent.

Many fraudsters very often use their solicitor's offices as a care-of address, particularly if the scam is close to collapse and arrears are beginning to accrue (see p 234, which is a standard letter used by many building societies). Building societies do check the position regarding properties, particularly if they are given a care-of address, as can be seen from the letter on page 235. The solution in this letter is probably a sensible one! Some solicitors do attempt to flannel the building society with spurious explanations as to why a sale of the property where there are arrears has been delayed. This alone may suggest that the sale will not be a genuinely arm's-length transaction, but simply a refinancing exercise.

Odd instructions

A telephone attendant's note like that of June 15, on page 238 should inspire an enquiry as to why a client is purchasing two flats in the same block, as should the letter at page 239. If this correspondence appears with the ledger card entry a transfer of a substantial sum from another property unrelated to the particular client. This should also provoke enquiry. It is sometimes genuinely the case that there are a number of abortive attempts to purchase the same property, or to purchase several properties, but there is a point where this becomes indicative of fraud and the investigator should cross-check other relevant ledger cards and files. The correspondence at pages 237–248 suggests that not only is the fraudster undertaking a commercial transaction in acquiring an item in a property portfolio, but moreover the solicitor is well aware of the situation. Sometimes the building society also will realise what is going on.

Acting for both seller and buyer

Page 249 of the specimen documents shows file extracts where the solicitor has acted for both the seller and buyer; again these are composites. Chapter 24 of the *Guide to Professional Conduct of Solicitors* principle 24.01 "Acting for Seller and Buyer", reads as follows:

"Principle (1) Without prejudice to the general principle of professional conduct that a solicitor should not accept instructions to act for two or more clients at once where there is a conflict of interests between the interests of those clients, a solicitor or two or more solicitors practising in partnership or in association shall not act for both seller and buyer on a transfer of land for value at arm's length, or for both lessor and lessee or the grant of a lease at arm's length, or for both lender and borrower in a private mortgage at arm's length.

(2) Provided no conflict of interest appears, and provided the seller or lessor is not a builder or developer selling or leasing as such, and provided the solicitor or any solicitor practising in partnership or association with that solicitor is not instructed to negotiate the sale of the property concerned, the rules set out in paragraph (1) of this rule shall not apply if:

(a) The parties are associated companies; or
(b) The parties are related by blood, adoption or marriage; or
(c) Both parties are established clients (which expression shall include persons related by blood, adoption or marriage to established clients); or
(d) On the transfer of land, the consideration is less than £5000; or
(e) There is no other solicitor or other qualified conveyance in the vicinity whom either party can reasonably be expected to consult; or
(f) Two associated firms or two offices of the same firm are respectively acting for the parties, provided that;

(1) The respective firms or offices are from different localities and
(2) Neither party was referred to the firm or office acting for him or her from an associated firm or from another office of the same firm; and
(3) The transaction is dealt with and supervised by a different solicitor in regular attendance at each firm or office.

The commentary to the principle goes on to say that the rule is mandatory, and if a particular transaction either falls outside the rule or is not covered by one of the exceptions to it, failure to observe the principle raises an issue of conduct. In particular, the exceptions do not apply where there is a conflict of interest (principles 15.01 and 15.02). If a conflict arises during the course of the transaction falling within part of an exception the solicitor must comply with principle 15.03 and cease to act for both parties unless he can do so without embarrassment. A solicitor may only continue to represent one of the clients in this situation if he is not in possession of confidential knowledge concerning the other. Even in such a case, consent should be obtained from the other client through his or her solicitors and the solicitor should proceed in the absence of such consent only if there is no good cause for refusal. The test of whether a person is "an established client" is an objective one, namely whether a reasonable and fair-minded solicitor would regard that person as an existing client. "Existing client" is not the same as an established client so that if the seller instructs the solicitor for the first time and it is subsequently discovered that the purchaser is an established client, the solicitor cannot act for both parties. The fact that a transaction is at market value does not necessarily mean it is at arm's length for the purpose of this rule. The letter on page 276 seeks instructions from someone who has no connection with the two ladies concerned and is in fact their vendor. The memo dated 15 March 1991, is not sufficient, since all of the transactions are being channelled through one office which has only one solicitor, the sole practitioner, to avoid a conduct issue. The documents at pages 249 *et seq* illustrate a transaction where a transfer is made from husband and wife to husband and wife using her maiden name and one only of her first names, as can be seen from the first page of the contract for sale. At no stage is the lender notified of what is going on. The transfer is duly registered and completion takes place with all the usual formalities. In the circumstances the solicitor is well aware that this is a fraud. The letter of 13 October 1990, last paragraph, is particularly silly.

Further examples appear at pages 256–257. Of course, a really accomplished fraudster would have included an attendance note or two which would have brought the matter squarely within one of the exceptions to the guiding principles.

Individual specimen documents have *aide-mémoire* notes in italics.

CHAPTER 5

The Practitioner's Viewpoint

Solicitors' conduct

The latest edition of the *Guide to the Professional Conduct Of Solicitors* was published by the Council of the Law Society in 1993. It sets out the professional standards which solicitors are expected to observe. Whilst part of the book is given over to the actual Rules of Conduct, most of it consists of guidance as to professional conduct which is not actually codified.

A former secretary of the Law Society, Sir Thomas Lund CBE, said:

"If I had to advise very briefly the young solicitor on the guiding principles of conduct when he comes into the profession, I think I should say to him that it is clear that only the highest conduct is consistent with membership of this profession of ours. Your client's interests are paramount—that seems to be clear—except that you should never do, or agree to do, anything dishonest or dishonourable, even in a client's interest, or even under pressure from your best and most valuable client: you had better lose him. Where you may be prevented by the rules affecting your client's privilege from disclosing something dishonourable which you clearly ought to disclose, you should refuse to take any personal part in anything which you yourself think is dishonourable; you should cease to act for that client even if he presses you to go on."

Much of the *Guide* relates to solicitors in private practice. Practice Rule 1 sets out the following principle:

"A solicitor shall not do anything in the course of practising as a solicitor or permit another person to do anything on his or her behalf, which compromises or impairs or is likely to compromise or impair any of the following:

(a) The solicitor's independence or integrity;
(b) A person's freedom to instruct a solicitor of his or her own choice;
(c) The solicitor's duty to act in the best interests of the client;
(d) The good repute of the solicitor or of the solicitor's profession;
(e) The solicitor's proper standard of work;
(f) The solicitor's duty to the court."

A solicitor must do his best for a client in the way he thinks is best for his client and use his utmost skill on his behalf, while acting with complete fairness. This involves complete honesty and frankness towards the client, both in the advice given and/or the solicitor's dealings with the client.

Fraud, dishonesty, failure to apply money received from the client for the specified purpose for which it has been paid, making untrue representations to the client or concealing material facts from him with a dishonest or improper motive cannot ever be consistent with the obligations which a solicitor owes his clients.

Conflicts of interest

A solicitor's duty may become more difficult where he acts for two clients and conflict arises between the interests of both those clients. Chapter 12 of the *Guide* deals with the retainer by the client. Conflict of interest is dealt with at 12.06 and the principle reads as follows:

> "A solicitor must not act, or must decline to act further where there is a conflict of interest between:
>
> (a) The solicitor and the client or prospective client;
> (b) The solicitor's firm and the client or prospective client;
> (c) Two existing clients; or
> (d) An existing client or former client and a prospective client."

This principle is clear. Whenever it becomes apparent that there is a potential conflict of interest a solicitor must consider whether he or she could continue to act or act at all. Disclosure of the conflicting interest of the client or potential client does not prevent conflict of interest even when the client consents. Chapter 15 of the *Guide* deals with conflict of interests in general. The principle stated at 15.01 is as follows:

> "A solicitor or firm of solicitors should not accept instructions to act for two or more clients where there is a conflict or significant risk of a conflict between the interests between those clients."

The commentary at 15.03 states that if a solicitor has already accepted instructions from two clients in a matter or related matters and a conflict subsequently arises between the interests of those clients the solicitor must cease to act for both clients unless he or she can without embarrassment and with propriety continue to represent one client with the other's consent.

Principle 15.04 reads as follows:

> "A solicitor must not act for both seller and buyer on a transfer of land or of interest in land or for a lender and borrower in a private mortgage unless he or she is able to do so in compliance with Rule Six, the Solicitors' Practice Rules 1990."

See above at page 8 and see also Annex 1A and Principle 20.01 of the *Guide*. Client confidentiality is dealt with in Chapter 16 of the *Guide*.

There is of course nothing obscure about these principles. They should be well understood by all practising solicitors. A solicitor is an officer of the court and advises his clients on the law. He should therefore be even more aware than most people of the possible danger of being perceived to be acting improperly. A solicitor should always be conscious of the fact that he may have to account for his actions in the future. If a matter is one which might give rise to criticism of the solicitor at a later date, whether from a professional, conduct or criminal point of view, he must take steps to protect himself. This protection is best done by obtaining written instructions from his client. It should be second nature for the solicitor to protect his reputation by making certain that anything he considers as untoward, or any strange or unusual instruction from the client, is confirmed in writing and detailed notes are taken of the advice given to the client and that advice is confirmed in writing. The necessity to make sure that his reputation is protected is particularly important for a solicitor who is acting for both parties in a conveyancing transaction.

As may be seen above, the Law Society generally prohibits a solicitor from acting for both vendor and purchaser; exceptions to this rule are set out above. In circumstances where a solicitor is acting for both parties, it may be that the solicitor has been instructed to do something detrimental, or that he becomes aware of something about his client which is detrimental to his other client. Under such circumstances the solicitor has to reconcile the professional principles that he has a duty to protect his client and is under an obligation to keep his client's affairs confidential, with the potential conflict of interest. In such circumstances it is clearly unacceptable for a solicitor to report to one client what the other client is doing, or what he thinks he is doing to that client's detriment. If it proves impossible to dissuade the offending client from an intended course of action, he should immediately withdraw from any transaction. Advice can always be obtained from the Law Society (see Chap 12).

Conveyancing and mortgages

Where a solicitor engages regularly in conveyancing work it is inconceivable that he should not understand the general operation of a mortgage advance. Whenever a solicitor is instructed by a building society it is common for the society to send a booklet or other document in which is explained the requirements of acting for the society in some detail. Solicitors are busy professionals and they do not always read through the full instructions every time. Although there are a number of variations between building societies, these tend to be in respect of fairly minor procedural points. For example, all building societies require advance moneys to be returned to them if the completion does not take place. There are variations between societies in respect of the timescale,which will vary typically between "immediately" and "seven days", but not as to whether or not the cheque should be returned. All solicitors should realise that under these circumstances they are obliged to return advanced moneys within a few days, from their experience of general practice.

Moneys advanced have to be secured by way of a mortgage on the property. No building society will make a mortgage advance without their loan being secured. Societies do not give permission for their funds to be used merely in anticipation of the loan being secured. Some building societies do now make unsecured loans, but these are not mortgages and are of comparatively small sums of money. These unsecured loans should not be confused with mortgage advances. The rates of interest are higher and the terms for repayment shorter.

Irregularities

On the question of conflicts of interest, it is unusual for a building society to do anything to the detriment of the borrower unless it is in connection with dealing with arrears of repayment/instalments. However, from time to time, there are borrowers whose intentions are not the same as those stated in the mortgage application form. On occasions it may be clear, either from their instructions, or from other information that is available, that they intend to do something of which the society would not approve. It is not a matter for the solicitor to make a judgement as to whether the society would make an advance if they were in full possession of the facts. If there is any doubt, the solicitor should notify the building society and let them make the decision. If a building society decides to allow an advance to proceed despite some irregularity in the application, then the solicitor should seek confirmation of this in writing, particularly if the matter is a material one. Exactly what is material is difficult to define comprehensively. For instance, if an applicant inadvertently states his age as 29 instead of 30, this may not be material as far as an ordinary repayment mortgage is concerned. However, if the purchaser states an intention not to live in the property but to put tenants in, then this would be very material because it might affect the building society's chance of realising the security. Those things which are likely to be material are facts which change the nature of the application, of the property or of the borrower's intentions towards the property.

In the extremely unlikely event that a building society would agree to the advance moneys being employed prior to completion, a solicitor would be expected to obtain confirmation of this in writing. It seems inconceivable that a building society would allow such a thing to happen, and it is for this reason that the solicitor should protect himself by obtaining written confirmation. In the specimen documents no such written confirmation occurs. None of the unusual instructions are confirmed in writing, particularly in cases where the solicitor was acting for both vendor and purchaser and their respective building societies.

Tenants

The question of tenants was mentioned above. This is an important matter as far as building societies are concerned. It is a fundamental principle in mortgage advances that the lender should be able to take possession of the mortgaged property in the event of the borrower falling into arrears. Therefore, it is important that the value of the property should be greater than the amount owing on the advance, so far as this is practical. Tenants of residential property enjoy a high degree of protection under the law and it is not possible to remove someone from their home without an order of the court. In certain cases, removal of a tenant may be difficult or nearly impossible. The principal market for residential properties is among people who wish to own their own property, and consequently the presence of a sitting tenant can have a serious effect on the value of the property. If a building society finds itself in possession of a property which has a tenant, it may be unable to recover the sum loaned out of the sale proceeds.

The solicitor's duty to the building society in respect of tenants is therefore quite clear up to the time of completion. If the borrower says, "I wish to purchase the property and put a tenant in, but I do not want the building society to know", there is an obvious conflict of interest if the solicitor is also acting for the building society. Similarly, if he says, "The property I am buying—can you draw up a tenancy agreement?", there is again a conflict of interest if the building society is not aware that this is the client's intention. The problem also arises where a purchase has been completed and the building society has ceased to be a client. At any stage the solicitor should advise his client to contact the building society and seek their permission. It would not be proper to assist the purchaser to arrange anything to do with the tenancy immediately after completion but it becomes more difficult to give clear advice on this matter if time progresses. However, the solicitor should not act naively. If the solicitor was aware of the fact that the purchaser had put tenants in every property he has purchased, then he should realise that it is likely to happen again. Consequently he should exercise his duty of care towards any new building society client in the light of this information prior to completion.

Building societies do sometimes make advances on properties which are to be let, and do sometimes agree to tenants being allowed into properties over which they have a normal residential mortgage. However, in these circumstances the society has made the decision itself and has been given the opportunity of weighing up all the circumstances before making that decision. It is improper for the solicitor to make a decision which should be made by his client, *i.e.* the building society.

Moneys held by the solicitor

Any moneys held by a solicitor for a client have to be placed in a client account. Whilst this account may be a single account as far as the solicitor's bankers are concerned, it is necessary for the solicitor to keep detailed records of the sums received and paid on behalf of each client. The traditional method of doing this is to maintain a separate ledger card for each client. Although individual systems may vary, particularly where computers are used, the principles are the same, namely that it should be possible to see what money is held on behalf of each client.

Although it is correct practice to maintain a separate account for each client, there are possible exceptions. Solicitors hold building society advance moneys for such a short time that it is a common practice to place the money in client accounts for the account of the purchaser until completion. There may be circumstances where a solicitor is legitimately acting for the purchaser and vendor and the purchase moneys may come from a third client. If completion was to occur simultaneously with the arrival of the funds it would be improper to pay the money into the vendor's account immediately. Paying the money into the vendor's account and then not completing for several weeks would obviously be wrong. This situation would be even worse if the money was employed by the solicitor on behalf of the vendor or for any other reason. The correct method of dealing with such cases would be to transfer the money from the purchaser's account to the vendor's on completion.

Where a solicitor is acting for two parties to a contract it may be necessary to check that the consideration on completion has changed hands. If a separate ledger is maintained for each client it should be possible to see when the transfer of funds took place. If the solicitor keeps only one ledger card for both clients, then at best it may prove difficult to show when the consideration changed hands and there would probably be a breach of the solicitors' accounts rules. In the context of keeping ledger cards, a solicitor has no authority to employ the building society's advance cheque without properly completing the purchase. By placing the money in the vendor's account, or in an account which may be the vendor's, in advance of completion, he is wrongly attributing ownership to the vendor. Quite obviously if the building society sends a cheque to the solicitor and the solicitor passes on money to his client in advance of completion, he has acted improperly. The situation may not be as simple as that, however. The solicitor may be involved in other business on behalf of his client and the money instead of going to the client may go to some other person on his client's behalf. It is logical in these circumstances to assume that the money has been misused in just the same way as if it had been sent directly to the client.

The need for caution

The green card has been discussed in some detail above. I should emphasise that it is possible that a specific point mentioned in the green card or in this book may be found in an innocent transaction. Failure to pay regard to the warnings may not be deliberate, but due to a mistake or inexperience. Neither lack of caution nor indeed a mistake or inexperience are evidence of a solicitor's participation in a criminal conspiracy. Anyone can make a mistake once, but repeated mistakes, or turning a blind eye, must give rise to a suspicion of co-operation with a dishonest client. Likewise, the failure to supervise and guide your staff is not an attractive defence.

It is important that solicitors remain alert to what is really going on around them. A line has to be drawn between thoughtless compliance with the vendor's or purchaser's instructions or the suggestions of the other conspirators' solicitors, and being unjustly accused of comparable participation in fraud. Because every property fraud requires a solicitor, then every solicitor involved may become a suspect. We market ourselves on the basis of our professional skills and integrity so inevitably we allow ourselves to be open to criticism where there has been any shortcoming in these qualities. Presumptions of innocence and suspicion of complicity might appropriately be drawn by comparing what a solicitor of average competence, experience and honesty would do or would not do in a particular set of circumstances with what actually happened. Because of the widespread knowledge in the profession of mortgage fraud which has been committed, the average level of prudence might be expected to rise. Many building societies in their instructions are now making it quite clear what precautions they require.

One of the greatest dangers to the profession is complacency. Mortgage fraud can happen anywhere. A member of staff may fail to understand the implications of an adjustment in the purchase price, or may simply fail to respond adequately to unusual features and question what they really mean. It is unpleasant to be under suspicion, it is even more unpleasant to have your files taken and your partners and staff questioned; it is still worse to incur the publicity of the court hearing, even if the case is dismissed. Prudent partners will wish to consider what they might be looking for in dealing with the introducer, or the client with other solicitors and with staff. Care should be taken on receipt of the original letters. I suggest that the first question one should consider is why the firm was instructed "out of the blue", and what the status and involvement of the introducer was. When dealing with a company a company search should be considered so that it could be established that there is no link between the shareholders or officers and the purchaser. You may also learn something from a company search about the introducer and perhaps also the vendor.

Indications of fraud

When receiving letters from a client in which they state that the deposit has already been paid to the vendor personally, it should be remembered that this is a common feature where fraud has taken place and it should always be questioned. You should insist on a deposit being placed with the vendor's solicitor as stakeholder. If the transaction is a scam, then that may immediately become apparent, especially if the purchaser clearly does not wish to meet his own solicitor. Solicitors should insist on meeting every client at least once. This is essential to protect yourself, and is the only way to establish a proper professional relationship. Building societies now require solicitors they instruct to satisfy themselves as to the identity of the client: it is difficult to see how this duty can be discharged except by personal meetings. Those solicitors who advertise that no personal attendances are required must be leaving themselves open to being utilised by a fraudster. The failure to establish the client's identity will give material for cross-examination at a criminal trial.

What happens if the fraudster has previously instructed another firm? It would be prudent to wonder why they are no longer acting, and that should always be a cause of enquiry. Unfortunately there are firms who smell a rat, refuse to act and just leave another less alert firm to fall into the trap. Where a vendor's solicitors tell you that their client has received a deposit of £X,000 and makes no further comment they may very well be turning a blind eye to the unusual a little too easily.

Suppose you learn that a house has more than one charge secured on it? Has the vendor mortgaged it to several lenders simultaneously? Will there be enough money at completion to discharge all the loans? Can you safely accept the vendor's solicitor's undertaking?

Suppose that a client, before contracts have been exchanged, announces that he has resold the property at a substantially higher figure. He wants all the transactions completed simultaneously. This illustrates several points that consistently recur in fraud cases. The sole purchaser is of course someone known to the seller. The property has been resold at a substantial profit, for which no explanation has been provided. There may well be another unusual arrangement about the deposit, which of course has in fact never been paid. It is not unusual when examining the documents in these cases to find that all signatories on the contracts, the transfer and the mortgage are identical. Some people do have very distinctive signatures. It is also not unusual for mortgage fraudsters to become careless. A sub-purchaser may never occupy the property. Conversion of houses into flats should also be watched.

What about allowances of the purchase price? These usually mean that the price actually paid is less than that shown on the contract on the transfers and on the building society's offer of advance. These allowances have been very common and are a cause of great concern to mortgage lenders, who have found that when they have repossessed the property it is worth a great deal less than what they believed to be the selling price. It is your duty when acting for a buyer and lender to report to the lender any arrangement between a buyer and seller which results in the price that is actually paid being less than the contract price. If your client will not permit you to report this to the lender then of course you should cease to act altogether. In fact the lender should decide whether the arrangement affects the decision to proceed with the loan. If acting for the buyer alone you must avoid being involved in any schemes which deceives a lender. Usually the allowance of the purchase type of fraud involves some degree of co-operation between the vendor and purchaser, although it is possible that the vendor does not understand what the arrangement is. Nevertheless he signs the contract, and must bear responsibility, as must the solicitors for both parties. Of course we are all used to attributing £200 or £300 to carpets and curtains where they are included if this brings the price of the house below the stamp duty limit. However, that practice may have led some solicitors to agreeing much larger allowances for alleged lack of repair, without giving the matter proper thought. It would be better now to refrain from adjusting purchase prices at all, even if the client then has to pay the stamp duty involved; it would certainly be a safer practice.

Due precautions

The way to prevent fraud is twofold. First make everyone in the office who is working on conveyancing fully and continually aware that the lender is an individual client, to whom obligations are owed which are quite separate from those due to the purchaser. It is a recurrent feature of mortgage fraud trials that the solicitors involved say that they had no concept of the nature of the obligations involved. Second, all conveyancing staff should know and understand the green form, the Law Society's guidance on allowances, and the relevant principles in the *Guides to Professional Conduct*.

It is important to know the client, whether vendor or purchaser; if in any doubt, a check with the voters' register may prove rewarding. You should keep a record showing what steps you have taken to identifying the new client and check the transactions are genuine.

Know the properties as best you can. If it is outside your local area, does it exist? Always ask for the agents particulars, with a photograph. At least, you then know it exists and it gives you some idea of the likely price range.

Consider the offer of the advance. Does it come from a building society branch outside the area of the property or the borrower's home or place of business? If so, why? Experience shows that this may indicate a dishonest manager conspiring with other criminals.

If the price for the house differs from the initial instructions, make sure that you know why. There must be a satisfactory explanation in a full note on your file. Consider your duties to the lenders at this point—you may have a purchaser who is trying out various lenders at different prices to see how big a mortgage he can get, with a view to the allowance fraud.

Do not accept any suggestion for allowances to be set off against the contract price. The full contract price must be truly paid. Be equally wary of proportioning the price, particularly if the sum is large and is alleged to be paid personally at completion.

Do not stand for any nonsense about the deposit. If it is alleged to have been paid to a party personally, insist that it be placed with a solicitor. Except in the case of a first-time buyer with a 95% mortgage, ask for a deposit of 10%. If you do not and there is subsequently an allegation that the transaction was fraudulent, you may have difficulties under cross-examination. It is a feature of the allowances given against price type of fraud that where a deposit is actually paid, it will often have been very small.

Insist that all documents leaving the office are fully and accurately completed in all respects. It is still common to find at exchange of contracts that the vendor's contract coming in has the date of completion omitted, and often figures at the foot of the front page are not correctly completed. That is slack practice but is also a feature found in fraud cases and it gives embarrassing cross-examination material to counsel.

Watch out for sub-sales. If your client is selling on, make sure you understand why. If he is a property dealer he could have picked up a bargain which he is selling on to make a quick profit, though that is not common in a recession. More likely than not your client is a rogue, you are now noticing something is up and had better take rapid steps to protect yourself and your clients, the lenders.

Be careful of simultaneous exchange and completion. There may be a good reason, but it is one of the characteristics of fraud and you will need to be sure that you are not being unwittingly involved in wrongdoing.

You must supervise the work of your staff, depending on their experience and qualifications. Insist that reports from title to lender are signed by a partner. That gives an opportunity of checking that there is nothing untoward, without appearing to be spying.

Your accounts department must report to you any unusual instructions for payments out of the purchase money. They should also tell you if several current transactions are going through for any particular client, because that could be an indication of the problems as well. The Law Society's Guidance on Mortgage Fraud appears at page 471 of the *Guide to the Professional Conduct of Solicitors.*

CHAPTER 6

The Law Society

The role of the Law Society

The Law Society's Property and Commercial Services Strategy was set out at the conference of the Council of Mortgage Lenders on 29 October 1992. It was as follows:

(a) Long term strategic planning on behalf of the profession;
(b) Advice for firms wanting to improve their performance and expand their main areas of practice:
(c) Promotion of the services of the profession; (*i.e.* Transaction and Will Power)
(d) Improving the procedures used in property transactions; (*i.e.* the National Conveyancing Protocol and standard business leases)
(e) Piloting experimental business matters particularly with information technology;
(f) Focusing on areas of law needing reform;
(g) Reducing the causes of incompetence and the opportunity for dishonesty;
(h) Monitoring government proposals affecting the profession;
(i) Identifying new areas of work;
(j) Ensuring practice rules protect clients, but also enable fair competition for solicitors;
(k) Collation and provision of statistical information;
(l) Introduction of measures to improve standards of work.

There is one important role which is not listed, however: that of acting to represent the interests of members, and it is in this capacity that the Law Society sometimes writes to mortgage lenders questioning their treatment of individual firms. Often complaints which the Law Society pursues go beyond this role and relate to monitoring and improving practice. It appears that most complaints relate to matters which are inhibiting efficient practice, such as the late arrival of advance cheques or unwarranted delay in receipt of form 53 from the lender. Such complaints will always be taken seriously.

The Law Society and mortgage fraud

The Law Society has consulted with the Council of Mortgage Lenders on work which its subcommittee on mortgage fraud has undertaken on standard instructions to solicitors relating to measures which are proposed to inhibit and detect fraud. The Society would like these instructions to be standard.

In-house solicitors employed by various lenders are of course Law Society members and are equally entitled to ask for guidance and support. The Law Society welcomes their input on the subject of fraud and any consultation on any changes in instructions which are to be issued to panel solicitors.

In recent articles in the *Gazette* or the *Legal Executive*, the Society has gone to great lengths to emphasise to members and legal executives that the lender is as much a client as the borrower sitting in front of him. It is, however, sometimes difficult for the solicitor to remember the lender is a client because of course the lender is not the one who is paying the solicitor's fee. The other side of the coin is that the lender client must treat the solicitor as a professional, and should not write in terms which do not acknowledge this.

It is easy for solicitors to assume that they are the first and last defence against fraud and that nobody else is taking responsible action to prevent fraud. What help does the Law Society give to members?

Representation

Solicitors in private practice are given support, which takes the form of representation to lenders if instructions to solicitors or the panel criteria for membership appear to be at variance with sensible or normal practice.

Ethical guidance

The Law Society gives advice on how to interpret the rules of professional conduct. In the Ethics Department of the Professional Standards Directorate there is a team of staff employed on telephone and written enquiries. If any solicitor suspects he has a conflict of interest or a case of suspected mortgage fraud he can contact this unit and receive instant guidance. A broadsheet has been prepared by the Professional Ethics Department which is distributed at local Law Society seminars on mortgage fraud.

Practice and procedure

The Legal Practice Directorate of the Law Society has an information office which can give guidance on procedures and which will send enquirers published information on the relevant subject. If there is a particularly difficult or practical problem then the telephone enquiry will be referred to the team, who will endeavour to provide a practical solution to the problem. Enquiries relating to potential frauds have increased considerably. This rise in the number of calls is comforting, as it shows that the profession is increasingly on the look-out for fraud.

The Solicitors Complaints Bureau also gives guidance to Law Society members and they have introduced a "Red Alert" telephone service, which enables lenders, local authorities and solicitors to put the Solicitors Complaints Bureau on notice that a particular firm is undertaking practices which appear on the face of it to require further investigation.

Communications

The *Gazette*, which is the Law Society's way of communicating with the profession, carries articles and guidance on practice procedure and has featured several articles on mortgage fraud. All of the contributions have been from the Law Society's staff, its committee members or members of the profession. There have also been a number of seminars organised by the Council of Mortgage Lenders and by local law societies. Mortgage fraud is also frequently a topic in commercially run fraud seminars.

The mortgage fraud working party

The Society has given members guidance on PACE orders and what to do when a police officer arrives at their offices and demands files. Although the onus is on the prosecution to prove fraud, in the experience of barristers and solicitors defending solicitors charged with fraud it is commonly assumed that the solicitor was actively involved in the fraud and it is virtually impossible to prove the solicitor's innocence merely by showing that he stood to gain nothing financially and that he has been innocently duped because he had not been sufficiently cautious. Specifically in relation to mortgage fraud a working party has been set up, chaired by Karen Aldred. This working party looked at ways in which mortgage frauds were perpetrated and practical measures which could be introduced to inhibit such frauds. One of the first things that the Society did was to establish the size of the problem of solicitor fraud. In 1991 twenty-nine cases were reported and in 1992 about the same number. The figures produced by the Solicitors' Indemnity Fraud also show that the figure is low. In recent years the size of frauds perpetrated by borrowers has increased. It is perhaps the case that in the past, when the property market was more buoyant, frauds were less likely to be detected.

The working party's work first came to wider notice in the spring of 1991, when the green card was issued. The green card is reproduced in the *Guide to Professional Conduct* and in the Law Society's *Conveyancing Handbook*. Further copies may be obtained from the Law Society, free of charge.

As part of the project on mortgage fraud the committee have also been looking at claims on the Compensation Fund and the Solicitors' Indemnity Fund to establish which of those were the subject of intentional rather than "innocent" fraud, and whether these cases, or those falling into the grey area between, could have been avoided by the use of different procedures. There has been much correspondence in the *Gazette's* correspondence columns about this. In addition, the committee has found that a large number of claims on the Solicitors' Indemnity Fund revolve around the use of undertakings which are either not specific or are badly drafted. A pink card has been produced giving guidance to solicitors on what undertakings should or should not be given in conveyancing instructions.

CHAPTER 7

The Lender

The lender's role in fighting mortgage fraud

The lender and the lender's staff have an important role to play in the prevention, discovery and recovery of mortgage fraud. Many lenders have in-house investigation and fraud departments. At the Council of Mortgage Lenders' mortgage fraud seminar on 29 October 1992, Peter Lilley, then Head of the Special Investigations Department at the Nationwide Building Society, threw down the following challenge:

> "I defy anybody in this room to categorically state that the financial institutions that they represent do not suffer from mortgage fraud".

He went on to say:

> "Fraud is carried out against *every* financial institution without prejudice. However, it must be said that the weaker the controls and procedures on acceptance and underwriting of mortgage business, the stronger the possibility of fraud."

The lending any financial institution carries out can be roughly divided into three categories: good lending, poor lending and fraud. Poor lending may occur because a lender has decided that the only way to maintain market share is actually to take up on lending which under other circumstances would be considered a poor risk. Poor lending also comes from badly trained, malicious or fraudulent employees subverting procedures and controls. The bulk of mortgage fraud, however, should not be confused with poor lending practice. Branch staff have a vital role in the discovery and prevention of mortgage fraud. Since an ounce of prevention is worth a pound of cure, a lender must be proactive, not reactive, and there must be a central point within the organisation for fraud prevention, detection and investigation.

Systems

All of the information that fraudsters use is collected by the lenders routinely. This includes false or genuine references, names and addresses, financial details, solicitors used and so on. This information can be analysed by the use of databases which can show previous fraudsters coming back for a second or third go, multiple applications where details such as phone numbers, addresses, accountants and work references are similar, together with inconsistencies in individual applications. A system can be developed to track staff members approving loans, solicitors involved and valuers, to highlight inconsistencies. (You may find it helpful to review the documents at pp 172–191 and at p 286 *et seq*.)

Validation

Validation means spotting the unusual, details that do not add up—not accepting anything at face value. In the case of a fraudulent mortgage application the areas which need to be examined are:

- the applicant's identity: is this a nominee? Is a maiden name used?;
- references which are provided or which the lender requests (see pp 172–191);
- the valuation report of the valuer (and whether the valuer is qualified);
- the applicant's home and work addresses—have they been used before? Do they exist?
- employers: are they in the telephone directory, in Yellow Pages?;
- estate agents selling the property: are they professionally qualified?;
- bank or accountants providing the reference: is the reference useful? (see p 172);
- the solicitors who are being used;
- the introducer who introduced the case: what is his business like? Is he a member of a profession? Is he regulated by a Financial Services Act Regulator?

Most of these things can be checked from a desk:

- by utilising such tools as the BT on-line telephone directory and enquiry system;
- by telephoning Companies House or requesting company searches;
- by getting in touch with professional bodies and associations to check that the valuer is actually professionally qualified, or that the solicitor is a solicitor;
- by checking with the police;
- credit searches, which should give evidence of the existence of the borrower at the stated address;
- information sharing.

It is important to report dubious practices to the police and professional bodies.

Discovery of fraud

What can be done if the mortgage application has not been prevented from getting through? There are various tools which can be used, and a variety of ways in which a fraud may be detected:

- arrears can be monitored;
- the local police may be able to help;
- staff in branches or mortgage processing centres, or underwriting teams who have been trained in fraud prevention and fraud identification, may be able to help;
- information may be received from informants;
- technology may be used to analyse transactions to identify frauds.

Recovery of property

Fraud recovery falls into two categories:

1. civil actions (see next chapter) to recover the mortgage debt, arrears or the property;
2. criminal proceedings following a police investigation. It has to be said that compensation orders in favour of building societies are uncommon;
3. claims on any insurance which the lender may have.

CHAPTER 8

Mortgage Fraud – Civil Litigation Fall-out

Lawyers provide an all-round service, so far as mortgage fraud is concerned. Some prosecute and some defend in the criminal cases which result. Others pursue and resist the civil claims which arise from it, while a third group supplies work for the other two by carrying out mortgage fraud or failing to prevent it. This chapter deals with the civil claims to which mortgage fraud gives rise, and aims to consider:

1. the purpose and place of civil litigation in the context of mortgage fraud;
2. the emergency remedies available to lenders attempting to recover funds;
3. some of the factors which have to be taken into account when deciding which civil remedies to pursue following a fraud;
4. the different types of action which can be taken and what they can achieve;
5. steps which lenders can take to maximise recovery.

The purpose and place of civil litigation

The civil courts are not a substitute for trial by battle. The vital point to remember about civil litigation resulting from mortgage fraud is that its purpose is the recovery of money. This may sometimes involve establishing that someone has acted dishonestly, but this is not by any means necessary and is most certainly not the main object of a civil claim. Civil litigation is an expensive process in terms of both legal costs and management time, and unless its true function is kept firmly in mind, there is a real risk of substantial costs and a great deal of management time being spent to no practical benefit. Mortgage frauds are complex. While lawyers may be tempted to try to pursue a line of enquiry to the bitter end, regardless of recovery prospects, lenders will be well advised to take a strictly commercial view of post-fraud litigation, as with any other area of their business. Solicitors conducting claims should regularly ask themselves whether, in the event of the action being successful, the costs of all the enquiries they are pursuing are likely to be recoverable from the defendant as having been reasonably incurred for the purpose of the proceedings. A lender client will not continue to employ a solicitor whose costs and disbursements are excessive.

Emergency remedies

Speed is of the essence in using emergency remedies. It sometimes happens that a lender is alerted to a fraud very shortly after parting with the advance. The lender therefore has a chance of recovering the money before the fraudster can make off with it. It is a simple matter to issue proceedings claiming the return of an advance procured by fraud, but the issue of such proceedings does not itself achieve very much—the plaintiff is faced with the problem that unless something is done to safeguard the position, service of the proceedings upon the defendant is very likely to lead to the swift disappearance of both fraudster and the advance moneys. In situations such as this a plaintiff should also consider making an *ex parte* application for a Mareva injunction at the time of issue of proceedings.

Mareva injuctions

A Mareva order is an interlocutory injunction usually made until trial or further order, which restrains the defendant from removing his assets from the jurisdiction, or from disposing of or otherwise dealing with those assets within the jurisdiction, save of course for assets the value of which exceed the plaintiff's claim. For a practical guide to law and procedure in civil proceedings, in particular Mareva orders, see Stuart Sime, *A Practical Approach to Civil Procedure*.

This is an area where the case law is added to on a daily basis. The remedy is very popular in intellectual property disputes. Similar orders are granted as part of confiscation proceedings.

A Mareva injunction will be granted by the court if it appears from the evidence produced by the plaintiff that the plaintiff is likely to recover judgment against the defendant, and that there is reason to believe both that the defendant has assets within the jurisdiction and that, unless restrained, he will conceal or dissipate the assets abroad. Typically such an injunction takes the form of an order forbidding the defendant from dealing with any of his assets within the jurisdiction, in so far as those assets exceed the stated figure representing the amount of the claim plus an allowance for the plaintiff's legal costs. In recognition of the fact that even fraudsters have to live and are entitled to legal representation, the order will also name a figure for the defendant's committed legal expenses which will include an allowance for legal costs of the proceedings. In fraud cases the courts are very ready to infer that a defendant will seek to conceal or export his assets, and there is seldom any difficulty about obtaining a Mareva injunction at the time of issue of the writ.

It is a punishable contempt of court for a third party knowingly to assist a defendant to breach the terms of an injunction; once obtained, therefore, the injunction should not simply be served on the defendant but further copies should be forthwith supplied to any third party who is thought to hold any of his assets—for example, his bank, building society or solicitors. Notice of the injunction should also be given to anyone it is thought might possibly be involved in dealings with his property—for instance a possible purchaser of his house, or his solicitors.

Giving clear notice of the grant of the Mareva injunction to third parties of the type referred to above is of considerable importance in fraud cases, as it is unlikely that a person who has already obtained money by fraud will baulk at breaching an injunction in an effort to hold on to it. In reality, therefore, the effectiveness of the Mareva injunction often depends not on the defendant's innate respect for the law, but upon the determination of third parties not to fall foul of the courts. For this reason it is suggested that when giving notice of the injunction to third parties they should be supplied with the full copy of the order and with a solicitor's letter giving full details laying out the effects of the injunction and giving clear warning of the consequences of assisting the defendant to breach it. This latter may have to be settled by counsel. Consideration should also be given to having the documents handed personally to third parties instead of simply sending them by post, as this minimises the chances of any subsequent argument as to whether proper notice was served. When giving notice to institutions such as banks or building societies the documents should always be served at any branch at which the defendant is thought to hold an account, as well as at the head office. Working out which third parties should be sued may require a diligent reconstruction of files by lenders' staff.

In recognition of the fact that many defendants cannot be relied upon to comply with the terms of a Mareva injunction, the courts are prepared when granting the main injunction to make ancillary orders directing the defendant to swear an affidavit and to disclose the documents giving details of his assets within the jurisdiction so that the plaintiff can give notice of the injunction to any appropriate third parties. Failure by the defendant to comply with an ancillary disclosure order constitutes a contempt of court for which he can be imprisoned. Ancillary orders are very useful, but they have their limits:

- except in exceptional cases the disclosure order is limited to the defendant's assets within the jurisdiction, it will not cover off-shore companies;

- it has been made clear in several cases, most recently in the judgment in *AT&T Istel Ltd and another* v *Tully* [1992] 2 All ER 28, that a defendant under civil action for fraud is under no compulsion to comply with the disclosure order, if to do so might infringe his privilege against self-incrimination.

A full explanation of the complexities of the rules relating to provision against self-incrimination is mercifully outside the scope of this book. For present purposes it is sufficient to say that whilst considerable inroads have been made into the rules against self-incrimination, principally section 31 of the Theft Act 1968 and section 72 of the Supreme Court Act 1981, the privilege can still be invoked by a defendant in civil proceedings who is at risk of a prosecution for conspiracy to defraud. As can readily be imagined, the privilege is regularly claimed by defendants in fraud actions in order to minimise the affect upon them of disclosure orders.

Despite enduring continuous attempts, the courts have not found a satisfactory way around the problem but a consultation paper has recently been published by the Lord Chancellor's Department which proposes that the privilege against self-incrimination should be withdrawn in civil proceedings and replaced by a form of secondary privilege which would prevent self-incrimination evidence given in civil proceedings being used against the person concerned in criminal proceedings. If, as seems likely, this proposal is adopted it will greatly enhance the efficiency of the Mareva.

It is not the function of this book to give a blow-by-blow account of court procedures relating to the obtaining of a Mareva injunction, but it is worth drawing attention to the following practical points which anyone who applies for such an order will need to bear in mind.

1. As a result of the County Court Remedies Regulations 1991, the county court no longer has jurisdiction to grant Mareva injunctions. All applications for such orders should therefore be made to the High Court.
2. Applications should always be made as swiftly as possible after the fraud has come to light. In cases of emergency the court will grant an injunction prior to the issue of the proceedings, and sometimes on the basis of a sworn affidavit or even simply following information supplied by a barrister as to the proposed contents of an affidavit.
3. As Mareva injunctions are usually granted without any notice being given, the plaintiff is under a duty to the court to make the full and frank disclosure of all relevant facts when applying for an order. Failure to do so can lead to the subsequent discharge of the injunction obtained. This duty involved differs from case to case but it would, for example, require a plaintiff to notify the court of any defence which he

is aware the defendant may seek to assert.

4. Any plaintiff seeking a Mareva injunction will have to give two undertakings to the court:
   i. to pay the defendant the damages which the court awards if it subsequently decides that the injunction should not have been granted and that the defendant has suffered loss as a result of it; and
   ii. to pay the reasonable costs and expenses incurred by any third party to whom notice of the injunction is given in ascertaining whether he has any assets subject to order in his possession and otherwise in complying with the order, and indemnify any such party against any loss, damage or liability suffered or incurred in complying with the order.

   In some cases a plaintiff will be required to provide security for such undertakings, but this is most unlikely if the plaintiff is a bank or building society of substance operating within the jurisdiction.

   When giving the undertakings the plaintiff should always remember that they can prove to be expensive, particularly if the effect of the injunction is to damage or destroy the defendant's business, or if the plaintiff serves notice of the injunction indiscriminately on all the banks and building societies in the country. The moral therefore is to seek Mareva relief only when the case against the defendant is a reasonably clear one, and then to give notice of the injunction only to those third parties who are reasonably suspected of having control of the defendant's assets.
5. In order to ensure that the injunction takes full effect as quickly as possible and that the expenses incurred by the third parties are kept to a minimum, the plaintiff should identify as precisely as possible all assets and accounts of the defendant of which he is aware. In the case of bank and building society accounts, the account numbers and the branches at which they are held should be given wherever possible.
6. It is for the plaintiff in the first instance to put forward a figure for the defendant's permitted weekly living and legal expenses. This figure should be a realistic one, taking into account the defendant's known lifestyle. If a figure is inserted in the order which the plaintiff should have known was unrealistic, the plaintiff is likely to be ordered to pay the costs of any application made by the defendant for an increase and if the court takes the view that a low figure has been made in order to bring pressure on the defendant the injunction could well be discharged.
7. Any Mareva order granted will almost certainly include a provision entitling any bank on which it is served to exercise any right of set-off which it may have in respect of overdraft facilities made available to

the defendant before the making of the order.

8. It should always be borne in mind that the Mareva injunction simply freezes assets pending judgment. It does not give the plaintiff any security for his claim, which could therefore be frustrated by the defendant's bankruptcy. If therefore, as is often the case, the defendant is being pursued by a number of creditors, it is vital that the plaintiff proceeds as quickly as possible with the action with a view of obtaining an enforcing judgment against the affairs and assets at the earliest possible moment.
9. It should never be forgotten that a Mareva injunction granted on the issue of the proceedings will automatically expire when the judgment is obtained. The court, however, has power to grant further injunctions to cover the period between giving judgment and the enforcement of it, and care should be taken to apply for a second injunction in appropriate cases.
10. Once a Mareva order has been granted the onus is on the plaintiff to proceed with the main action expeditiously.

Anton Piller injunctions

Although the Mareva injunction is at present the most effective remedy available to a plaintiff seeking to abort a fraud, a brief mention should be made of the Anton Piller injunction. Whilst this is a very rare order and at present seldom, if ever, available to victims of mortgage fraud, it may become useful to plaintiffs if the rules relating to privilege against self-incrimination are modified in the manner proposed by the consultation paper mentioned above. The Anton Piller injunction, which like the Mareva injunction is normally applied for *ex parte* and before the service of the proceedings on the defendant, was originally devised to deal with cases of copyright piracy. It takes the form of an injunction which restrains the defendant from disposing of the specified items or business records, and requires him to permit persons authorised by the plaintiff to have access to named premises for the purpose of searching out and removing items or records of the specified type. Clearly such an injunction could be a very great assistance to victims of multiple mortgage fraud who wish to know how extensive the defendant's fraud has been and who else was involved.

Unfortunately, in *Cate Access Floors Inc.* v *Boswell* [1990] 3 All ER 303 the court held that because the effect of an Anton Piller would be to end the defendant's privilege against self-incrimination, they are at present worthless. Such injunctions will not be granted in cases where the court considers that execution of the order might result in the uncovering of documents exposing the defendant to the risk of prosecution for conspiracy to defraud. In the circumstances, the remedy will not be discussed in detail here but those who pursue civil claims arising from mortgage fraud should keep an eye out for legislation implementing the current proposals.

Finally, on the subject of injunctions, it should be made clear that although most often used as an emergency remedy at the start of legal proceedings, Mareva and Anton Piller injunctions may be applied for at any stage of an action.

Selecting the remedy

When considering what legal proceedings should be brought following a mortgage fraud, the following matters require consideration:

- What has become of the advance moneys?;
- Whether the property which is to be the security (assuming it exists) is occupied, and if so by whom and on what basis. Proceedings can cause extreme hardship to innocent tenants;
- The likely value of the security, especially in recessionary times;
- Whether the security is the subject of a valid charge in favour of the lender, and thus the role of the lender's solicitor;
- Whether the borrower can be found and whether he is likely to be worth suing;
- Whether it is possible to identify those involved in the fraud, and whether they are worth suing;
- Whether the solicitor and valuer instructed by the lender acted honestly and competently and whether any financial reference for the borrower was supplied negligently.

Information on some of these points can usually be obtained fairly easily by making enquiries at the property and by instructing a valuer. An enquiry agent can often help upon matters such as the present whereabouts of the borrower and his financial situation. Consideration of the other topics, however, involves an enquiry into the history of the fraudulent transactions. Fortunately land transactions usually involve a number of people and generate a good deal of paperwork, with the result that helpful material can often be obtained from some or all of the following sources:

- the lender's file relating to the mortgage application;
- the contents of the deeds (if the deeds have been surrendered);
- the Land Registry which, if the information is required as part of the fraud investigation, is always willing to provide copies of relevant documents such as transfers and mortgage deeds and to supply details of the history of any relevant transaction, including information such

as the names of solicitors who acted for the parties. The Land Registry is now open for public searches;

- the valuer who inspected the property may be able to supply useful details such as the name of the person through whom he made arrangements to inspect the property and whether the property was occupied at the time of his visit. He may help with tenancy details;
- if the borrower was introduced through brokers, the brokers will sometimes supply information and copies of the paperwork;
- it is worth seeking information from any innocent party or parties involved in the transaction as such people are very often willing to assist by producing statements and by authorising their solicitors to produce their files for inspection. If the whereabouts of the innocent parties or the identity of their solicitors is not known, the Land Registry is usually able to supply details at least about the solicitors;
- the lender's solicitors;
- any tenants in occupation who may be able to help with details as to who collects their rent.

The lender's solicitors are, of course, in possession of a great deal of information concerning the transaction, but obtaining access to it can often be a problem. The difficulties stem from the fact that they will usually have acted for the borrower as well as the lender and prima facie are under a duty to the borrower to keep his affairs confidential unless lender or borrower permits disclosure. This prima facie duty of confidentiality, coupled on occasion with an understandable concern about their own position, sometimes prompts solicitors to refuse to supply lenders with any information or documents other than those which relate strictly to the completion of the mortgage. Lenders faced with such a refusal should not allow it to pass unchallenged if either there is already good evidence that fraud has occurred or if the solicitors concerned have not yet discharged their retainer by completing the registration of the charge at the Land Registry and surrendering the deeds. In the former case, the solicitor should be referred to subparagraph 1 of Principle 12.02 of the *Guide to Professional Conduct* and the judgment of Mr Justice Morritte in *Dubai Bank* v *Galadari* in April 1991. These make it clear the duty of confidence, and that legal professional privilege does not apply to communications between the client and his solicitor in furtherance of fraud or other crime. This is the case even if the solicitor was unaware of the client's criminal intention. If the solicitors have not yet discharged their retainer they should also be referred to principle 12.07 of the *Guide to Professional Conduct* which, subject to various irrelevant exceptions, states that a solicitor is under a duty to pass on to his client and use all information which is material to the client's business regardless of the source of the information. References should also be made to the judgment in *Moody* v *Cox* [1917] 2 Ch 71 and *Goody* v *Baring* [1956] 1 WLR 50 which make it plain that if a solicitor chooses to represent two parties in the transaction he must accept that he is placing himself in a position in which an irreconcilable conflict may arise between his duty to one client to keep certain information confidential and his duty to his other to disclose that information. Both judgments state clearly that if such a situation arises it is the solicitor's fault for acting for both clients and that the law will not assist him in extricating himself by permitting him to comply with his duty to one client at the expense of the other. Although both cases involve a solicitor who acted for vendor and purchaser, the judgments are equally applicable to the situation of solicitors who act for mortgagor and mortgagee.

Whilst arguments along these lines will not always produce co-operation, they do produce useful results in a reasonable proportion of cases, particularly so if the solicitors are presented not with a generalised request for relevant information but with a list of specific questions about the transactions. Occasionally the lender's solicitors fail to supply documents to which the lender, under any analysis, is clearly entitled *e.g.* the deeds to the property. If following suitable warnings these are not produced the Solicitors' Complaints Bureau should be informed and proceedings should be taken also against the solicitors under section 68 of the Solicitors Act 1974 for the delivery of the deeds or documents in question.

Categories of remedy

Post-fraud litigation can, by and large, be divided into salvage claims and compensation claims. A single fraud often gives rise to claims of both types.

Salvage Claims

Salvage claims are actions aimed at:

1. **Tracing and recovering the advance moneys.** The rules relating to tracing are complex; it is not proposed to go into the main detail here, suffice it to say that tracing action can be useful if the money received by the fraudster has either been invested in identifiable property or it has been laundered by third parties who have either knowledge of the fraud or who did not give consideration for the payment received by them. The attractions of the tracing remedy are that:

   - it is not a simple debt claim but a proprietary claim in respect of the fraud on the property being traced. The result of this is that the plaintiff is also able to claim priority to other professionals into whose hands the property has been traced, and the claim is unaffected by the defendant's insolvency;

- if a third party assists the fraudster or any of his nominees to dispose of the fund or property with the result that it becomes incapable of being traced, and he does so in circumstances which would have indicated to an honest and reasonable man that a fraud was being perpetrated, that third party can be held liable for the full amount disposed of: *Agip (Africa) Ltd* v *Axon* [1991] 3 WLR 116.

There are, however, limitations to tracing remedies which mean that they are likely to assist only in a small minority of cases:

- a fund or property cannot be claimed back from an innocent purchaser for value who has no notice of the fraud;
- a plaintiff has to be able to point to a fund into which the advance moneys actually have been paid, or a property which has been bought with those advance moneys. If, as is very often the case, the advance moneys have been dissipated by the fraudster, it is not possible to rely on a tracing claim against other property belonging to him.

2. **Obtaining a money judgment against the borrower.** An action for a money judgment can take the form either of a claim against the borrower under the covenants in the mortgage deed, or if the mortgage deed was not properly completed but the advance money was none the less released to the borrower, an action for money had and received. Such actions are worthwhile if there is clearly going to be a shortfall following the sale of any security and it is thought that the borrower may have sufficient assets to make the proceedings worthwhile.
3. **Enabling the lender to take possession and sell the security.** If the property exists and is vacant and is properly charged, no proceedings are necessary. Likewise possession proceedings are not appropriate if the property is occupied by persons other than the borrower who have rights of occupation clearly binding on the lender—*e.g.* a tenancy which was granted by a person who was at the time the legal owner of the property and which demonstrably began before the date of the mortgage. In such a situation, the best course is usually to appoint a receiver at an early stage to collect the rents payable. If the property is occupied by the borrower or by third parties whose rights of occupation are not accepted by the lender as binding, this is the standard point of possession on which an action can be taken.

4. It frequently happens in fraud cases that the property has not been properly charged—*e.g.* there may be no mortgage deed. In such cases proceedings may be taken for a court order declaring the lender has some form of equitable charge over the property and directing a sale of it. There are various bases for asserting the existence of an equitable charge and it is not possible to go into them all here. It would, however, be a reasonably accurate generalisation to say that if it can be demonstrated that a mortgage offer was made and accepted, and that the advance moneys or part of them were used in the purchase of the property that was to form the security, the courts are normally anxious to assist. Problems of defective security can also arise in the case of the husband who remortgages the house which he owns jointly with his wife and forges her signature on mortgage deeds. In such cases the mortgage deed is invalid and any registration of it at HM Land Registries is therefore negated. The lender, however, is often able to salvage a fair slice of the advance by claiming declarations first that the whole of the property, including the wife's interest, is subject to an equitable charge in its favour to the extent that the advance moneys were used to pay off prior valid legal charges, and secondly that the husband's share in the property is subject to an equitable charge to the whole value of the loan.

Compensation Claims

Compensation claims can for present purposes be divided first into actions for fraud against those who were parties to deception, and secondly actions for breach of contracts/negligence against professionals retained by the lender or in negligence alone against any institution which supplied a financial reference for the borrower.

Fraud Actions

In deciding whether there are any advantages to mounting a fraud action as opposed to any other form of proceedings, the following matters should be considered.

1. In order to succeed in a claim for fraud it is necessary to prove in the balance of probabilities, first that the defendant has made a full statement of fact or of professional opinion (*e.g.* a valuation figure in a mortgage valuation report) without an honest belief in its truth, and intending the plaintiff to act upon it, and secondly that the plaintiff did so act and suffered damages as a result. It should be noted that it is not sufficient proof of lack of honest belief simply to demonstrate that the statement concerned was wildly inaccurate. It has to be shown that it

was made with the knowledge of falsity, or without belief in its truth, or recklessly, careless whether it could be true or false. That is a very high burden of truth and in the case of mortgage fraud there are usually remedies available with less exacting requirements, such as claims against the borrower under the personal covenant in the mortgage deed or for money had and received; and against the professionals for negligence and/or breach of contract.

2. Fraud claims tend to be more bitterly contested and are usually considerably more expensive than other forms of action. Because of the implications for their future careers, this is particularly so in the case of fraud claims against solicitors, valuers and accountants. It is probably also fair to say that, because of the stigma attached, the courts are normally reluctant to make a finding of fraud without compelling evidence.
3. If an action for fraud succeeds against a professional who is a sole practitioner, his insurers will not indemnify him (see Chap 2). In the case of a solicitor, the Compensation Fund will no doubt step in if the defendant is unable to pay the full amount of the damages awarded, but the fund is the last resort and it may therefore not pay up immediately upon judgment being given.
4. The measure of damages awarded for fraud is the amount required to compensate the plaintiff for all of the actual damages directly flowing from a fraud to the extent that such damage may have been increased by the unreasonable conduct of the plaintiff—*Doyle* v *Olbey (Ironmongers) Ltd* [1969] 2 QB 158. In theory, this may be a more advantageous measure of damages than that available from an action for negligence or breach of contract, where the damages are limited to such loss as was reasonably foreseeable. In practice, however, there is rarely likely to be any significant difference.
5. The damages awarded to a plaintiff in an action based on negligence may be reduced if the court considers the plaintiff was partially responsible for the loss suffered *(e.g.* if a lender failed to comply with its own vetting procedures before making a mortgage offer to a fraudster). This defence of contributory negligence does not apply in fraud cases.
6. Financial references for borrowers sometimes contain a provision excluding liability for their contents. Whilst such a disclaimer may be effective if the writer was merely negligent, it will be wholly ineffective if he was fraudulent. (See Case Study 1.)

As will be gathered, it is likely that the occasions on which it is to the plaintiff's advantage to mount a fraud claim will be few, but lenders should always notify the relevant regulatory bodies if they consider a professional has been a party to fraud.

Professional negligence actions
When considering whether there are grounds for taking proceedings for professional negligence against the valuer or solicitor following a mortgage fraud, it is necessary to consider two preliminary points:

1. whether he is in breach of specific contractual duty;
2. whether he is in breach of any legally implied duty of care owed to the client.

The starting point for consideration of both matters is the terms of a solicitor's or a valuer's retainer. Neither the solicitor nor valuer is under a general duty of care to consider all aspects of his client's interest. As Oliver J. said in *Midland Bank* v *H Stubbs and Kemp* [1979] Ch 384:

> "The expression 'my solicitor' is as meaningless as the expression 'my tailor' or 'my bookkeeper' in establishing any general duty apart from that arising from the particular matter for which his services are retained. The extent of his duty depends on the terms of that retainer and any duty of care must be related to what he is apt to do.... I think the court must be beware of imposing upon solicitors or upon professionals in other spheres which go beyond the scope of what they are requested to undertake. It may be that a meticulous and conscientious practitioner would, in his client's general interests, take it upon himself to pursue a line of enquiry beyond the strict lines comprehended by his instructions but that is not the test. The test is what the reasonably competent practitioner would do having regard to the standards normally adopted in his profession."

The terms of a solicitor's or a valuer's retainer are to be found in the written instructions given to them by the lenders. In the case of the valuer the instructions normally require a valuation in accordance with mortgage valuation guidance notes published by the profession's regulators. There is no similar standard form setting out the duties of the solicitor, and some members' instructions are skimpy with the result that the solicitor's performance has to be judged by applying the somewhat uncertain test of what a reasonably competent solicitor would have done in the circumstances.

There are two particular cases which are relevant when considering the state of the solicitor's duty in the context of mortgage fraud:

1. It was decided in *Scholes* v *Brooks* [1891] 63 LT 837 that whilst a lender's solicitor was not under a general duty to advise on the adequacy of the security, he should report if, when investigating title,

he discovers something which indicates that the security is insufficient. In general, however, it will be sufficient if he raises the matter with the valuer, and he is not under an obligation to report to the client as well.

2. In *Anglia Hastings and Thanet Building Society* v *House and Son* [1981] 260 EG 1128 it was held that the lender's solicitor is under an obligation to report to the lender if there are grounds for doubting the bona fides of the mortgage transaction.

In addition to these authorities, it must also be borne in mind that the Professional Conduct Rules require that if a solicitor is acting for two clients in the same transaction, and becomes aware of a conflict of interest between them, he should cease to act.

Once the relevant duties owed by the valuer and solicitor have been identified, the next issue is whether any of those duties has been breached. This is an issue of fact to be decided in each case.

So far as the valuer is concerned the first step should be to obtain a report from another qualified valuer, who should be asked to provide a valuation figure for the property as at the date of the original valuation report and on the assumption that the property was then in precisely the state identified in the original report, together with a considered view as to whether at the date of the original inspection of the property it was in the condition described by the original valuer, and if it was not, the effect of any difference on the valuation figure.

In deciding on the basis of the new report whether the original valuer was negligent, it must be borne in mind that valuation is not an exact science and there is plenty of scope for legitimate difference of professional opinion. In *Mount Banking Corporation Ltd* v *Brian Cooper and Co* [1992] 35 EG 123 it was held that the correct course is to consider what figure a valuer adopting a competent approach would have come up with and then to see whether the actual valuation figure is within a reasonable margin of error (a reasonable margin of error in an ordinary case appears to be about 10% either way).

The following points may assist in forming a view as to whether a solicitor breached his duty to report matters reflecting on the bona fides of a mortgage transaction:

1. The solicitor is to be judged on the basis of the circumstances known at the time, and not with the benefit of hindsight.
2. The Law Society's green card was sent to every solicitor in April 1991 drawing attention to some of the features of mortgage fraud. A separate warning on variations in purchase price was published in the *Law Society Gazette* in December 1990. Both those warnings also now

appear in the Law Society's *Conveyancing Handbook* and in the *Guide to Professional Conduct*, and it can be assumed that any reasonably competent solicitor should be aware of and would comply with those warnings.

3. Both the warnings referred to above are *reminders* to solicitors of their existing obligations and do not purport to impose any new duties. Prima facie, therefore, if a solicitor became aware of matters of the type referred to in the warnings and failed either to report them or to cease to act for the lender, he may be negligent regardless of whether the failing occurred before or after publication of the warnings. It is probably fair to say, however, that in a border-line case the courts may take a less rigorous view if the fraud occurred before publication of the warnings.
4. Solicitors who specialise in litigation tend to suffer from a serious failing: namely, a willingness to insist upon a perfection in others which they themselves fail to attain. The judgement of a litigation solicitor on the performance of a conveyancer should therefore be treated with caution, and in any sort of borderline case the views of an experienced independent conveyancer should always be sought.

The next issue to be considered in relation to professional negligence actions is the measure of damages. The aim of any award will be to put the plaintiff in a position in which he would have been had it not been for negligence of the defendant. If the solicitor was negligent in failing to give warning of the possible fraud, the chances are that but for that negligence the mortgage advance would not have been made at all. In those circumstances the plaintiff is entitled to recover the difference between the full amount advanced, plus a sum to compensate the plaintiff for the interest that would have been earned on the money had it not been paid over to the fraudster, and, secondly, any sum actually recovered (net of the expense of recovery)—*e.g.* stock, from the fraudster or from the sale of the security. In *Swingcastle Ltd* v *Gibson* [1991] 2 WLR 1091, it was decided that the interest element in the damages should be calculated on the basis of the interest charged by the plaintiff to its customers only if the plaintiff can demonstrate that at the relevant time there was an unsatisfied demand for loans and that had the loan to the fraudster not been completed, the money could have been advanced to a bona fide non-defaulting borrower. If the plaintiff cannot prove this, the court will award a range of interest which it feels appropriate. Depending on the period to which this relates, this is likely to be around the 10–15% per annum mark.

The measure of damages against the valuer will be approached by the courts in precisely the same way, so that if the court concludes that the valuer had not been negligent, a loan would still have been made but for a lesser amount. The starting point of the calculation will be the difference between the amount actually advanced and the lesser sum which should have been lent in the event.

In the context of damages it is also necessary to look at the plaintiff's obligation to take reasonable steps to mitigate his loss, and the question of contributory negligence. A plaintiff who is suing for breach of contract or negligence is obliged to take whatever reasonable steps may be open to him to reduce the loss which he suffers and to give credit for the net amount of each reduction. If the court considers that the plaintiff has not taken proper steps to mitigate, it will reduce the damages awarded by an appropriate amount. Precisely what steps the plaintiff should take to discharge his obligation will vary from case to case. In *Pilkington* v *Wood* [1953] Ch 770 it was held that the application did not require a plaintiff to "embark on a complicated and difficult piece of litigation against a third party". Subject to that qualification it is probably sensible to assume that, save where the circumstances make it inappropriate, the plaintiff lender should enforce the borrower's personal covenant and take reasonably prompt steps to take possession of the security and sell it.

The general rule is that if the plaintiff brings a claim of professional negligence against a solicitor or valuer and the court concludes that whilst the defendant was negligent the damage suffered by the plaintiff as a result was partly his own fault, the damages awarded may be reduced by a suitable percentage. This rule is, however, subject to a qualification that if the plaintiff negligently makes a statement upon which he intends the plaintiff to rely, the damages awarded will not be reduced simply because the plaintiff relied on the statement and carelessly failed to make other enquiries which would have revealed the truth—*Gran Gelato Ltd* v *Richcliff (Group) Ltd* [1992] 1 All ER 865. The significance of this to claims of professional negligence following mortgage fraud is that if a valuer negligently overvalues the property in his report and valuation, the damages awarded to the plaintiff should not be reduced, even if it appears that had further checks been carried out the overvaluation would have come to light. Likewise, the solicitor cannot complain about the acceptance of his report on title. There would seem to be no reason in principle, however, why the court should not reduce the damages if the plaintiff negligently failed to comply with its own procedures when approving the mortgage application in the first place, if the vetting procedures were themselves inadequate.

Maximising recovery

As indicated at the beginning of this chapter, the purpose of civil litigation following fraud is the recovery of the maximum sum in the shortest period of time and in the most cost-effective manner. In order to achieve these ends the following points should be borne in mind.

1. If the fraud is discovered at a stage where there is still a chance of recovering the advance, solicitors should be asked to take proceedings to seek a Mareva injunction straightaway. Papers relating to the loan should be delivered to the solicitors forthwith and someone with the knowledge of fact should be made available to swear any necessary affidavits. The solicitor should also be told that the necessary undertakings may be given in the course of any application for a Mareva injunction and they should be given as much detail as possible about any bank accounts or other assets which the proposed defendant is believed to possess. This will save enquiry agents' costs too.
2. Immediate consideration should be given to the state of the security, its potential market and, if possible, possession should be taken and it should be sold. When doing so, however, it should be ensured that proper provision and valuations are obtained from outside valuers, which will demonstrate that the sale price is a proper one. The history of the marketing of the property should be fully documented. If there is any possibility of professional negligence claims either against the solicitor or the valuer, the potential defendant should be offered the opportunity of obtaining his own valuation report on the property before it is sold.
3. Solicitors should be asked to investigate the background to any mortgage fraud as promptly as possible and should be requested to advise fully on the salvage and compensation claims which can be pursued.
4. If solicitors advise that there are salvage claims which can be pursued with a reasonable prospect of success and at reasonable cost, those proceedings should be taken promptly and pursued vigorously in order to enable the lender to demonstrate in any subsequent negligence proceedings that proper steps were taken to mitigate the loss.
5. Professional negligence claims often involve lengthy arguments as to whether any, and if so what, report would have been made by a hypothetical reasonably competent practitioner had he been faced with the circumstances which confronted the defendant. Much of this could be avoided if lenders could revise their standard forms of instructions to solicitors and set out examples of the types of matter

which should always be reported—if, *e.g.* a portion of the purchase price is allegedly being paid by the purchaser to the vendor. In doing this, however, care should be taken to stress that the matters quoted are examples only, and that the lender looks to the solicitor to report any matter reflecting on the bona fides of the transaction.

6. If the plaintiff's mortgage succeeds in a claim for one reason or another he is not in a position to add his legal costs to the security, although costs can still be recovered from the defence. It is unlikely, however, that these costs will amount to a full indemnity. A close eye should always be kept on legal costs which are being incurred, and care should be taken to ensure that solicitors are not asked to pursue investigations more appropriate to the police.
7. Always be prepared to pursue and negotiate a settlement.

CHAPTER 9

Fraud Prosecution

Introduction

Apart from those members of the profession who specialise in representing clients who are alleged to have committed offences, most solicitors do not imagine that they will ever become involved in the criminal justice system. Solicitors tend to specialise, even at high street level. Except in one-man-band practices, criminal advocacy and conveyancing are not dealt with by the same person. Just as prosecutors, defence lawyers and policemen tend to be a little scornful of solicitors who are involved in mortgage fraud, however innocently, so conveyancers tend to feel they have enough to do keeping up with changes in conveyancing law and need not, therefore, even bother to read articles in the legal press on crime-related topics. Conveyancers tend not to want to become familiar with court procedure. It is therefore a rude shock when they are confronted by police officers requesting files or, worse still, police officers who require assistance with their enquiries, The worst case scenario is for a member of staff or a partner in a firm of solicitors to be arrested, charged and convicted.

We have all been brought up, during our professional education, to believe that professional confidence is one of the foundation stones of the relationship with our client. But is this, in fact, the case? Under what circumstances are we, as solicitors, obliged to co-operate with the police or even, perish the thought, to turn informer?

Like any other learned profession, as well as being called as witnesses of fact, solicitors may also give evidence as expert witnesses, either for the prosecution or for the defendant.

Investigations

Investigations are, of course, initially the province of the aggrieved lender and the lender's staff. The majority of investigations into cases of mortgage fraud are conducted by the police (see below), though a few cases have been prosecuted by the Serious Fraud Office (SFO) (see below for details of the SFO's powers under section 2 of the Criminal Justice Act 1987). Another prosecuting agency which regularly investigates mortgage fraud is the Inland

Revenue. Mortgage fraud involving domestic residential property almost invariably involves a fraud on the Inland Revenue in respect of the tax allowances permitted under the MIRAS scheme for mortgage relief at source in respect of a mortgagor's principal residence.

Building society investigations

Fraud control measures by lenders can be divided into preventative steps taken at the application stage to weed out bogus applications (see Chap 7 above), and measures taken once an existing application is seen to be fraudulent.

Fraud control, from the point of view of the lender, is both a financial services market hazard and a balance sheet cost against which they have to both budget and insure, if their lending risk is to be secure. Lenders derive a substantial degree of security from the protection afforded by employing members of the solicitors' profession in the conveyancing process. As we have seen above, it is the solicitor's job to ensure that the loan is sound, in respect of both the borrower and the identity of the property and its value as a security. The valuer is responsible for confirming that the property is worth the sum paid for it, and therefore the amount lent by the lender.

Both banks and building societies tend to have fraud investigation departments or members of staff who combine responsibility for fraud with their other duties. The fraud section is not normally based at branch level. Branch staff, of course, will have a responsibility for applications made to ensure that the applicant is financially eligible for the loan requested and capable of servicing a loan as well as being willing to do so. They will have to assess whether the applicant's circumstances may suddenly change, particularly having regard to the locality in which they are operating. It is also to be expected that branch staff will be more aware of local property prices and values than staff at head office, and it is to be hoped that branch staff will be able to spot whether there is anything fundamentally odd about an application (see Chap 7 above and specimen documents, especially pp 172–191).

Head office staff become involved in fraud control usually either when the lender receives information from the police that a fraud is being perpetrated, or when a loan "goes bad" and investigation reveals that the application was fraudulent all along.

All lenders who have business introduced to them by independent providers of financial services are, to a certain extent, open to abuse. How this system can be abused is illustrated by Case Studies 2 and 3. Lenders maintain records of individual brokers' track records which can be interrogated if necessary. Even though an individual broker only produces limited business, overall such small brokers can provide a substantial proportion of a lender's entire business.

The two most common locations for mortgage fraud control departments are audit or a special security unit. The latter usually has responsibility for other sorts of fraud, such as credit card fraud, and also for physical security of society premises and items such as documents, cash and information. These units are usually staffed and headed, to a large extent, by former police officers. As might be expected, the role played by fraud control staff is determined by the number of frauds reported to the lender, organisational politics and the lender's financial and other priorities. Fraud investigation tends to be a self-perpetuating activity. The more fraud that you find, the more you will find. Lenders attempt to seek a balance between the costs of fraud management and investigation and the amount that they lose from fraud. It is obviously crucial to detect fraud at the application stage (see Chap 7 above) rather than later in the process, and particularly once the application has been accepted and arrears have accrued. Lenders are only too well aware of the cost of recovering properties offered as security, particularly during a period of falling house values, when the value of the security may not be as great as that of the outstanding loan. Many societies carry insurance to cover the difference. However, providing staff to give evidence in criminal trials and to provide statements to police, together with the necessary documentary evidence support, is a substantial and irrecoverable cost. Most fraud investigations begin with information supplied to the lender by the police, or when staff or solicitors discover, on investigating arrears of a loan, that the application was fraudulent.

Readers who are interested in building societies' practice and policy should consult Michael Clarke *Mortgage Fraud*.

Police investigations

The majority of mortgage fraud prosecutions begin with a police invetigation. Each major police force has a fraud squad. The Metropolitan and City fraud squad has a specialist mortgage fraud team.

Like other defendants the treatment of a solicitor defendant should ideally be in accordance with the provisions of the Police and Criminal Evidence Act 1984 (PACE) and in particular the codes of practice issued under section 66 of that Act. It is not unusual for a potential defendant in a fraud case to assist the police as a volunteer, without being arrested. PACE would not then apply, though the volunteer may leave the police station when he wishes. He will not have to be advised of his right to legal representation, but what he says cannot be used in evidence. Once the police officer suspects that an offence has been committed the suspect must be cautioned in the usual way, and PACE comes into effect. Unlike the subject of a DTI investigation, at the moment the suspect may exercise his right to silence though failure to mention a potential defence may lead to adverse comment at trial.[1]

Other prosecuting authorities do not have the same powers as the SFO has under section 2 of the Criminal Justice Act 1987, though there has been much discussion as to whether these powers should be extended to all serious fraud trials. Reluctant witnesses may have to be compelled to attend court by witness summons. In practice, however, a prosecutor will be reluctant to call a witness whose evidence is an unknown quantity.

Fraud cases are remarkable for the number of documents which they generate. These documents will be obtained by court order or by search. The production of documents may be obtained by the police by the Banker's Books Evidence Act 1879 (as amended by the Banking Act 1987), or under PACE.

The Banker's Books Evidence Act provides that (by section 3) "a copy of any entry in a banker's Book shall in all legal proceedings be received as prima facie evidence of each such entry, and of all the matters, transactions, and accounts therein recorded"

Sections 4 and 5 require that statements must be made by a partner or officer of the bank to ascertain that:

1. the relevant book was "one of the ordinary books of the bank";
2. the entry was made in the usual and ordinary course of the business;
3. the book is in the custody or control of the bank.

Section 6 states that a banker may not be called to produce his books or give evidence without order of a judge made for a special cause. The procedure is set out in section 7. An application cannot be made until charges are laid, and may have to be made *ex parte*. It should be served at least three clear days before it is to be obeyed, unless the court or judge otherwise directs. Applications on notice are encouraged.[2] Straightforward applications are usually made to a magistrates' court, though if in difficulty the justices can refer the application to the High Court. "Fishing expeditions" are discouraged. The Crown should not apply in the hope of obtaining evidence if it has no other evidence against a defendant. There should also be a time limit on disclosure. Legal proceedings are widely defined in section 10 of the Act, and would include proceeding before a solicitors' disciplinary tribunal.

The definition in section 2 does not appear to include the daily notes kept by bank managers, employees, bank correspondence files[3] or cheques and paying-in slips. The bank manager's notes may be particularly useful to the

[1] See The Royal Commission for Criminal Justice Proposals, p 54 *et seq.* The police caution includes reference to potential defences.

[2] *R* v *Marlborough Street Magistrates' Court Metropolitan Stipendiary Magistrate, ex p Simpson* (1980) 70 Cr App R. 291.

[3] *R* v *Dadson:* see Archbold (44th ed) para 9-128.

prosecution. A defendant may have expressed his intention to acquire a property portfolio, or may be financially overstretched, thus providing a motive.

To obtain access to material which is not covered by the Banker's Books Evidence Act and which is subject to a duty of confidentiality, it will be necessary for an application to be made before or after charges are laid under PACE section 9 and Schedule 1. This material is classified in the act as "special procedure material" which is defined in section 14(2) as:

> "material other than items subject to legal privilege and excluded material in the possession of a person who–
>
> (a) acquired or created it in the course of any trade business, profession, or other occupation or for the purpose of any paid or unpaid office: and
>
> (b) holds it subject to an express or implied undertaking to hold it in confidence."

An application must be made by a constable to a circuit judge. The constable must satisfy the judge that one of the two sets of access conditions have been complied with. Applications are made ***inter partes***. The access conditions are set out in the schedule to PACE. The first set of conditions are those more usually applied.

There must be reasonable grounds for believing that a serious arrestable offence has been committed, that special procedure material exists, that the material is likely to be of substantial value to the investigation and relevant, that other methods of obtaining the material have been tried without success or would be bound to fail, and that it is in the public interest that the material should be obtained.

The second set of conditions is that there is a reasonable belief that excluded or special procedure material is on the premises, a warrant to search could have been issued prior to the enactment of PACE, and it would have been appropriate to issue such a warrant.[4]

If these conditions are satisfied a judge may make an order requiring a person in possession of the material to produce it to the constable for removal, or give him access within a period not more than seven days from the making of the order. A person aggrieved by such an order may contest it.

The Divisional Court made a number of observations about section 9 applications in *R* v *Central Criminal Court, ex p AJD Holding*.

1. It was important before any warrant was applied for, that careful consideration was given to what material the police hoped to find in

[4] s 9 (2).

any search, because this could affect the legality of the search were its ambit to be questioned.

2. The material had to relate to the crime under investigation.
3. Officers conducting the search should be briefed as to both these matters and should clearly understand the limits of the search and seizure operation.
4. A note should be taken of anything which was said in support of the application beyond what appeared in the written application.
5. Finally the court emphasised the safeguards set out in sections 15 and 16 of PACE.

In summary, a search is only legal to the extent that it is covered by the warrant the court has issued. Evidence seized other than lawfully may be excluded.[5] There is no provision in the Act for the person who is the subject of the investigation to be notified of an application. Banks do not have to tell their customers that such an application has been made.[6]

The party against whom the order is made should know before the order is made what he has to produce or allow access to, and the nature of the offence which is being investigated,[7] though this information could be oral. The respondent to an application has to be supplied with the evidence on which the application is made.[8] Some information as to what material the police wish to obtain must be supplied.[9] The police do not have to produce full details to the hearing—the courts do take account of the fact that too much information may lead to the destruction of the documents.

Section 10 of PACE defines items subject to legal privilege (and see p 86 below).

Items held with the intention of furthering a criminal purpose are not items subject to legal privilege. The provision of legal services such as conveyancing does not attract legal privilege, unless a communication actually contained legal advice.[10]

In *R* v *Central Criminal Court, ex p Francis and Francis*,[11] the House of Lords decided that documents which were otherwise privileged, and which were held without any criminal intent by a solicitor, could lose that protection if a third party other than the solicitor's client intended that the documents should be used for furthering a criminal purpose. In this case the solicitor and

[5] See also *R* v *Chief Constable of Lancashire, ex p Parker and McGrath*, *The Independent*, 1 April 1993.
[6] *Barclays Bank* v *Taylor* [1989] 3 All ER 563; *Trustee Savings Bank of Wales and Border Counties* v *Taylor* [1989] 3 All ER 563.
[7] [1988] 2 All ER 769 *R* v *Manchester Crown Court ex p Taylor* [1988] 2 All ER 769, [1988] 1 WLR 705.
[8] *R* v *Inner London Sessions Crown Court, ex p Baines* [1988] QB 579, [1987] 3 All ER 1025.
[9] *R* v *Central Criminal Court, ex p Adegbesan* [1986] 3 All ER 113, [1986] 1 WLR 1292.
[10] *R* v *Inner London Sessions, ex p Baines*, *R* v *Guildhall Magistrates' Court, ex p Primlaks*.
[11] [1989] AC 346.

his client were being used as dupes in a conveyancing transaction which was in reality a money laundering exercise. The criminal intent has to exist at the time the documents enter the solicitor's possession.

For material which is not excluded, or special procedure material, application has to be made under section 8 of PACE in the usual way to a magistrate. Material which is the subject of legal privilege or a duty of confidentiality must be the subject of an application under section 9 and Schedule 1 of PACE.[12] An application under these provisions should never be treated as routine; all the access conditions must be met.[13] It is always preferable that applications should be heard *inter partes*.

The position of the solicitor *vis-à-vis* his client is dealt with in Chapter 12 of the Law Society's *Guide to Professional Conduct of Solicitors*, which suggests that a prudent solicitor should insist on a court order before he hands over client's papers.

A warrant to search for and seize special procedure material requires an application to a circuit judge, and should be made on notice, save in very exceptional circumstances.[14] The reader is reminded of the provisions relating to arrest, entry to premises and search after arrest contained in sections 17–23 of PACE. After seizure, the occupier of the premises is allowed access to the papers seized and to take copies, although access may be supervised and copies will be charged for. The officer in charge of the investigation may refuse access and taking of copies if he believes, on reasonable grounds, that these would prejudice the investigation. Section 22 provides for the retention of the material for so long as is necessary.

Third parties involved in related civil litigation will not be allowed access to the material.[15] There is *obiter dicta* in Marcel to support the supply of documents to another prosecuting agency,[16] quite apart from the provisions of PACE.

Professional privilege and the solicitor's duties of confidentiality

The position before April 1994

The solicitor-client relationship involves two aspects: so-called "legal professional privilege" and the obligation of professional confidence. These

[12] *Ex p Primlaks Holdings Co* [1990] 1 QB 261, [1989] 2 WLR 841.

[13] *R* v *Maidstone Crown Court, ex p Waite [1988] Crim LR 384.*

[14] *Ex p Waite.*

[15] *Marcel* v *Metropolitan Police Commissioner* [1992[Ch 225, [1992] 1 All ER 72, [1992] 2 WLR 58.

[16] *Ibid* 1125.

two aspects of the relationship must be differentiated. In *Parry-James* v *The Law Society* [1969] 1 Ch 1, the then Master of the Rolls, Lord Denning, said:

"As between solicitor and client, there are two privileges. The first relates to legal proceedings—commonly called 'legal professional privilege'... The second privilege arises out of the confidence subsisting between solicitor and client... the law implies a term into the contract whereby a professional man is to keep his client's affairs as secret..."

Legal professional privilege

Legal professional privilege is a branch of the law of evidence. It prevents a solicitor from producing or disclosing in any legal proceedings any of the communications between himself and his client without the client's consent. It has been held to cover the following items:

1. instructions given by the client to the solicitor;
2. instructions given by the solicitor to a barrister;
3. counsel's opinion taken by a solicitor (*Bristol Corporation* v *Cox* (1884) 26 Ch D 678);
4. documents brought into existence by a party for the purposes of instructing a lawyer (*Anderson* v *Bank of British Columbia* (1876) 2 Ch D 644);
5. copies of documents, the originals of which were brought into existence for the purpose of instructing a lawyer (*R* v *Inland Revenue, ex p Goldberg* [1988] 3 All ER 248); or
6. a selection of pre-existing documents which themselves are not privileged but which have been copied or assembled by a solicitor and betray the trend of advice given to the client (*Lyell* v *Kennedy* (1984) 27 Ch D 1).

In criminal cases, legal professional privilege is now governed by the Police and Criminal Evidence Act 1984 (PACE). Legal privilege is defined in section 10 of that Act:

"(1)... Item subject to legal privilege means:

(a) communications between a professional legal adviser and his client or any person representing his client in connection with the giving of legal advice to the client;

(b) communications between a professional legal adviser and his client or any person representing his client or between such an adviser and any other person made in connection with or in contemplation of legal proceedings and for the purpose of such proceedings; and

(c) items enclosed with or referred to in such communications and made:

(i) in connection with the giving of legal advice; or

(ii) in connection with or in contemplation of legal proceedings and for the purpose of such proceedings they are in possession of a person who is entitled to possess them.

"(2)... Items held with the intention of furthering a criminal purpose are *not items subject to legal privilege*."

In the case of *R* v *Central Criminal Court, ex p Francis and Francis* [1989] AC 346, the House of Lords held that the reference to "intention" in section 10 (2) of PACE can be the intention of the solicitor or any other person.

Both the Police and Criminal Evidence Act 1984 and the Drug Trafficking Act 1994 (DTA) allow an application to a Circuit Judge for an Order to compel production by a solicitor of papers or files, if there is a prima facie case that the client has used the solicitor's services for criminal or fraudulent purposes.

The *Guide to the Professional Conduct of Solicitors* gives guidance to solicitors concerned about applications made under PACE or DTOA. Commentary 5 to Principle 16.04 provides:

"Occasionally, a solicitor is asked by the police to give information or to show them documents which the solicitor has obtained when acting for a client.... If the request is made by the police under the terms of the Police and Criminal Evidence Act 1984, then... the solicitor should, where appropriate, leave the question of privilege to the Court to decide on the particular circumstance."

The duty in confidentiality

A solicitor's duty in confidentiality is broader than the concept of professional privilege. Principle 16.01 of the *Guide* provides:

"A solicitor is under a duty to keep confidential to his or her firm the affairs of clients and to ensure that staff do the same."

The commentary to that principle distinguishes the duty in confidentiality from the concept of legal professional privilege. It says:

"Legal professional privilege protects communication between a client and solicitor from being disclosed, even in a court of law. There are, however, certain communications which are not protected by legal privilege and reference should be made to an appropriate authority on the law of evidence. Such non-privileged communications remain subject to the solicitor's duty to keep the client's affairs confidential until a court orders disclosure."

It would appear that the duty of confidentiality applies to "informal or quasi clients", that is, persons who are not strictly clients of the firm (per Parker LJ, *Re a firm of solicitors* [1992] 1 All ER 353 at p 363).

The Law Society accepts that the duty of confidentiality can be overridden in certain circumstances, including:

1. where the communications are made before the commission of the crime for the purposes of being guided or helped in the commission of it;
2. where the client expressly consents to disclosure;
3. where the court orders that matters are to be disclosed;
4. where the matters are on public record.

In addition, confidentiality may be affected by statute. The Drug Trafficking Act 1994 and the Prevention of Terrorism (Temporary Provisions) Act 1989 affect solicitors because they create money-laundering offences. The Drug Trafficking Act 1994 has replaced the Drug Trafficking Offences Act 1986.

Section 50 of the Drug Trafficking Act 1994 makes it an offence to assist another to retain the benefits of drug trafficking. The offence occurs where, for example, a solicitor is concerned in an arrangement whereby the retention or control by or on behalf of a client of the client's proceeds of drug trafficking is facilitated (whether by concealment, removal from the jurisdiction, transfer to nominees or otherwise), or where the client's proceeds of drug trafficking are used to secure that funds are placed at the client's disposal or are used for the client's benefit to acquire property by way of investment.

To be guilty, the solicitor in the above example must know or suspect that his client is a person who carries on or has carried on drug trafficking or has benefited from drug trafficking.

A disclosure to a constable of a suspicion or belief that any funds or investments are derived from or used in connection with drug trafficking can amount to a defence for any accused, provided the disclosure is made before the prohibited act is committed with the consent of the constable or after the act, but made on the accused's own initiative and as soon as it is reasonable for him to make it. It is necessary for the defence to show that the accused intended to make the disclosure but that there was a reasonable excuse for his failure to do so. (See section 52(4).) The Act specifically provides "that disclosure shall not be treated as a breach of any restriction upon the disclosure of information imposed by contract".

Under section 11 of the Prevention of Terrorism Act 1989, an offence is committed where, for example, a solicitor enters into an arrangement whereby the retention or control by or on behalf of another person of terrorist funds is facilitated either by concealment, removal from the jurisdiction, transfer to nominees or otherwise. Section 12 of the Act allows a defence where a disclosure is made to a constable of the accused's suspicion or belief or where the disclosure is made after he enters into the transaction, the disclosure is made on his own initiative and as soon as it is reasonable for him to do so. The Act provides that disclosure can be made notwithstanding restrictions imposed by contract; again, "by contract" is replaced by the words "by statute or otherwise" by the Criminal Justice Act 1993, section 49(3).

Commentary 9 of Principle 16.04 of the *Guide* provides:

> "Under section 24 of the Drug Trafficking Offences Act 1986 and section 12 of the Prevention of Terrorism (Temporary Provisions) Act 1989, a solicitor may, in certain circumstances, notwithstanding the duty of confidentiality, disclose to the police a suspicion or belief that certain moneys are derived from or used in connection with drug trafficking or that certain money or property is derived from terrorist funds and, in certain circumstances, such disclosure may prevent the solicitor from committing an offence under these provisions."

In April 1994, yet further inroads were made into the solicitor-client relationship. Specific new money-laundering offences were introduced into the Criminal Justice Act 1988 by the Criminal Justice Act 1993. These are now contained in Part VI, section 93 A–D of the Criminal Justice Act 1988.

Section 7 of the Criminal Justice Act 1988 provides:

> "In this part [ie, Part VI] of the Act -... (c) references to an offence to which this part of the Act applies are references to any offence which –
>
> (i) is listed in Schedule 4 to this Act; or
> (ii) if not so listed, is an indictable offence other than a drug-trafficking offence or an offence under Part III of the Prevention of Terrorism (Temporary Provisions) Act 1989."

Section 93A creates a new offence of assisting another to retain the benefit of criminal conduct. This is a similar crime to those under the Drug Trafficking Act and the Prevention of Terrorism Act and is applicable to proceeds of general criminal conduct which, of course, includes mortgage fraud.

An offence is committed where a solicitor, for example, is concerned in an arrangement whereby the retention or control by or on behalf of a client of the client's proceeds of criminal conduct is facilitated (whether by concealment, removal from the jurisdiction, transfer to nominees or otherwise) or where the client's proceeds of criminal conduct are used to secure that funds are placed at the client's disposal or are used for the client's benefit to acquire property by way of investment.

To be guilty, the solicitor in such a case must know or suspect that his client is a person who has been engaged in criminal conduct or has benefited from criminal conduct.

A disclosure to a constable of a suspicion or belief that funds or investments are derived from or used in connection with criminal conduct can amount to a defence for any accused, provided that the disclosure is made before the prohibited act is committed with the consent of the constable, or after the act but made on the accused's own initiative and as soon as it is reasonable for him to make it.

It is also a defence to show that the accused intended to make the disclosure but that there was a reasonable excuse for his failure to do so. Section 93A (3) (a) provides expressly that "the disclosure shall not be treated as a breach of any disclosure of information imposed by statute or otherwise."

In regard to employees, a defence exists where disclosure (as noted above) is made to the appropriate person in accordance with the procedure established by their employer. The penalty for this offence is imprisonment for up to 14 years and/or a fine. The reader is referred to the Money-laundering Regulations and to recent guidance provided by the Law Society including, in particular, the blue money-laundering card.

It is an offence for anyone under section 93B to acquire, use or have possession of any property which is or which directly or indirectly represents another's proceeds of criminal conduct, knowing that the property is the proceeds of criminal conduct.

There is a defence to show that the property was acquired by the accused for adequate consideration. There are also similar defences available where disclosure is made or the accused intends to disclose to a constable. The employee defence is also available if disclosure is made according to established procedures. (See again the Money-laundering Regulations, and Law Society Blue Card.)

An offence of concealing or transferring the proceeds of criminal conduct is created by section 93C. The offence is committed if a person conceals or disguises property which is or which directly or indirectly represents his proceeds of criminal conduct or converts or transfers that property or removes it from jurisdiction for the purpose of avoiding prosecution for an offence under Part VI, or by making or enforcement of a Confiscation Order. This offence is aimed at the offender who attempts to money-launder. However, if a person is guilty of an offence where he knows or has reasonable grounds for suspecting that the property is or directly or indirectly represents another's proceeds of criminal conduct and he conceals or disguises that property or converts or transfers or removes the property for the purpose of assisting a person to avoid prosecution for a money-laundering offence.

Section 93D creates three "tipping-off" offences:

1. It is an offence for a defendant who knows or suspects that an investigation into an offence of money-laundering is being conducted or is about to be conducted to divulge that fact, or other information, which is likely to prejudice such an investigation.
2. If a disclosure of a suspicion or information has been made to a constable under sections 93A or 93B, an offence is committed if that fact is disclosed to another where it is likely to prejudice investigation.
3. If the disclosure is by an employee to an appropriate person, it is an offence to disclose to another where it is likely to prejudice an investigation.

An exemption is provided for "professional legal advisers", who may disclose any information to a client or to his representative in connection with the giving of legal advice to the client, or to any person in contemplation of or in connection with legal proceedings and for the purpose of those proceedings.

CHAPTER 10

Evidential Matters in Mortgage Fraud Trials

Introduction

The purpose of this chapter is not to give a comprehensive dissertation on the rules of evidence, but to draw attention to those matters which are particularly important in fraud trials, namely documentary evidence and the use of expert evidence. Evidence is also important in the context of trial preparation and presentation. It is generally accepted that fraud trials are too long. Unless carefully prepared, the issues at stake may remain a mystery to many jurors; the volume of paper used is recognised as a threat to the world's forests.[1]

Chapter 5 of the Roskill Report, page 64, recognised that there should be changes in the existing system as it related to fraud trials:

> "We have thought it right to devote a separate chapter to the vexed question of the rules of evidence as they apply in criminal cases, because we have concluded that the rigidity and artificiality of the present rules are an obstruction to the just and expeditious disposal of fraud cases."

Even at the time that the Roskill Committee sat, many of those who gave evidence pointed out the time and money wasted in calling witnesses to testify to the genuineness of routine documents.

Serious fraud cases place burdens of a particular kind on all involved in their preparation and presentation. Even after conscientious sifting of the evidence, the prosecution can give the impression on the day that trial starts that they are still painting the roses, like the card soldiers in *Alice in Wonderland*. The issues involved may well be outside the experience of most jurors.

As the Roskill Committee pointed out, there is a marked divergence between the view of fraud trials taken by lawyers and by laymen.

Lawyers will argue vehemently that unless the prosecution case, in the absence of admissions which themselves have only been permissible as evidence since 1967, satisfies every requirement of evidential proof, an acquittal, however unmeritorious should follow.

[1] Michael Levy—Research paper for the Royal Commission on Criminal Justice No 27.

The layman undoubtedly regards this attitude as evidence of the law being an ass. Even in the rarefied areas of high finance and computer science, the educated layman reaches decisions on the basis of evidence which would be ruled inadmissible in any court as not being "best evidence" or as being hearsay: "You mustn't tell us what she told you—it's not evidence. Now an affidavit from a thunderstorm or a few words on oath from a heavy shower...".[2] Laymen rely on the word of a trusted subordinate, even when that subordinate has no personal knowledge of the matter. A layman will also attach more weight to a contemporary document than is usually given to testimony by a witness whose memory may be affected by time and the inevitable subjective element in any human recollection.

Background

The English criminal trial is based on the oral testimony of witnesses who attend at the trial and give evidence from their own first-hand personal knowledge of the offence. Oral testimony used to be the main and, in some cases, the only form of evidence which could be presented before a court. As the witness gives evidence in chief, he can be seen as he appears in person, and the credibility of his evidence can be tested in cross-examination. Juries sit as a body of independent people who have not been involved in the investigation or the preparation for trial, and who know nothing of the background of the case until the trial starts. Documents are treated with suspicion by the law; their importance tends, therefore, to be undervalued.

Evidential problems in fraud cases

The rules of evidence in civil cases were modernised and reformed by the Civil Evidence Acts 1968 and 1972. As a result, though it has been said that the rules of evidence are the same broadly in both civil and criminal cases, in reality, at the time that the Roskill Committee sat, the position was very different.

The Criminal Law Revision Committee created controversy in its eleventh report, which would have gone some way to assimilating the rules of evidence in criminal cases to those in civil cases. Most of its recommendations remain unimplemented, though some have been revived by the Runciman Commission. It remains to be seen which of the proposals contained in this later report are implemented. The provisions regarding documentary hearsay

[2] Gilbert and Sullivan, *Iolanthe.*

contained in the Police and Criminal Evidence Act 1984 were less radical in their approach than those envisaged by the Criminal Law Revision Committee and the Civil Evidence Act, though the Criminal Justice Act 1988 goes some way towards mitigating the problem.

The main problems in mortgage fraud cases caused by the existing rules of evidence, at the time that the Roskill Committee sat, were those relating to documents and opinion or expert evidence.

Hearsay and documents

The evidence which a witness gives must be first hand. If all he can do is recount what another witness has said, then that other witness should give evidence; the second-hand version is not acceptable. As applied to documents this rule, which is known as the hearsay rule, means that it is not sufficient to produce a cheque: the drawer of the cheque, the bank clerk and the payee should each come to court, because they alone can give evidence of the transaction: the cheque cannot speak for itself. It does not take a very vivid imagination to see how this principle can prolong a trial.

The Criminal Evidence Act 1965 and the Police and the Criminal Evidence Act 1984 relaxed the hearsay rule in certain particular cases. These relaxations applied to classes of documents compiled as records by persons acting under a duty. The 1965 reform applied to records compiled by persons acting under a duty in the course of a private business, and PACE simply extended the relaxation to records kept by anyone acting under a duty, whether in the public or private sector. But the reforms are framed as exceptions to the general rules of evidence and are subject to a code of conditions which stipulate in effect that oral testimony as to the contents of the documents must not be available. The conditions are that the person who supplied the information contained in the document is either dead, ill, or cannot be traced or is outside the United Kingdom and cannot reasonably be expected to come to court or that having regard to all the circumstances he cannot be expected to have any recollection of the subject matter.

These exceptions to the general hearsay rule were, it must be admitted, of great assistance to the prosecution at least. The maker of routine entries in statements of account, ledger records and entries in financial books need no longer be called to court. Foreign government and overseas business records could be produced in court without the requirement that their authors should appear in court to prove them.

There remained, however, a number of areas where documentary evidence was not admissible and where oral testimony had to be produced. First, there were those documents which were not records compiled by a person acting under a duty. The Roskill Committee thought the distinction between records and non-records was artificial and of doubtful value. Secondly, there were those documents which were within the definition of a record but where the author or supplier of the information was still alive, within the country, and might have some recollection of events. If personal attendance was possible, this was obligatory, even though there might be very little that the author could add to the contents of the documents, except to confirm that, to the best of his recollection, the document accurately recorded the transaction.

Copies of documents

The common law rule was that copies of documents were not admissible in evidence; the original was required, because it was the "best evidence". Since this rule predates the photocopier or carbon papers, the amelioration by PACE was overdue. Where a document is admissible under sections 68 or 69, it may be proved:

1. by the production of that document; or
2. whether or not the document is still in existence, by a production of a copy of that document or of the material part of it, authenticated in such manner as the court may approve.[3]

This section only applies to documents admitted in evidence under PACE.

Foreign evidence

In large-scale fraud cases it is common for the prosecution to have to obtain evidence abroad in the form of documents or witnesses or both. The Roskill Committee noted that the system of letters of request then in force was cumbersome and unreliable. Though evidence taken in criminal proceedings in this country could be used abroad, since the Evidence (Proceedings in Other Jurisdictions) Act 1975 the reverse position did not obtain. The Criminal Law Revision Committee decided against recommending that provision should be made for obtaining oral evidence by commission in criminal trials because they thought it would open a door to evidence which could not be tested by cross-examination. They also decided against the procedure whereby documents in the possession of a person within the jurisdiction of a foreign court could be used. Of course there would still be no way of compelling the attendance of a foreign witness.

There were two main consequences of these evidential problems. The first was that some prosecutions could not be brought, because of the strictness of the rules of evidence. Investigative journalists did not then ask themselves when questioning why a prosecution had not been brought when there was evidence aplenty, whether that evidence was available and could be given in a form which was admissible at a criminal trial.

[3] PACE, Sched 3 para 13.

The second consequence was that:

"They permit—indeed they encourage—the skilled fraudster with no real defence to obstruct the administration of justice in the hope of gaining some advantage. Where the defendant has a substantive defence to put forward, for example that he was not acting dishonestly, the defendant clearly has no interest in prolonging the trial and possibly alienating the jury by requiring the attendance of witnesses whose evidence will be uncontested. But we have been informed of a sufficient number of instances where defendants have not been prepared to agree documents where the only possible motive for their being unwilling to do so was a desire to prolong the trial, to confuse the jury and take advantage of every conceivable opportunity to play the system. There have been cases where defendants have required every cheque, every bank statement, every account entry to be identified and explained by a series of hapless witnesses who have then been subjected to prolonged cross-examination about their history and methods of work in the hope that a weak point will emerge."

The Roskill Committee also felt it was undesirable that a speedy trial could only be achieved by the co-operation of those on trial.[4]

Expert evidence

As has been mentioned above, fraud trials tend to involve issues and working practice which require expert evidence to explain them to the jury. Alternatively, expert evidence may be called to establish the distinction between normal working practices which although not ideal nevertheless do not amount to criminal behaviour, and criminal behaviour. The Roskill Committee saw no reason why a trial judge should not have power to order that a report should be admissible in evidence, leaving it to the jury to decide how much if any of it they accept as correct.

"The report must be open to challenge and since the maker of the report is likely to be available to give evidence, it seems to us absurd that everything should be dragged out orally and the jury never see the report on which in many cases the prosecution was founded."

[4] 5.27 Roskill Report.

The Reforms Contained in the Criminal Justice Act 1988

Vital reforms were made in the Criminal Justice Act 1988.

Section 23

Section 23 admits first-hand hearsay documents where the maker is unavailable to testify. The material provisions are:

- Section 23(1): "a statement made by a person in a document shall be admissible in criminal proceedings as evidence of any fact of which direct oral evidence by him would be admissible if:
  (i) the requirements of one of the paragraphs of subsection (2) below are satisfied ;or
  (ii) the requirements of subsection (3) below are satisfied."
- Section 23(2): "the requirements mentioned in subsection (1)(i) above are—
  (a) that the person who made the statement is dead or by reason of his bodily or mental condition unfit to attend as a witness; or
  (b) that
    (i) the person who made the statement is outside the United Kingdom
    and
    (ii) it is not reasonably practicable to secure his attendance
    or
  (c) that all reasonable steps have been taken to find the person who made the statement, but that he cannot be found."
- Section 23(3): "The requirements mentioned in subsection (1)(ii) above are—
  (a) that the statement was made to a police officer or some other person charged with the duty of investigating offences or charging offenders; and
  (b) that the person who made it does not give oral evidence through fear or because he is kept out of the way."
- Section 23(4): "Subsection (1) above does render admissible a confession made by an accused person that would not be admissible under section 76[5]."

"Statement" and "document" are defined as for the Civil Evidence Act 1968, section 10 (see above) which means that statement includes any representation of fact, and document includes graphs, photos and films.

[5] of PACE.

Section 24

Section 24 admits "business etc." documents whether or not the supplier of the information is available to testify, unless the document was prepared with proceedings in mind, in which case the document is only admissible where the supplier is unavailable to testify.

It will be noted that this section overlaps with section 23, but is wider in that it is not limited to first-hand hearsay. The extra scope of the section is justified because of the likelihood that documents admitted under it will be reliable.

The material parts of the section provide:

- Section 24(1): "a statement in a document shall be admissible in criminal proceedings as evidence of any fact of which direct oral evidence would be admissible, if the following conditions are satisfied—
  (i) the document was created or received by a person in the course of a trade, business or profession or other occupation or as the holder of a paid or unpaid office; and
  (ii) the information contained in the document was supplied by a person (whether or not the maker of the statement) who had or who might reasonably be supposed to have had, personal knowledge of the matters dealt with."
- Section 24(2): "subsection (1) above applies whether the information contained in the document was supplied directly or indirectly, but if it was supplied indirectly, only if each person through whom it was supplied received it—
  (i) in the course of a trade, business, profession or other occupation or as
  (ii) the holder of a paid or unpaid office."
- Section 24(3): "subsection (1) above does not render admissible a confession by an accused person that would not be admissible under section 76 of the Police and Criminal Evidence Act 1984."
- Section 24(4): "A statement prepared... for the purposes—
  (a) of pending or contemplated criminal proceedings; or
  (b) of a criminal investigation shall not be admissible by virtue of subsection (1) above unless
  (i) the requirements of one of the paragraphs of subsection (2) of section 23 above are satisfied ; or
  (ii) the requirements of subsection (3) of that section are satisfied; or
  (iii) the person who made the statement cannot reasonably be expected (having regard to the time that has elapsed since he made the statement and to all the circumstances) to have any recollection of the matters dealt with in the statement."

Both sections 23 and 24 are subject to section 25, which provides a structured discretion under which a court may refuse to admit evidence. The "test" is whether the court considers it to be in the interests of justice to admit the evidence.

Section 25

Section 25 applies where the court:

- Section 25(1): "is of the opinion that in the interests of justice a statement which is admissible by virtue of section 23 or 24 nevertheless ought not to be admitted, it may direct that the statement should not be admitted."
- Section 25(2): "Without prejudice to the generality of subsection (1) above, it shall be the duty of the court to have regard— (a) to the nature and source of the document containing the statement and to whether or not, having regard to its nature and source and to any other circumstance that appear to the court to be relevant, it is likely that the document is authentic;
  (b) to the extent that the document appears to supply evidence which would not otherwise be readily available;
  (c) to the relevance of the evidence that it appears to supply to any issue which is likely to have been determined in the proceedings; and
  (d) to any risk, having regard in particular as to whether it is likely to be possible to controvert the statement if the person making it does not attend to give oral evidence in the proceedings; that its admission or exclusion will result in unfairness to the accused, or if there is more than one, to any of them."

This structured exclusionary discretion can be exercised against the defence as well as against the prosecution.

Section 26

Section 26 also applies to documents tendered by either side. It comes into play in respect of statements which appear to have been prepared for pending or contemplated criminal proceedings, or a criminal investigation.

It provides that the statements to which it applies:

- Section 26(1): "shall not be given in evidence without the leave of the court, and the court shall not give leave unless it is of the opinion that the statement ought to be admitted in the interests of justice; and in considering whether its admission would be in the interests of justice it shall be the duty of the court to have regard—

(i) to the contents of the statement;
(ii) to any risk, having regard in particular to whether it is likely to be possible to controvert the statement if the person making it does not attend to give oral evidence in the proceedings, that its admission or exclusion will result in unfairness to the accused or, if there is more than one, to any of them; and
(iii) to any other circumstances that appear to the court to be relevant."

Recent case law

There has been extensive recent case law on these sections. The reader is referred to Archbold and to the *Criminal Law Review*.

Documentary hearsay and the interests of justice

Documents admissible under sections 23 and 24 are subject both to a general discretion to exclude provided by section 25, and to the similar but stronger requirement to obtain the leave of the court to admit documents prepared for criminal proceedings/investigations imposed by section 26. The sections direct the court to have regard to slightly different factors, according to which section is in play, but in both cases the court is allowed to consider any relevant matter, the ultimate question being whether the interests of justice are best served by admitting or excluding the evidence.

Sections 25(2)(d) and 26 (ii) require the court specifically to have regard to any risk of unfairness to the defence arising out of difficulties in contraverting the statement if the person making it does not attend to give evidence, and it is this provision which has been the focus of much of the early case law concerning witness statements or depositions tendered by the prosecution.[6] However, there is no equivalent provision dealing specifically with unfairness to the prosecution where evidence is tendered by the defence. Are the principles any different?

In *R* v *Patel*,[7] P's defence to an incident involving false imprisonment and criminal damage was alibi. Two alibi witnesses gave evidence but were uncertain about the date to which their evidence related. A third witness, L, who had made a statement supporting the alibi had left the country, and it was held that the trial judge was right to exclude L's statement under section 26. Two points were made:

[6] The most important is *R* v *Cole* (1990) 90 Cr App R 478 (CA).
[7] [1993] Crim LR 291 (CA).

1. with regard to its contents (a matter which the court must consider under section 26(i)), it was a very "bald statement" and had L been cross-examined he might have proved as uncertain as the other witnesses (the outcome might have been different if the police had had the opportunity to interview L);
2. the fact that the statement went to a crucial issue was not necessarily something going against admission: it might make it all the more important to admit it.

With regard to point (2.) in *Patel*, it may be the case that a different attitude to the introduction of crucial evidence in documentary form may be taken where the only piece of evidence available to the prosecution is a witness statement: thus in *Neill* v *North Antrim Magistrates' Court*[8] the House of Lords considered it doubtful whether it could be in the interests of justice to admit in untested documentary form evidence of identification which formed the principal element in the prosecution case.

Warning from the trial judge where evidence is of poor quality

The weight to be given to the inability to cross-examine depends, in part, on the quality of the statement. The court is required to consider how far any possible unfairness can be counteracted by a warning from the trial judge. In many cases the warning may have to be developed by pointing out the features in the documentary evidence which conflict with other evidence in the case.[9] An example of a case where the warning was not developed in the required manner is[10] where the statement of W, an alcoholic and alleged victim of a police beating, was admitted even though it conflicted with other prosecution evidence. It was held that it was not improper to admit the evidence, even though there was other prosecution evidence of the assault. However, the warning was not developed to draw attention to the inconsistencies.

[8] [1992] 1 WLR 1221 (H of L for Northern Ireland).
[9] Cole, *op cit n.* 6. above.
[10] *Kenally* [1994] Crim LR (Jan) (CA).

Computer evidence

Computer evidence is common in mortgage fraud cases. It can range from bank records to a solicitor's word processing files. Much computer evidence is also hearsay. Where this is the case, the courts have always accepted that the evidence must fulfil two criteria:

1. the conditions of a relevant hearsay exception (usually section 24 Criminal Justice Act 1988); and
2. the conditions of section 69 of PACE 1984, which in brief require proof that the computer was working properly and has not been tampered with.

- Section 69(1): "In any proceedings, a statement in a document produced by a computer shall not be admissible as evidence of any fact stated therein unless it is shown—

1. That there is no reasonable grounds for believing that the statement is inaccurate because of improper use of the computer
2. That at all material times the computer was operating properly, or if not, that any respect in which it was not operating properly or was out of operation was not such as to affect the production of the document or the accuracy of its contents and;
3. That any relevant conditions specified in rules of court under subsection (2) below are satisfied."

- Section 69(2): "Provisions may be made by rules of court requiring that in any proceedings where it is desired to give a statement in evidence by virtue of this section such information concerning the statement as may be required by the rules shall be provided in such form and at such time as required."

There was further difficulty where evidence, though computer-generated, was not hearsay. The Court of Appeal in *Minors* v *Harper*[11] regarded section 69 as inapplicable, despite section 69's clear provision that "a statement in a document produced by a computer shall not be admissible as evidence of any fact stated therein unless it is shown...". In spite of criticism from Professor Smith in *Criminal Law Review* commentaries, the fallacy persisted *e.g. Spiby.*[12] Fortunately, the House of Lords have now taken a hand. In *R* v *Shepherd*,[13] the central question concerned the expertise required of a witness giving oral

[11] [1989] 1 WLR 44 (CA).

[12] (1990) 91 Cr App R 186 (CA).

[13] [1993] 1 All ER 225 (HL).

evidence to prove the conditions of admissibility of a computer printout under section 69(1) of PACE 1984. In an important aside, however, the House of Lords considered that section 69 applies to all computer evidence, whether hearsay or not.

The case concerned the admissibility of Marks and Spencer's till rolls. The rolls were adduced in evidence by a store detective for the purpose of showing that goods found in S's possession had not been sold to her, the inference being that she had stolen them. The tills were linked to a central computer which fed in the date, the time, customer number and till number on each roll. The rest of the information was provided by the till operator punching in an item's price or product code number. The store detective was no expert in computers but was thoroughly familiar with the day-to-day operation of the equipment in question.

It was held that the degree of expertise to be expected of a witness giving oral evidence under section 69(1) to prove that the computer was operating reliably at the material times, varied according to the needs of the case, but in the vast majority of cases it would not be necessary to call an expert. Instead, the burden could be discharged by calling a person such as the store detective who is familiar with the operation of the computer in the sense of knowing what the computer is required to do and who can say that it is doing it properly.

It would be premature to say that computer evidence no longer poses a problem, but the decision in *Shepherd* was a step in the right direction. However, certain problems are still likely to be encountered; for example over the definition of a computer, when expert evidence is required, and how far bank and building society staff can be relied upon to satisfy the criteria in section 69.

Expert witnesses—the importance of expert evidence

Introduction

The preparation and use of expert evidence is a matter of great practical importance in fraud trials. According to the Roskill Committee Report:[14]

> "if the meat of a complex fraud case is an accountant's report we can see no reason why a trial judge should not have power to order that that report should be admissible in evidence leaving it to the jury to decide how much, if any of it, they accept as correct. It must of course be open to challenge and since the accountant,

[14] P 77, para 5.47.

unlike the foreign witnesses, is likely to be available to give evidence, it seems to us absurd that everything should be dragged out orally and the jury never see the report on which in many cases the prosecution is likely to have been founded."

This quotation emphasises an important truth about fraud trials. The prosecution is very often based on an expert's report, whether it be a general report upon the practises of a particular market place or a minutely detailed analysis of how a particular defendant's conduct not only fell short of that which could be expected from that defendant if he wished to avoid a claim for professional negligence, but how that conduct crossed the line between negligence and criminal conduct.

In *Whithouse* v *Jordan*,[15] counsel had assisted in the writing of a report by a medical expert. The involvement attracted judicial criticism both in the Court of Appeal and in the House of Lords Lord Wilberforce said:

"While some degree of consultation between experts and legal advisers is entirely proper, it is necessary that expert evidence presented to the court should be, and should be seen to be, the independent product of the expert, uninfluenced as to form or content by the exigencies of litigation. To the extent that it is not, the evidence is likely to be not only incorrect but self-defeating."

This dictum, as was pointed out in a recent article by Andrew Bartlett QC in *Counsel,* has caused confusion as to counsel's role. In practice, it is almost impossible to comply with it and at the same time properly prepare a case for trial. It is the duty of lawyers, not just counsel, conducting litigation to ensure that experts' reports are suitable both in form and content for the needs of the litigation. To the extent that an expert's report is not influenced in form and content by the needs of the litigation, it is likely to hinder the due administration of justice and to result in costs being wasted. Everyone involved in fraud trials sees this occur.

Lord Wilberforce's remarks were only dicta. Of the other four members of the court, only Lord Fraser expressed agreement.

Points in practice

It is suggested that the practical requirements of an expert's report in a fraud trial are as follows.

1. The contents of the report must not be dishonestly or recklessly devised, slanted or massaged for the purpose of supporting the case of the party calling the expert. Solicitors should be very wary of an expert recommended by a lay client or quasi-client.

[15] [1981] 1 WLR 246.

2. Within the limits of propriety, the expert is entitled and indeed ought to receive guidance from the party's legal advisers as to the form and content of the report. Guidance from the parties or from those conducting the investigation is likely to be partisan or capable of being presented as such to a jury.
3. In all but the simplest cases the form of an expert's report should not be left to chance or to the personal views of the expert. Some witnesses, while experts in their own field, have no practical experience of litigation and will require detailed guidance as to a suitable form for their report.

It is the legal adviser's duty to see that the report is in a form which is easy to assimilate for both the judge and jury. If it is not, time and costs may be wasted and the client's case may suffer.

Form of expert's report

Experts who are inexperienced in fraud trials may not be aware of matters which are obvious to an experienced prosecutor or defence lawyer:

- The report should be dated and signed.
- There should be a table of contents at the beginning.
- The report should commence with an introduction of the author, and his CV should be contained either in the introduction or in an appendix at the end.
- The report should be laid out clearly, preferably in short numbered paragraphs, and paginated.
- The contents should be presented in a logical order and broken down into whatever separate sections are appropriate for the particular case.
- Supporting items such as calculation sheets, test results and extracts from professional journals and codified principles of professional conduct, such as the *Guide to Professional Conduct*. should be contained in appendices.

Contents of expert's report

In relation to the content of an expert's report, lawyers also have very important functions to perform. They should vet the report to ensure it contains and only contains the material which it ought to contain.

- Does it clearly indicate the scope of the report? The expert should state exactly what he has been asked to report on by indicating the nature of his terms of reference.

- Does it adequately identify the material on which it is based? Differences of opinion between experts often stem from their being given different facts or assumptions from which to work. If the court is to weigh conflicting opinions from different experts, it is vital that it should know the factual basis for each opinion.[16]
- Is the report properly researched ? If the data available to the expert are insufficient for him to be confident of his opinion, he should indicate the areas of uncertainty and state explicitly where his opinion is provisional.[17]
- Does the report properly acknowledge the limits of the writer's expertise? The expert should make clear the extent to which the questions considered fall within the area of his special expertise. For an example see *The Ikarian Reefer*.
- Where a report contains evidence or expertise contributed by persons other than its apparent author, those persons, and their contributions, should be identified so that at the very least they can be tendered for cross-examination.[18]
- Has there been any change of view by the expert which requires explanation. Sometimes experts express views in meetings or in reports and subsequently change their minds and express a different opinion. Where this occurs it should be dealt with in their latest report, giving any necessary explanations. Otherwise they may lay themselves open to damaging cross-examination.[19]
- Does the report go too far in usurping the role of the judge? The traditional wisdom was that the expert should not express his view whether of fact or law on any matter which had to be decided by the judge or jury. Today this rule tends to be acknowledged more in the breach than in the observance. In a professional negligence case it is impossible for an expert to state his opinion without expressing a view on the very issue of negligence, and the same applies to fraud trials. It may, however, be appropriate for the witness to say something along the lines of, "In my opinion, the defendant adopted a course which a skilled practitioner acting honestly would not have adopted".
- What can be omitted from the report?[20]

[16] See the remarks of Cresswell J in *National Justice Compania Naviera SA* v *Prudential Assurance Company Limited* (*The Ikarian Reefer*) [1993] 2 Lloyd's Rep 68.
[17] *Re J (a minor)* (expert evidence) [1990] TLR 568, and see again the *Ikarian Reefer* case.
[18] *University of Warwick* v *Sir Robert McAlpine* (1988) 42 BLR 1,23.
[19] *University of Warwick*, above.
[20] See below.

So much for the expert's report and its contents. There remains the question of what constitutes an expert, how one finds an expert in a fraud-related field, and what procedural considerations apply to the admission of his report.

General points on experts' reports

There are many situations in which the issues the court is required to determine are so far removed from the court's experience, and indeed that of the jury, that it needs to obtain the opinion of experts to help it determine the issue in question.[21] When such a need arises the opinion of an expert is admissible. It is not possible to list all the matters in respect of which expert evidence is required—some matters are obvious, for example scientific and medical matters. In some matters the line between when to call expert evidence and when not to call it is very fine.

In *R* v *Turner*[22] Lawton LJ said: "The fact that an expert witness has impressive scientific qualifications does not by that fact alone make his opinion on matters of human nature and behaviour within the limits of normality any more helpful than that of the jurors themselves; but there is a danger that they may think it does."

Many of the cases on expert evidence do not in fact relate to fraud cases. Examples of matters where expert evidence might be called are:

- the practice in a solicitor's office in respect of conveyancing (mortgage frauds);
- the practice of a solicitor, banker or accountant on a reverse take-over (breaches of the Financial Services Act and section 151 of the Companies Act 1985);
- accountancy practice (thefts by an accountant);
- computers (whether or not the computer was working properly, or what was found on the computer hard disk of a defendant charged with offences under the Computer Misuse Act 1990).

Most professions have recognised professional standards for their members and may even prescribe what constitutes an expert. While the principle of "he who pays the piper calls the tune" is a commercially admirable one, it is part of the function of the prosecution or defence lawyer to ensure that the expert is indeed an expert, and this will involve enquiries of professional organisations,

[21] See generally *Folkes* v *Chad* (1782) 3 Doug KB 157.
[22] [1975] QB 834 at 841.

a detailed CV and a careful check to ensure that there is nothing in the expert's previous history which devalues his opinion, such as a professional negligence claim or involvement in an ongoing criminal enquiry as a witness of fact or, worse still, as a potential defendant.

Who is an expert?

Where a matter does call for expert evidence, only a suitably qualified expert can give it. Indeed the starting point in examining in chief an expert witness is to establish his or her expertise. This does not necessarily mean formal qualifications.[23] It will not be easy to satisfy a judge that a witness is expert in a field if he lacks formal qualifications.

The status of expert witness evidence

As Diplock LJ said in *R* v *Lanfear*[24]: "Expert evidence should be treated like the evidence of any other witness and it will be a misdirection to the jury that they must accept it." However, in *R* v *Anderson*[25] it was held that it would equally be a misdirection to tell a jury that it could disregard expert evidence which had been given by only one witness and which, if accepted, dictated one answer.[26]

Nature and content of expert evidence

An expert opinion will be based on much more than the facts of the particular case he is considering. It will be based on the expert's experience and any information that he has obtained from textbooks, articles and journals. Such information, often referred to as secondary facts, is not treated as hearsay but simply forms part of the basis for the expert's opinion. Obviously the facts on which the opinion is actually based, the primary facts, should be proved by admissible evidence, whether or not by the expert. For example, in *English Exporters (London) Ltd* v *Eldonwall,*[27] valuers gave evidence on the value of property on the basis of comparisons of valuations for similar properties. Necessarily this evidence relied on the opinions of other people as to valuations of other properties. Megarry J said, obiter, that such evidence is permissible, recognising that it is inevitable that experts will rely on what they research when forming their opinions.[28]

[23] See, for example, *R* v *Silverlock* where a solicitor had studied handwriting as a hobby for many years [1894] 2 QB 766.
[24] [1968] 2 QB 77.
[25] [1972] 1 QB 304.
[26] See also, to the same effect, *R* v *Bailey* (1977) 66 Cr App R 31.
[27] (1973) Ch 415.
[28] *R* v *Bradshaw* (1985) 82 Cr App R 79, where as a concession to the defence a psychiatrist was allowed to base his opinion on the accused's mental state upon statements made out of court by the accused, *i.e.* on hearsay.

A good example of the difference between primary and secondary facts is *R* v *Abandon*.[29] The defendant was charged with robbery. A forensic expert gave evidence that glass found on the defendant's shoes came from a window which had been broken during the robbery, samples of glass from both locations having the same refractive index. The expert stated that according to statistics produced by the Home Office Research Establishment, the chances of the glass being from two distinct sources were minimal. The defendant was convicted, and appealed on the grounds that the HORE statistics were hearsay. The Court of Appeal held that the statistics were secondary facts supporting the expert's opinion. So long as the primary facts—that the glass compared was (a) the glass on the defendant's shoes and (b) the glass from the robbery scene—were proved by admissible evidence, the expert could and indeed should state why he arrived at his opinion on those facts.

In the absence of an expert's report, a defendant cannot use referrence to a medical journal to help his defence.[30]

Advance notice of expert evidence in criminal cases

The prosecution is obliged to disclose expert evidence to the defence on general principles. However, there used to be no obligation on the defence to disclose expert evidence, even in cases where the defence carried a legal burden of proving a matter calling for expert evidence, such as insanity or diminished responsibility. This has been changed as regards Crown Court cases, by the Crown Court (Advance Notice of Expert Evidence)Rules 1987 (SI 1987 No 716) made pursuant to PACE 1984, section 81, which require any party proposing to adduce expert evidence to furnish the other parties with a statement in writing of the expert finding or opinion. Such party then, on request in writing by any other party, must provide a copy of the record of any observation, test or calculation on which the finding or opinion is based.

If the rules are not complied with, expert evidence can only be admitted with the leave of the court, but a party may elect not to comply with the rules if that party has reasonable grounds for believing that compliance might lead to intimidation or attempted intimidation of an expert witness, or to interference with the course of justice (but such party must give notice of the grounds for non-compliance to the other parties).

[29] (1983) 76 Cr App R 48.
[30] *Dawson* v *Lunn* [1986] RTR 234.

Opinion evidence and the hearsay rule

By the Criminal Justice Act 1988, section 30:

"**1.** An expert report shall be admissible as evidence in criminal proceedings, whether or not the person making it attends to give oral evidence in those proceedings.

2. If it is proposed that the person making the report shall not give oral evidence, the report shall only be admissible with the leave of the court.

3. For the purpose of determining whether to give leave the court shall have regard:

(i) to the contents of the report;

(ii) to the reasons why it is proposed that the person making the report shall not give oral evidence;

(iii)to any risk, having regard in particular to whether it is likely to be possible to controvert statements in the report if the person making it does not attend to give oral evidence in the proceedings, that its admission or exclusion will result in unfairness to the accused or, if there is more than one, to any of them; and

(iv)to any other circumstances which appear to the court to be relevant

4. An expert report, when admitted, shall be evidence of any fact or opinion of which the person making it could have given oral evidence.

5. In this section 'expert report' means a written report by a person dealing wholly or mainly with matters on which he is (or would be if living) qualified to give expert evidence."

The effect of this section, which applies to statements of fact and opinion, is clear: a hearsay exception specifically directed at expert reports is created. However, it represents a significant change in the law and it remains to be seen how strictly the courts apply it, particularly where the expert is not available as a witness (and the court's leave to admit the report is required).

The effect of evidential problems in fraud cases—Roskill's proposed reforms and how far have these happened

To some extent the problems of evidence which so vexed the Roskill Committee have now been remedied. The procedures for dealing with documentary hearsay have been clarified, though it remains to be seen how much use will be made of these. Certainly, shortly after the Criminal Justice Act became law, prosecution lawyers were not making the anticipated use of these provisions. One of the longest fraud trials ever, to date, was *Britannia Park*: a prosecution of the organisers of a theme park in Derbyshire prosecuted by the Fraud Investigation Group after the SFO had decided (admittedly shortly after it was set up) that the case was neither sufficiently serious nor sufficiently complex for the SFO to deal with it. One of the reasons which Professor Levy gave in his evidence to the Royal Commission for the length of the trial was that everyone was still learning to cope with the then new Criminal Justice Acts of 1987 and 1988, and accordingly the prosecution called 158 witnesses, some of whose evidence would now no doubt be dealt with differently. This case was not reported.

The rules regarding expert evidence have been clarified. However, many problems with experts are practical ones which are not capable of legal solutions. There are still professional organisations which either do not define in their code of professional conduct what qualifications an expert should have, or which alternatively provide no means of assessing what constitutes an expert in that profession. Of course the ultimate sanction for relying on an inadequate witness is to lose the case.

Problems of presentation of evidence

Schedules, charts and bundles of documents—how far technology can help

The one matter which everyone, however ill-informed, remembers and comments on about mortgage fraud trials, other than their length, is the number of documents involved in the trial.

It is accepted that the provision of adequate document handling, both pre-trial and during the trial, depends ultimately upon the funds made available for the prosecution and defence of fraud cases, and this may be, as Professor Levy has pointed out in his evidence to the Royal Commission and in his earlier book *Regulating Fraud*, a matter of political will.

In the Roskill Committee Report it was pointed out that much of the evidence in fraud cases is likely to be of such a nature that it lends itself to being summarised or put in the form of schedules. Examples given are the relevant features of a series of transactions, or the structure of a group of companies. Useful though such documents may be, their use at trial in summary form will depend upon the defence agreeing to their use. Failing such agreement, the documents will remain working documents only, and will have to be proved point by point in the usual tedious way. The Roskill Report also recommended that the judge should have power at a pre-trial review to order, where there is no genuine challenge to the documents upon which such a schedule is based, that the schedules should be admitted in evidence. Such a provision now only exists in respect of those cases where there has been a preparatory hearing.

Schedules, charts and other visual aids depend upon two other matters—a proper understanding of the complex documents involved in a fraud case and the ability to reduce those to a meaningful summary form, and whatever document-handling aids the prosecution team, in particular, has access to.

Some of the skills necessary to sift and rationalise the evidence in a fraud trial would apply to any complex trial. What follows is intended to be an *aide-mémoir* only. Fraud trials are a field-day for the computer-literate.

Initial handling of the evidence

The initial handling of complex data in a fraud case is made much more useful by the use of spreadsheets, or better still a simple database.

An advantage of data base packages such as Fox-Pro and Data Ease is that the very tedious job of scheduling transactions in date order, alphabetical order and in order of named applicant can be achieved by the use of standard report forms.

Once all the details of each transaction have been entered on the computer, searches can be made, for example to ascertain how many times and for what purpose a particular name or address has been used.

There are a number of specialist evidence analysis packages which are tailor-made for the legal profession and directly available as either proprietary software or through shareware houses. The Law Society publish a review of legal software, and there are regular articles in the trade magazines and in the *Journal of the Society for Computers and the Law.*

The handling of vast quantities of documents remains a problem in fraud trials. A computer-generated image of a document has no status, and until further research on this point has been done, it is likely that any document-handling system will remain no more than a tool for the lawyers involved, but will give place to the original documents at trial, with perhaps an improved system of presentation such as the rostrum camera system used at the *Blue Arrow* trial.

Both the Serious Fraud Office and the Crown Prosecution Service Fraud Investigation Group have pioneered the use of computers for a variety of purposes during the course of fraud cases.[31]

In an address to the Society for Computers and the Law, the then Barbara Mills, first director of the Serious Fraud Office, listed six ways in which computers could be used:[32]

1. For the management of documents—to preserve the source and integrity of documents. The SFO may have to prove two years later precisely where a document was found. A system has been developed in conjunction with the Metropolitan and City police which uses a combination of manual procedures and computer support. Documents which were seized during a search are sealed and removed to the SFO. There, they are entered into the computer. At any later stage in the investigation the document can be retrieved and its origin traced.
2. To facilitate access to the information contained in the documents or in a seized computer. Each document is put through an image scanner which converts the image of a document into digital representation. The software then converts that image into computer text. An index is created of every word in a document so that a large number of words can be searched quickly. Finally the operator can interrogate the text and display it. The prosecuting authorities seize large numbers of computers in their investigations. Computer contents are copied onto optical disks which cannot be altered, thus preserving them from any corruption. Sometimes it is necessary to recover material which has been wiped either deliberately or accidentally. Computer-generated material can be indexed and searched. Statements, exhibits and transcripts are added to the index in the same way as the case develops.
3. To retrieve information in a usable form. There is no point in storing and indexing unless the material can be retrieved in a useful form. By using keyword searches, all the dealings in shares in a particular company, for example, can be traced and easily presented. A chronology can be important. This is an extremely tedious task if done manually, but can be done very easily by computer. The SFO use a system called Topic.

[31] Mark Tantum, "The Lawyer and the War" 1991, *Yearbook of Computers and Technology* p 71.
[32] Barbara Mills, "The Use of Information Technology in Serious Fraud Trials" (1991) 2 *Computers and Law*, p 5.

4. For the preparation of evidence for court. The SFO has developed a simple system to allow an index of statements and documents to be created by an individual reference to a statement or exhibit. As a result, it is easy to prepare a list of unused material as well as committal bundles. If the reforms in prosecution disclosure proposed as a result of Judith Ward's appeal become law, this will be vital.
5. For the presentation of evidence for use in court. Simple multicolour block diagrams and bar charts can be produced with most graphics packages. An example of SFO work appeared in the *Blue Arrow* trial to show the share take-up rate and the timescale over which shares had to be taken up for the issue to be a success.

   - Concept graphics—sometimes fraud trials involve concepts with which the jury will not be familiar, such as trading in futures or unit trusts. (For an example of these, see Mark Tantum's article in *The Year Book of Law and Computers*.[33]
   - Fact graphics—these illustrate the accepted facts in a case, such as the structure of a company or interlocking structure of a group of companies.
   - Graphics which show the basis of an allegation, such as fraudulent trading.[34]

   So far as the production of schedules and charts is concerned, any standard computer graphics package will make the process much easier, particularly when last-minute alterations have to be made. Software Packages such as Harvard Graphics and Lotus Freelance all have their devotees. Much depends on the quality of printer on which the final result is produced as to how effective it really is. For the production of schedules and chronologies, each of the major word processing packages has its advantages. Those who are interested in this aspect of fraud trials may find the journal published by the Society for Computers and the Law of assistance.
6. Trial use. It goes without saying that for the computer to be used as a successful court room aid, the court room itself has to be fitted out appropriately. This has been the case with the new courts at Chichester Rents, used for the *Blue Arrow, Barlow Clowes* and *Maxwell* trials. The SFO use a central court display unit which provides images to the VDUs in front of the jury, counsel, witnesses

[33] 5 (1991), p 70. This article shows examples of all three sorts of graphic. The concept graphic is for trading in unit trusts.
[34] *Ibid.*

> and defendants and all other interested departments. At the moment the SFO use a rostrum camera to display documents, which has the advantage that the defence, who may not be as technically skilled, can put in documents manually in the usual way. The computer can be used to show on the VDU moving or static graphics of the sort referred to above. Transcripts are produced daily on a disk which is fed into the index central—this has proved to be of particular help, as there is of course a search facility which means a recollected piece of evidence can easily be referred to and used later in the trial.[35]

It would be wrong to suggest that technology in trial preparation is the sole prerogative of the SFO, or indeed of the prosecution, or to suggest that the use of such technology is without problems. Judges, lawyers and jurymen are used to having their own hard copy of documents, on which they can make notes.

Information technology is still in its infancy as a legal tool, but some problems in day-to-day use have already become apparent. Scanners work well with clean typed copies, but they are not so accurate with handwritten documents or poor photocopies, which have to be carefully checked after they have been scanned into the system, if they are to have any value. Text retrieval, data base, scanning software and hardware and any conversion software package all have to work smoothly together. The storage space has to be adequate and must operate both smoothly and quickly.

The cost of this type of technology is seen as prohibitive for many cases, and even modest systems may be too expensive for small legal aid firms, especially those which specialise in crime. Investment in systems is discouraged by the legal aid authorities and by lenders, even though the systems would reduce the cost of litigation and save expensive and scarce court time.

There is dispute as to who should pay for technology which makes court rooms more efficient, as illustrated by the recent dispute over the CRANS system. CRANS was a network system to notify barristers' chambers of the state of the court lists. Although hailed as a success by the profession, the Lord Chancellor's department is not prepared to continue using the system because it would lead to dependence on one software house.[36] Should it be the clients, the court, or the law firms who pay? What about compatibility and should the court provide the hardware and data base facilities? This might resolve the problem of inequality of resources between large and small firms.

In the trial of serious fraud cases, the SFO and CPS have funded the use of technology in trial preparation, notably in the *Guinness* case, but aim to

[35] Source: Nicholas Parnell, who appeared for the Crown, and Oliver Sells, who appeared for the defence.
[36] *Computer Weekly*, various articles during 1991 and 1992.

redress any imbalance by ensuring that the defence has full access to the computerised case. There is, however, the problem that the defence may not master the technology to the same extent as the prosecution, or may refuse altogether to deal with the computerised documents, insisting on hard (paper) copy. There is no obligation on defence lawyers to accept a computerised case, and some firms even insist on printouts of the contents of their client's computers, code and all.[37] It remains to be seen whether the sanction of costs in criminal proceedings can be used to meet genuinely obstructive behaviour.

It is sometimes forgotten that the SFO only deals with a tiny fraction of all fraud cases. Most are dealt with by the Fraud Investigation Group or by the CPS branches. Funds for computerisation would have to come from the Treasury, requring political will, particularly since fraud is only part of the CPS work. Wearing a different hat, the Treasury is keen to reduce the amount spent on legal aid for criminal cases.

The legal status of duplicate documents in image form is unclear. There is no precedent on the point in this country as yet. In the USA, duplicate records may be admitted in evidence if they "accurately reproduce the original". A recent case in California and quoted by Tina Bondy,[38] illustrates another aspect of the problem. Witnesses there were reluctant to identify documents shown on screen. This is not so much a legal issue as a psychological one.

Our criminal justice system is an adversarial one. The provisions of the Code for Crown Prosecutors do place an obligation on the prosecutor to consider the public interest. Whether this obligation has been successfully shouldered by what is still a relatively new service is a matter of debate, though curiously the recent academic research has dealt only with branch prosecutions[39] and not with the work of the FIG, CPS HQ or the SFO. One thing is certain, there is no obligation on defence lawyers to ensure that fraud trials are quick and effective—this may not even be in their clients' interest.

Abuse of process is an argument which has become fashionable in recent years in big fraud cases. The courts are only just beginning to accept that fraud cases, and particularly mortgage fraud cases, take time and manpower to investigate. There is as yet no obligation on the defence to consider the public interest, though an advocate for plaintiff or defence who wastes court time in civil proceedings may find himself at the other end of a personal order for costs, or sanctioned on taxation. Yet one thing which did come over from jurymen in the *Guinness* and *Britannia Park* cases was that the prosecution's efforts to summarise and to use concept graphics do seem to have been appreciated and that the jurymen felt that the defence were sometimes

[37] The author's personal experience—but none has yet insisted on code printouts being included in a fraud trial jury bundle!
[38] Tina Bondy "A Future for Courtroom Technology" (1991) 2 *Computers and Law* 5.
[39] McConville, Sanders and Leng, *The Case for the Prosecution* (Routledge, 1991).

deliberately obscuring the issues in the case, against the interests of justice. *Blue Arrow* illustrated this point still further. The transcripts show that the prosecution, who do after all have to prove their case beyond all reasonable doubt, occupied just over a quarter of the total court time.[40]

Perhaps the only way in which the tension between public interest and defendant's interests can be resolved is for the facilities at Chichester Rents to be expanded and for there to be Treasury support for fully computerised trials to take place, so that a study can be done to see what the advantages and disadvantages are. Only by imposing the system *ex cathedra* can the courts avoid the expense of retrial.

The real issues in making full use of information technology in the court room are not related to technology itself, but are organisational and human issues inherent in our criminal justice system. For instance, the design of any court room system will need careful thought. Portability is important—juries will need to have some way of taking copies to the jury room and of making notes on an exhibit which will remain confidential. Professional privilege must be preserved as well. There could be injustice if standards of computer literacy vary—there would have to be thorough training of counsel and skilled support. The same goes for the judiciary.

Mortgage fraud trials

There are four basic types of mortgage fraud (see Chap 1). The nature of this type of fraud is that for it to succeed at all but the very simplest level, there will have to be a solicitor or licensed conveyancer involved, and possibly also a valuer and a building society manager. The *dramatis personae* may also include either providers of false references, or legitimate businesses which are prepared for one reason or another to "expand" their payroll to include non-existent employees.

To quote Sir John Smith: "The courts have been much troubled recently with mortgage fraud—cases in which a bank or building society is induced to make a mortgage advance by deception."

The prosecutor has to decide whether to opt for substantive charges, or whether to charge statutory or common law conspiracy. One of the crucial problems is the variety of ways in which a mortgage advance may be paid, and the way in which the applicant expects the advance to be paid. A variety of substantive changes may be possible. The reader is referred to Professor Smith's many articles in *Archbold News* and in the *Criminal Law Review*.

[40] I am grateful to the SFO *Blue Arrow* court room support team for this information

Obtaining services by deception

By section 1(2) of the Theft Act 1978, obtaining services by deception "... is an obtaining of services where the other is induced to confer a benefit by doing some act, or causing or permitting some act to be done, on the understanding that the benefit has been or will be paid for." It has always been understood that this constitutes an exhaustive definition of the relevant words.[41]

A mortgage advance is the loan of money secured on property. The borrower seeks and obtains a loan because he wants it; it constitutes a benefit. He will pay for this benefit in the form of interest (plus any arrangement fee). In *Halai*[42] the appellant had been convicted of obtaining a service, namely a mortgage advance, by deception by falsely representing his employment details. In allowing the appeal on this count of the indictment, O'Connor LJ said:

> "In our judgment a mortgage advance cannot be described as a service. A mortgage advance is the lending of money for property and can properly be charged under section 15 of the 1968 Act, if the facts support it. This count should never have been in the indictment."

In *Widdowson*[43] the Court of Appeal distinguished *Halai* but added no helpful explanation beyond saying, obiter, that a hire purchase agreement can constitute a service.

Professor Smith's commentary in the *Criminal Law Review* includes the following passage:

> "The Court distinguished *Halai* but did not explain that puzzling decision. Services is very widely defined in section 1 (2) of the Theft Act 1978.... It can hardly be said that making a mortgage advance is not an act and any suggestion it is not to be 'paid for' would be greeted with cynical laughter by any mortgagor struggling to keep up his repayments including the high rate of interest required. A hire purchase agreement is obviously services for the purposes of the section; and so it is respectfully submitted is a mortgage advance. *Halai* is surely wrongly decided."

Obtaining property by deception

Perhaps, as Professor Smith has suggested, the reason that the court thought that obtaining the mortgage advance could not be obtaining services was because it was obtaining property. This is not an attractive charge because in practice lenders transfer funds to borrowers or solicitors by electronic means,

[41] See Smith and Hogan, *Criminal Law* (Butterworth), 7th ed (1992) p 574-5.
[42] [1983] Crim LR 624.
[43] (1985) 82 Cr App R 314.

telegraphic transfer, CHAPS[44] or a variation, not by cheque. There is no pre-existing property for the defendant to obtain.[45]

The Court of Appeal considered this point in *Williams and Crick*,[46] where the appellants were charged with conspiring together and with others in dishonestly obtaining property; namely money in the form of mortgage loans from lending institutions with the intention of permanently depriving the lending institutions thereof by deception. Macpherson J said:

"A point taken before the trial judge and before this court is that there was no obtaining of property in this case, because the transfer of money from the lending institution to the account of the mortgagor at the mortgagor's solicitors was by way of electronic transfer and not by cheque. The submission is that the creation of a positive balance in the solicitor's client account of the mortgagor and the reduction in the appropriate account of the lending institution was not an obtaining of property, but obtaining of services."

The point did not arise for decision in this appeal because some of the mortgage loans involved the sending (by the lending institutions to the mortgagor's solicitors) of cheques to the amount of the mortgage loan, so that in those cases property was obtained. Further there was no evidence that the conspirators contemplated that the mortgage loans would be effected by way of electronic or telegraphic transfer. The judge reviewed the criticisms of *Halai* including Professor Smith's article and the criticism by Lord Lane CJ in *R* v *Teong Sun Chuah and Anor*, decided on 19 February 1991. At page 4B of the transcript Lord Lane said:

"We have accordingly heard no argument on the question which was troubling the judge and has troubled others, namely whether the decision of the court in *Halai* was correct or not. The one sentence which we have already related, in which the court expressed their views on this matter, seems to us very likely to have been expressed *per incuriam*. Whether this is so or not, a decision on that point must wait for another occasion for review. Suffice it to say, so far as we are concerned that decision seems to have all the hallmarks of a decision *per incuriam*."

"... Mr Tyrell has submitted that where the mortgage advance is effected by way of electronic transfer there has been no obtaining of property. In our opinion, that submission is incorrect.

The matter turns on the meaning of 'obtaining' and the meaning of the word 'property' in the 1968 Theft Act. Section 4 (1) provides the general definition of

[44] Clearing House Automatic Payment System.

[45] See Griew (6th ed) para 7-06, Professor Griew's article at [1986] Crim LR 265 and Professor Smith's commentary on *R* v *Dhillon* at [1992] Crim LR 891.

[46] 29 July 1993 — transcript numbers 91/3265/W3 and 91/3266/W3, (1993) *The Times* 8 August 1993.

property for the purpose of the Theft Act 1968. It reads:

'Property includes money and all other property, real or personal including things in action and other intangible property.'

'In our opinion the sum of money represented by a figure in an account falls within the phrase 'other intangible property'. The reduction of the sum standing in the lending institution's relevant account; and the corresponding increase in the sums standing to the credit of the mortgagor in his solicitor's client account, although the transaction is effected by electronic means, is nevertheless the obtaining of intangible property. Those facts, in our view, fall within the terms of section 15(2) of the 1968 Act."

Identical considerations would probably preclude a charge of theft, even after the House of Lords' decision in *R* v *Gomez*.[47]

Procuring the execution of a valuable security: Theft Act 1968, section 20

A mortgage advance may be made by cheque, a CHAPS order or telegraphic transfer. A cheque is certainly a valuable security. Where the applicant expects to receive a cheque this seems a very appropriate charge. It accurately reflects the fraud involved—deceiving the lender into signing a cheque and thus creating a right against itself. It was held in *King*[48] that a CHAPS order was a valuable security, even though the primary executor of the security was the defendant himself—it was also signed by bank officials, and their signatures were procured by deception. In *Bolton* the judge's direction that a telegraphic transfer was capable of being a valuable security was held to be wrong, in the absence of any evidence as to how it works. In *Manjdadria*[49] it was held that neither the telegraphic transfer nor the computerised ledger account of the solicitors making it was a valuable security.

Of course a mortgage deed could be a valuable security, but in modern conveyancing practice the mortgage deed is only signed by the mortgagor, which may make Woolf LJ's suggestion in *Bolton* at pages 78-79 difficult to apply. As Professor Smith has said:

"In these cases it seems that the applicant generally does not know how the advance will be made. If he expects a cheque and gets a CHAPS order or vice versa he is presumably guilty. He causes the *actus reus* he intended to cause so the doctrine of transferred intent should apply. But if he procures a telegraphic transfer that is not the *actus reus*. If however he believed the advance would be made by cheque or CHAPS he might be guilty of an attempt to commit an offence under section 20."

[47] [1992] 3 WLR 1067.
[48] [1991] 2 WLR 246.
[49] [1991] Crim LR 73.

Conspiracy to defraud

Conspiracy to defraud has the same advantage as a charge under section 1 of the Theft Act 1978. It does not matter what method of making the advance was anticipated by the applicants, nor what method was actually used. The lender will be equally defrauded whether he makes the advance by cheque, CHAPS or telegraphic transfer. Much then depends on when the conspiracy occurred (as in *Bolton* and *Manjdadria*) before 20 July, 1987. If it did, the rule in *Ayres*[50] still applies and a conspiracy to defraud will not lie if the carrying out of the agreement would necessarily amount to the commission of a specific offence. It must then be charged as a statutory conspiracy. If the agreement was made or continued[51] after that date it may be charged as a conspiracy to defraud as well as a statutory conspiracy.[52]

Conspiracy to procure the execution of a valuable security

This was the offence charged in *Bolton* and in *Dhillon*. Under the Criminal Law Act 1977 there is a conspiracy only if the carrying out of the agreement "will necessarily amount to or involve the commission of an offence." It was argued in *Bolton* that if the transactions might in fact have been carried out by telegraphic transfer they would not necessarily amount to the commission of an offence under section 20. The court held that "in the case of conspiracy as opposed to the substantive offence, it is what is agreed to be done and not what is in fact done which is all important." It is therefore sufficient if the jury were satisfied that at the time of the agreement the defendants contemplated that the execution of a valuable security would necessarily be in one or more of the 34 transactions. But they had been misdirected that a bank statement and a telegraphic transfer were valuable securities.

In *Dhillon* the judge left it to the jury to decide on the basis of their own experience whether advances were generally paid by cheque and whether the defendants must have expected and intended that they would be so paid. It is submitted that that was wrong. This is not a matter on which juries have the necessary experience to decide.

Dishonesty

Whatever the offence charged, dishonesty must be proved as well. In *O'Connell*, the defendant obtained mortgages on residential properties which he intended to let and then sell off at a profit when prices rose. He used false names because he knew that the building societies would not make multiple mortgage advances in this way for commercial purposes. The judge ruled as inadmissible his testimony that because the building societies had good

[50] [1984] AC 447 HL.
[51] *Boyle and Mears* (1992) 94 Cr App R 158.
[52] See *Dhillon* [1992] Crim LR 889.

security for their money and he intended to repay in accordance with the contract, he did not regard the conduct as in any way dishonest. It was held that the evidence should have been admitted and the jury could then have been directed in accordance with *Ghosh*.[53] However, because it was such a prolonged and extensive scheme, involving so many properties, the court was in no doubt that a jury properly directed would have convicted, and dismissed the appeal, applying the proviso.

There are a number of particular factors which should be borne in mind in sentencing for mortgage fraud. These were outlined by Leggat LJ, in giving the judgment of the court in *Stevens* (see Chap 1).

Practical problems with mortgage fraud trials

Documents at trial

Mortgage fraud trials tend to involve very large numbers of similar documents which relate to similar transactions. The prosecution should give thought early in the proceedings to the form of trial and jury bundles. Much of the evidence can be reduced to a more palatable form for presentation to the jury. Schedules should be prepared to show:

1. the chronology of individual transactions;
2. the parties involved—vendors, purchasers, mortgagors, solicitors and estate agents—correlated with each property;
3. addresses used for correspondence, references and addresses to which correspondence is sent after completion.

Documents will be obtained from a number of sources—the parties' solicitors, the defendants and the mortgagors. These should be sorted according to property address, with their source indicated, perhaps by the use of colour coding. If a solicitor is involved then the client's ledger card should be matched to the property and with the bill and statement of account.

The jury will find it easier to follow the trial if supplied with a simple explanation of the conveyancing process, perhaps illustrated with specimen documents and a flow chart.

[53] [1982] QB 1053.

CHAPTER 11

Prosecuting Bodies

The Crown Prosecution Service

The majority of fraud cases are prosecuted by the Crown Prosecution Service, either at branch level or by Crown Prosecution Service Headquarters. The Crown Prosecution Service was created by the Prosecution of Offences Act 1985 to be an independent prosecuting service. Staff were recruited largely from the old county prosecuting solicitors' departments and from the DPP's office. The latter, in particular, had always had a few fraud specialists. In 1985, the Fraud Investigation Group (FIG) was created. Its structure and its guidelines were set out in Home Office Circular No 16/1985 to Chief Officers of Police, which appears as an annex to the Roskill Report at page 233.

The two main objectives of the FIG were to be as follows.

> "first to ensure the speedy investigation and institution of proceedings in those cases where the course is justified, and second early identification of those cases where an investigation is unlikely to result in criminal proceedings so that the investigation may be discontinued and valuable manpower and other resources deployed to other investigations. It will be an essential function of FIG, and a matter over which the Controller will exercise close supervision, to avoid wastage of time on minor offences, minor offenders, blind alleys and peripheral matters."

It was intended that the FIG should handle the following sorts of frauds:

- frauds upon government departments and local authorities;
- frauds which include large-scale corruption;
- frauds involving large shipping and currency offences;
- frauds discovered by Inspectors appointed pursuant to section 109 of the Companies Act 1967 or section 165 of the Companies Act 1948.[1]

It was envisaged that the FIG would also handle :

- frauds upon the governments of other countries;
- frauds with an international dimension;
- frauds involving nationalised industries and public limited companies;
- frauds by persons connected with Lloyd's of London, the Stock

[1] Now ss 446 and 447 CA 1985.

Exchange and other commercial exchanges;

- frauds involving well-known public figures, for example Members of Parliament, captains of industry.

FIG lawyers and accountants were intended to play a major role in the investigations.[2] It was also intended that counsel should be involved at an early stage in very complex cases. At the time that the Roskill Report was compiled, four weeks was seen as a long trial. Trials lasting many months, and even years, such as *Blue Arrow*[3] and *Britannia Park*[4] were the stuff of nightmares for court administrators.

At the time that Lord Roskill's Committee reported, the FIG was a new department. Even then three important factors were recognised :

1. "fraudsters are skilful and well organised and the number of cases is increasing year by year";
2. in the investigation of frauds, a number of government departments are involved in the same area of work. The committee said that though they had been told that it was accepted that one department should have a co-ordinating or overseeing role, they did not accept that this was the case;
3. the role of the FIG in supervising and advising on investigations conflicted with the rationale of the independent Crown Prosecution Service.

It was these considerations which led to the committee's recommendation that the Serious Fraud Office be set up. At the time of writing, the definition of a Serious Fraud Office case is that:

1. the facts and/or the law are complex; or
2. there is great public interest or concern; and
3. in judging referrals, account will need to be taken of the need to use the Serious Fraud Office's section 2 powers, whether the value of the alleged fraud exceeds £1 million and, for marginal cases, the availability of resources. The financial limit has recently been revised downwards: the previous limit was £5 million.

The FIG, now known simply as Headquarters Fraud, has more complex selection criteria. The sums at risk should not be taken as the sole factor for deciding which fraud cases should be referred to the FIG. As a general rule, one or more of the following should be present:

[2] Roskill, p 236.
[3] *R* v *County Nat West and others.*
[4] *R* v *Kellard and others* (unreported).

1. the facts and/or the law should be of considerable complexity;
2. the sums at risk are substantial—in excess of £250,000;
3. there is considerable public interest and concern;
4. the need for expert (in-house) financial guidance and investigative assistance;
5. the proposed defendants are personally known to the local area chief crown prosecutor or his senior staff, or it would cause embarrassment for the proposed defendant to be prosecuted by the local area CPS.

Cases falling under the following guidelines have been found to respond well to the FIG process, according to the Roskill Report:

1. frauds on government departments and local authorities (and sponsored agencies which are supported by public funds);
2. those which involve large-scale corruption;
3. those involving large shipping and currency offences;
4. frauds upon governments of other countries;
5. frauds with an international dimension;
6. frauds involving nationalised industries and very large public limited companies (most cases of multiple share applications fraud would not be referred to CPS HQ on financial criteria alone);
7. frauds by persons connected with stock exchanges and other commercial exchanges and City institutions;
8. frauds involving well-known public figures.

Frauds falling within the following categories which meet the general criteria should be reported to CPS HQ at the first instance:

1. frauds discovered by Inspectors appointed pursuant to sections 432 or 447 of the Companies Act 1985 and reported to the DTI;
2. frauds discovered as a result of police investigations into alleged contraventions of the Insolvency Act 1986, the Insurance Companies Act 1982, the Financial Services Act 1986, the Building Societies Act 1986, the Lotteries and Amusements Act 1976 and the Local Government Act 1972;
3. reports by liquidators relating to delinquent officers and members of companies pursuant to section 218 of the Insolvency Act 1986;
4. reports by Official Receivers;
5. frauds which require banking evidence to be obtained from Switzerland, Liechtenstein, Andorra or Austria;
6. frauds which require the services of an investigating accountant or other investigating expert;
7. frauds reported by the Law Society or other professional bodies;

8. frauds which are likely to require extradition;
9. frauds which the DPP has designated as serious and complex and has issued a notice of transfer pursuant to section 4(2) of the Criminal Justice Act 1987.

There has been much media and ministerial discussion as to the respective roles of the SFO and the CPS. It seems likely that the rivalry between what are after all two government departments, unless it is to become destructive, will be resolved at ministerial level—and in the present economic climate, on financial grounds.

This rivalry was to some extent fuelled by the transfer of Mrs Barbara Mills from the SFO to the CPS, where she commissioned a review of the prosecution of fraud by CPS Headquarters.[5] The Royal Commission on Criminal Justice has recognised that the present state of affairs is unsatisfactory. The two departments were carrying out very similar work, but the CPS department did not have the same powers or resources available as the SFO:[6]

> "Unfortunately practical considerations preclude us from recommending either an immediate amalgamation of the FIG with the SFO or an extension of section 2 powers to the FIG. The two bodies work quite differently. The SFO mounts highly resourced team investigations; the FIG advises on investigations which are carried out almost exclusively by the police. The Director of the SFO told us in oral evidence that he was concerned that any amalgamation should not dilute the resources available to the SFO to cope with its existing workload. We accept that that risk must be avoided. But we are seriously concerned that the powers and resources which are held to be necessary for the effective investigation and prosecution of serious and complex fraud are not available to all those who are charged with that task, particularly at a time when the number of offences and amounts of money involved are both increasing. It cannot be regarded as satisfactory that the present state of affairs should continue indefinitely and we therefore recommend that the government conduct a study of the feasibility of merging the SFO and the CPS's Fraud Investigation Group as a matter of urgency."

The Royal Commission were aware that this would still mean that a large number of cases would still fall to be investigated by the police under their ordinary powers, but doubted whether in the short term it would be practical to aim for more than the proposed amalgamation.

The Royal Commission were principally concerned with investigations undertaken by the police though they expressed the broad hope that their

[5] Source: *Independent on Sunday*, 3 July 1994.
[6] Para 73.

recommendations would be taken up by other relevant agencies such as Customs and Excise.[7]

The Code for Crown Prosecutors

The Code for Crown Prosecutors is issued pursuant to section 10 of the Prosecution of Offences Act 1985 and is included in the DPP's annual report to the Attorney-General. Amendments to the Code can be made from time to time. It was revised in 1994.

When considering the institution or continuation of criminal proceedings, the first question to be determined is the sufficiency of the evidence.

The Crown Prosecution Service does not support the proposition that a prima facie case is enough,[8] but will apply the test of whether there is a realistic prospect of conviction. Obvious matters to which a prosecutor should apply his mind are set out in the text of the code.[9] The second criterion, once the evidential sufficiency hurdle has been cleared, is the so-called public interest criterion.

Having satisfied himself that the evidence can justify proceedings, the Crown Prosecutor must then consider whether the public interest requires a prosecution. The Crown Prosecution Service will be guided by the view expressed in a House of Commons debate by Lord Shawcross when he was Attorney-General and subsequently endorsed by his successors:

> "It has never been the rule in this country—I hope it never will be—that suspected criminal offences must automatically be the subject of prosecution. Indeed the very first regulations under which the Director of Public Prosecutions worked provided that he should... prosecute 'wherever it appears that the offence or the circumstances of its commission is or are of such a character that a prosecution in respect thereof is required in the public interest.' That is still the dominant consideration."[10]

He concluded by saying that regard must be had to "the effect which prosecution, successful or unsuccessful as the case may be, would have upon public morale and order, and with any other considerations affecting public policy."

Although the public interest will be the paramount consideration, the interests of the victim are an important factor in determining the balance of the public interest. Decisions of the Crown Prosecutor were expressly

[7] s 114 of PACE is concerned with the application of PACE to HM Customs and Excise. The Act applies to the extent directed by Treasury Order.
[8] Para 6.
[9] Code for Crown Prosecutors, para 5.
[10] H.C. Deb, vol 483, col 681, 29 January 1951.

excluded from judicial review, in the Prosecution of Offences Act.

Factors which are referred to in the Code which may be relevant to fraud cases are:

1. the likely penalty;
2. staleness;
3. old age and infirmity: in the context of serious fraud trials infirmity usually means whether or not the defendant is fit to stand trial. This is a difficult area, because a defendant may have become mentally disturbed or depressed by the mere fact that his conduct has been discovered. Some defendants have made miraculous recoveries, either when the prospect of prosecution has receded, or after an appeal has been heard.

Paragraph 13 of the previous edition of the Code reminds prosecutors of the Practice Direction at [1977] 2 All ER 540, which states that where an indictment contains counts alleging substantive offences and a related conspiracy count, the prosecution must justify the joinder of or be required to elect to proceed on the substantive or conspiracy counts.

The effect of *R* v *Ayres*,[11-12] which effectively abolished common law conspiracy to defraud, has been reversed by section 12 of the Criminal Justice Act 1987. The Act also provides a maximum penalty for the offence, of ten years' imprisonment. Where substantive offences are no more than steps in the achievement of a dishonest objective, prosecutors may concentrate on the objective and charge a single count of conspiracy to defraud. This single charge is also used by prosecutors where it is felt that substantives will not meet the case by adequately reflecting the degree of criminality involved in a course of conduct.

The provisions of the Criminal Justice Act 1992 as to which offence may be taken into account in sentencing have led many prosecutors to charge conspiracy to defraud where prior to the Act substantives might have been considered more appropriate. It has sometimes been forgotten that the elements of the conspiracy still have to be proved.

The Attorney-General has expressed a wish that the Code should be applied *mutatis mutandis* by the SFO.

[11-12] [1984] AC 447.

Inland Revenue

The Inland Revenue exists to recover tax, not to prosecute:

"In the main the department deals with the tax evader not by prosecution but by money penalties graded according to the gravity of the offence.... Criminal Prosecution for tax offences is undertaken only in a small minority of cases... a selection of the most serious cases of fraud."[13]

Criminal proceedings are undertaken as a last resort and the decision to prosecute may therefore not be made until long after an investigation has been instigated. Investigations will be subject to the Taxes Management Act 1970, section 20. Once the decision to prosecute has been made, the normal rules of criminal procedure apply. The decision to prosecute is entirely at the discretion of the Revenue, as is any decision to compromise. The Code for Crown Prosecutors is not mandatory.[14]

Investigation

Taxpayers may be invited for interview at any stage of an Inland Revenue enquiry. The taxpayer cannot be compelled to attend or forced to answer questions. Interviews are not taped, though if the taxpayer agrees that an interview is accurate, it may subsequently be used against him.

In answer to a House of Commons question on 5 October 1944, the then Chancellor of the Exchequer said:

"The Commissioners have a general power under which they can accept pecuniary settlements instead of instituting criminal proceedings in respect of fraud or wilful default alleged to have been committed by a tax payer. They can, however, give no undertaking to a tax payer in any such case that they will accept such a settlement and refrain from instituting criminal proceedings even if the case is one in which the tax payer has made full confession and has given full facilities for the investigation of the matter. They reserve to themselves complete discretion in all cases as to the course which they will pursue, but it is their practice to be influenced by the fact that the tax payer has made a full confession and has given full facilities for investigation into his affairs and for examination of such books, papers, documents or information as the Commissioners may consider necessary."

The *Hansard* statement used to be given to taxpayers, and any statement made in response to it would be ruled inadmissible by the courts, on the basis

[13] The Committee on Enforcement Powers of the Revenue Departments, Cmnd 8822.
[14] See Inland Revenue policy as set out in the *Hansard* statement.

that it had been induced by the promise to consider not instituting criminal proceedings in exchange for full disclosure from the taxpayer. Books and records produced in response to it were treated in the same way.[15] This position has now been reversed by section 105 of the Taxes Management Act 1970. Statements and documents produced in response to a *Hansard* statement are now admissible. After arrest in a revenue case, the provisions of PACE and the Codes of Practice apply.

Production of documents

The Inland Revenue can demand the production of documents under section 20 of the Taxes Management Act; taxpayers may also be required to furnish particulars. The taxpayer has to be given the opportunity to produce documents and furnish particulars voluntarily, before a formal demand is made.[16] The documents have to be in the power or control of the taxpayer and the tax inspector must reasonably be of the opinion that the documents relate to the taxpayer's business affairs in the UK or another member state of the EC.[17] The Board of Inland Revenue can make similar requests if they reasonably believe that the taxpayer has committed or will commit a serious breach of the tax rules.[18] The particulars relate to answering questions, not to interview. The questions will be set out in the notice and answered in writing. A notice can be served on a third party, such as a professional adviser, with the consent of a general or special commissioner. The name of the taxpayer must be included and should relate only to such documents as may be in the third party's possession or power and, as in the reasonable opinion of the tax inspector, contain or may contain information relevant to any tax liability to which the taxpayer is or may become subject. There is no provision for the furnishing of particulars. Confidentiality is overridden by the duty to furnish particulars but not legal privilege. Only if the taxpayer is suspected of fraud will he not be sent a copy of the notice.

The courts will find the tax inspector's opinion reasonable unless strong evidence can be adduced that the documents sought do not relate to the tax affairs of the taxpayer.

There are further powers to obtain information in sections 745 and 788 of the Income and Corporation Taxes Act 1988, with sanctions for failing to comply which may be enforced by proceedings under section 98 of the TMA.

Powers of search

Powers of search are contained in section 20C of the TMA which require an *ex*

[15] *R* v *Barker* [1941] 2 KB 381, [1941] 3 All ER 33.
[16] Tax Management Act 20B(1).
[17] s 125 Finance Act 1990.
[18] TMA s 20A (7).

parte application to a circuit judge. There is no right for the taxpayer to be heard. It is usual for a police officer to be present at an Inland Revenue search. Such a warrant can only be applied for if there are reasonable grounds for suspecting that a serious fraud offence is involved.

The offence has to involve substantial financial gain or serious prejudice to the proper assessment or collection of tax, or be part of a course of conduct which is, or would but for its detection be, likely to involve serious prejudice to the proper assessment or collection of tax.

Items may be removed during a search[19] if the officer has reasonable cause to believe that they may be evidence for the purpose of proceedings. The officer may also conduct a search of any person found on the premises whom he has reasonable cause to believe to be in the possession of such things. A record of items seized must be supplied.

The case of *IRC* v *Rossminster*[20] examined the issue of warrants generally. The House of Lords held that the description "an offence involving fraud in connection with or in relation to tax had been committed" was sufficient for the warrant to be upheld as valid. The taxpayer did not have to be told the precise nature of the offences alleged against him nor of the reasonable grounds upon which the judge who had originally heard the *ex parte* application had been satisfied that the application was a proper one.

Professional privilege

A legal advisor is not obliged to deliver up any document in his possession for which a claim to professional privilege can be maintained.[21] This protection does not extend to the material in the possession of the taxpayer. Similarly, documents which are at the lawyer's premises may not be removed.[22] The definition of legal privilege in a tax case is extended to legal advice generally, whether or not given in contemplation of legal proceedings. Section 20B creates a quasi-legal privilege for auditors and tax advisers. It only protects documents which are the auditor's property and were created by him or on his behalf for or in connection with the performance of his functions.

The Serious Fraud Office

The origins of the SFO

When the Roskill Committee reported, in January 1986,[23] it expressed the concern that:

[19] s 20C (3).
[20] [1980] AC 952, [1980] 1 All ER 80.
[21] s 20B (8).
[22] s 20C.
[23] The Report of the Fraud Trials Committee (1986).

"The public no longer believes that the legal system in England and Wales is capable of bringing the perpetrators of serious frauds expeditiously and effectively to book. ... In relation to such crimes, and to the skilful and determined criminals who commit them, the present legal system is archaic, cumbersome and unreliable. At every stage, during investigation, preparation, committal, pre-trial review and trial, the present arrangements offer an open invitation to blatant delay and abuse. ... Self-regulatory mechanisms designed to encourage honest practices are now coming into force. Where those mechanisms are abused, the law must deliver retribution, swift and sure."[24]

The Roskill Committee's principal recommendation that the "need for a new unified organisation responsible for all the functions of detection, investigation and prosecution of serious fraud cases should be examined forthwith".[25] The Criminal Justice Act 1987 Part I established the Serious Fraud Office and conferred its powers of investigation and prosecution of offences of serious or complex fraud.

The SFO became fully operational in April 1988. Its immediate objectives included:

- the development of a coherent approach to the investigation of serious fraud;
- the development of expertise in specialist areas, such as stock exchange fraud, insurance fraud and computer fraud;
- the more efficient use of the new procedures established by the 1987 Criminal Justice Act for prosecuting complex fraud cases;
- the presentation of cases in new and more accessible ways so that ordinary members of juries could understand the issues.

The SFO is accountable through its Director to the Attorney-General and to Parliament. The Director of the SFO is required to make an annual report to the Attorney-General on the discharge of his functions.[26] The Annual Report provides an evaluation of the SFO's performance.

In addition to the Director, the SFO is staffed by a Deputy Director, Chief Accountant and a hierarchy of assistant directors (who are lawyers or accountants), other lawyers and accountants and administrative staff.

The SFO's caseload

The SFO receives cases from a variety of sources. Most frequent sources of referrals are the DTI and the police. Other sources include self-regulatory

[24] *Ibid*, at p 5.
[25] *Ibid*
[26] s 1(15) and Sched 1, para 3 of the 1987 Criminal Justice Act.

organisations, the CPS, Bank of England and others (such as members of the public, solicitors, accountants and companies). In that same period 5% of cases were generated internally from other investigations.[27]

Frauds involving banking, insurance, the investment of money or the management of funds, criminal offences committed during the course of mergers or acquisitions, shipping and currency frauds and frauds uncovered in the course of investigations, for instance under the Companies Act 1985, the Financial Services Act 1986 or the Banking Act 1987[28] have all been included in the SFO case load.

A number of large mortgage frauds have been prosecuted by the SFO.

The SFO's criteria for acceptance of a case are set out at page 124 above.

In deciding whether to accept a case, regard will also be had as to whether the SFO's special powers of investigation conferred by section 2 of the 1987 Criminal Justice Act and powers to transfer cases from the Magistrates' Court to the Crown Court conferred by section 4, will be required.[29]

At any one time the SFO handles approximately 60 cases. The type of cases has varied widely, from very substantial and well-publicised investigations and prosecutions like *Guinness*, *Blue Arrow/County Nat West*, *BCCI*, *Maxwell* and *Polly Peck/Nadir*, to much smaller and less widely known cases. The Annual Report carries full details.

Internal organisation

If a case is accepted for investigation a case team is appointed by the Deputy Director. This team is headed by the Case Controller, who will be an experienced lawyer. Other members of the team will include an investigating lawyer, accountants, police officers, information technology personnel and administrative support staff. The case team may also work closely with other experts, for instance bankers, stockbrokers and computer specialists, seconded to the SFO as required by the needs of a particular investigation. It is usual for prosecuting counsel to be instructed at an early stage of the investigation.

The decision to prosecute and charge

As an investigation progresses the Case Controller, either alone or with a more senior lawyer, reviews the evidence obtained and decides whether it is sufficient to justify a prosecution. A lawyer who has played an active part in the investigative process, for example by conducting section 2 interviews, will

[27] See Annual Reports.

[28] For more details see *An Introduction to the Serious Fraud Office* and *The Serious Fraud Office - What it does and How it works*, both published by the SFO, and the SFO's Annual Reports.

[29] See SFO Annual Report 1992-93 at p 25, and Staple, "Serious and Complex Fraud: A New Perspective" (1993) 56 MLR 127 at p 129.

not play a part in this process.[30] The SFO applies the Code for Crown Prosecutors in making decisions to institute and continue proceedings.[31] Whilst judicial review of the decision to prosecute is a theoretical possibility, in the absence of evidence of fraud, corruption or bad faith on the part of the prosecuting authority, such a challenge is highly unlikely to succeed.[32] Logically, this would also appear to apply to any challenge to the Director's power to "investigate any suspected offence which appears to him on reasonable grounds to involve serious or complex fraud" under section 1(3) of the 1987 Criminal Justice Act.

If a decision is made to lay charges, the police officers on the case team will arrest and charge the defendants. They are then taken to the magistrates' court where questions of bail are resolved.

Procedure in serious fraud trials

The special transfer procedure for use in serious fraud trials is to be found in the Criminal Justice Act 1987 and its accompanying statutory instruments (see Bibliography). It should be noted that by section 4(2)(d) of the Criminal Justice and Public Order Act 1994, this procedure is preserved.

Section 44 (1) of the 1994 Criminal Justice and Public Order Act abolishes committal proceedings and replaces them by an administrative transfer for trial procedure. The new procedure became effective on 10 July 1995. There is a helpful article on procedure during the adjustment period in *The Law Society Gazette* of 24 May 1995.

It remains to be seen whether any overlap between the two procedures causes practical difficulties.

[30] For a review of the SFO's powers, especially under s 2 of the 1987 Act see DM Kirk and AJJ Woodcock *Serious Fraud Investigation and Trial* (Butterworths, 1992).

[31] See Archbold para 1-296 to 1-297 and Appendix D to the Supplement.

[32] See *R* v *IRC, ex p Mead and Cook* [1993] 1 All ER 772; *R* v *Panel on Takeovers and Mergers, ex p Al Fayed*, *The Times,* 15 April 1992.

CHAPTER 12

A Checklist for the Prevention and Recognition of Mortgage Fraud

By now, this book should have made it quite clear that, for the average honest solicitor, mortgage fraud is expensive and stressful. The best preventative measures are education and advice. These should be coupled with an in-house reporting scheme, together with a more developed determination to prevent the dishonest members of the profession from flourishing.

The first source of education and advice has to be in-house. All staff should have access to a copy of the *Guide to Professional Conduct of Solicitors*, the *Professional Standards Bulletins* and the latest edition of the Green Card.

I make no apologies for including my own checklist for prevention and recognition of mortgage fraud and, indeed, other sorts of fraud common in solicitors' offices.

1. Take up references for staff. In particular, check with the Law Society before you employ admitted staff or solicitors' clerks.
2. Do not go on employing staff you know are dishonest. Small firms seldom survive intact after a mortgage fraud, and larger firms are irreparably damaged. Checking the names of firms involved in mortgage fraud with any of the professional directories two years after will illustrate the truth of this.
3. Meet your clients at least once.
4. Building societies are clients too. You should be familiar with the *Guide to Professional Conduct of Solicitors* and, in particular, with the provisions which relate to conveyancing.
5. When in doubt, ask someone who knows better—a partner, counsel, the Law Society Professional Ethics and Guidance Department, or even your insurers.
6. If you have been referred clients from a source which you do not know well, such as an estate agent, insist on meeting the client before you agree to act for them. You should also check introducers with their appropriate regulatory organisation.
7. Never take instructions from a third party without a valid power of attorney. Always confirm instructions in writing. Be very wary of the intermediary, be he financial adviser or estate agent, who claims to act for a number of clients. If the problem is language, use an interpreter —preferably an independent interpreter.

8. Multiple purchases and sales by the same client, especially through nominees or shelf companies, and especially over a short period, should be watched carefully. Check that a company exists. Check where you suspect that there is a connection between the company selling and your client; family members who are directors is the common example.
9. Watch the client who seems to have a lot of solicitors on stream at once. This is a practice that makes fraud easier.
10. Question instructions to show anything other than the true sale price in documents, especially if the cash price or other particulars differ from the mortgage offer.
11. Mortgage fraudsters seem to favour small suburban firms and larger firms with a number of staff solicitors who may be on a profit-related bonus. It is not unusual for two or three firms in the same area to be unwittingly involved in a fraud. In at least one case, if the solicitors involved had compared notes when they found that members of the same family were using a rota of solicitors, the loss to the compensation fund and SIF could have been prevented.
12. If you are faced with a number of clients with a very common name, you should seek to establish identities. Ask to see identification and make a note on the file with a copy of the identification supplied.
13. Never take instructions only by phone or letter.
14. Always keep an eye on the client's address. A client whose address does not change on completion is unlikely to be a genuine residential purchaser. A number of clients who use the same address should be questioned. It is a feature of mortgage frauds that addresses are recycled, both as residential addresses and as security. Only the building societies change each time, so that building society staff will not spot fraud.
15. Small-scale mortgage fraudsters use permutations of their own names, so look out for maiden names or diminutives of a first name. Rosemary, for example, will become Mary.
16. Organised "factory" mortgage fraudsters use nominees. Look to see where the deposit cheque comes from. Check the identity of the nominee as well.
17. There are no really good reasons for chains of roll-over transactions in residential conveyancing. They should be particularly suspect where there is a steady, or even marked, rise in price with a different source of finance every time. If this is happening, particularly with a different firm of solicitors in a different area for each step, you should take advice immediately. Solicitors in different areas are used on the theory that professional jealousy will prevent the firms concerned from

comparing notes. You must check the position of your client lender as well. Building societies do not specialise in short-term finance for property developers at preferential rates.

18. Check the use of the property. It is not unheard of for the enterprising fraudster to finance a chain of hotel purchases with loans from building societies and banks. This is still fraud.

19. When the property market slumps, the technique changes. Intermediaries, in particular, make money out of insurance commission and multiple chains of transactions. Use your common sense—is it really likely that a house would increase in value in a slump? If the purported reason is that there have been improvements, ask to see evidence of this—building regulation consents, fire certificates, planning permissions. Do bear in mind that it is only possible to get so many residential units out of a terraced house. There have been a number of mortgage frauds where the fraudsters have used tame builders, or even a company of their own, to carry out non-existent conversions.

20. Above all, ask yourself why a new client has selected you out of all the other solicitors in the area.

Education

It is crucial that all solicitors—not just those who are subject to the Continuing Professional Development requirements—should keep up to date with the law and with developments in practice and procedure. Increasingly, as well as offering courses on aspects of a new law, the providers of professional education are also offering practice-related courses which include courses on client-handling and, in particular, on the less attractive aspects of practice, such as a solicitor including fraud by clients and staff. These are advertised in the legal press. You will be familiar with the Law Society *Gazette*. A less well-known source of regular updates is LINK, the Legal Information Network, which is a software package providing an on-line electronic mail and information retrieval service for lawyers. It is easy to use and, at the time that this book went to print, the basic system is available without charge.

LINK provides an electronic document exchange. You can send messages and documents to other lawyers on the system free of charge. It provides access to thousands of pages of legal information, such as case transcripts, articles, legal updates and the latest legal news. It can be used to access specialist legal services, such as company searches, shelf companies, ordering textbooks and Lexis.

The system is not, however, designed to be a toy for PC wizards. It is designed to save money by providing information electronically to which, in particular, small firms would not normally have access. It is much cheaper to check a case through LINK than to send an articled clerk to the nearest law library! The vast majority of services, including electronic document exchange, can be used free of charge. Services which have to be paid for, such as company searches, are clearly marked. Lawyers in private practice will find the electronic document exchange extremely useful because of its speed. It can, for instance, be used to send urgent instructions to a barrister. The information service has obvious benefits. In addition, many lawyers in private practice will want to join in conference and discussions on-line, both with other private practice lawyers and with in-house lawyers. For the small firm and for sole practitioners, this provides a valuable additional source of advice. LINK software can be obtained by faxing their systems administrator on headed notepaper, on 0171 396 9300.

The majority of solicitors will, by the time that this book is published, have become familiar with the reporting procedures required by the Money Laundering Regulations 1993. The Law Society has sent a pack containing the guidance card (it's a blue card this time), together with a suggested form of report and general advice on preventing money-laundering and setting up a reporting system. Money-laundering is often allied to mortgage fraud and both sorts of fraud can be equally devastating to a solicitor's practice. Common sense would suggest that the same reporting system can be used by staff to alert the partners to circumstances which they find suspicious. Quick, Easy and Written should be the key words in respect of a reporting procedure. A report should include date, circumstances giving rise to suspicion, and relevant documentation—because a decision may have to be made about either retrieving documents from storage or their preservation. The identities of the reporter and reportee should be given and the action to be taken should be recorded. It is a sad fact that smaller firms can be better at supervision and reporting procedures than larger ones, simply because the partners tend to be more accessible. The *Guide to Professional Conduct* does spell out responsibilities which partners have towards their staff and to their clients; see above. These have a better chance of being fulfilled if the partner responsible for receiving such a report is perceived by the staff as being approachable and willing to listen.

Sources of help outside the firm

Outside the firm, sources of help tend to be classified not by their quality but by whether or not the solicitor concerned will have to pay for them. The Law Society's Professional Ethics and Guidance Department is one obvious source. A less well-known source of assistance is the Solicitors' Assistance Scheme. The Scheme was set up in 1972 to help solicitors who might find themselves in difficulties in obtaining guidance and advice from an independent and sympathetic solicitor on a confidential basis. The Scheme is administered by the Law Society's Professional Ethics and Guidance Department, which is quite separate from the Solicitors' Complaints Bureau. A list of Scheme members is, however, sent out by the SCB to those who are invited to provide an explanation with regard to their conduct by the Bureau. Members are nominated by local law societies usually and are neither officers nor council members of the local society. The Scheme is operated on a completely confidential solicitor-and-client basis. No charge is made for the first interview. It is not unusual for solicitors in difficulties to contact a Scheme member from outside their own area. Often, Scheme members help by acting as a source of referral to specialist help; for example, the Lawyers' Support Group provides help with alcohol and drug abuse problems. Professional Ethics and Guidance will also provide to scheme members details of appropriate sources of help. Local law societies can also provide a source of both education and advice. Many local societies—an example is the Holborn Law Society—have provided a series of lectures on mortgage fraud and, of course, their functions provide an opportunity for solicitors to meet other members of the profession.

Lastly, SIF will provide assistance over the telephone, particularly on claims avoidance. Those solicitors who are unfortunate enough to find themselves involved in a claim for professional negligence will be referred to one of the panel solicitors specialising in professional indemnity work.

Barristers who specialise in professional negligence and fraud work can be traced easily from the directory published annually by Chambers & Partners, or through the Law Society.

Some useful names, telephone numbers and addresses are listed below:

Professional Ethics and Guidance
Ipsley Court
Berrington Close
Redditch
Hereford & Worcester
B98 0TD
Telephone: 0171 242 1222, local calls 01527 517141

Fax: 01527 510213
DX: 19114 REDDITCH

Lawyers' Support Group
c/o St Giles's Church
Off Wood Street
Barbican
London
E2

Telephone: 01202 734488
0181 870 1601
01895 833245

Solicitors' Indemnity Fund Limited
100 St John Street
London
EC1M 4EH

Telephone: 0171 566 6000
Fax: 0171 566 6006
DX: 46601 BARBICAN EC1

Chambers & Partners Publishing
74 Long Lane
London
EC1A 9ET
Telephone: 0171 606 2266

Bibliography

General books

Archbold, *Criminal Pleading, Evidence and Practice* (Sweet and Maxwell, updated annually).
Blackstone's Criminal Practice (Blackstone Press, annual).
Griew, *Theft Acts 1968 and 1978* (Sweet and Maxwell, 1992).
Kirk and Woodcock, *Serious Fraud Investigation and Trials* (Butterworths, 1992).
Levy, *Regulating City Fraud* (Tavistock Publications, 1988).
Levy "Serious fraud", research paper 27 (Royal Commission on Criminal Justice).
The Fraud Trials Committee Report (Chairman, The Lord Roskill PC) (HMSO, 1986).
Smith and Hogan, *Criminal Law* (Butterworths, 1992).

Expert evidence and other evidential problems

Clarke, *Mortgage Fraud*, (Chapman and Hall, 1991).
Evidence and Casework Skills (Inns of Court Law School, updated annually).
Hodgkinson, *Expert Evidence Law and Practice* (Sweet and Maxwell, 1990).
Jackson and Powell, *Professional Negligence* (Sweet and Maxwell, 1992).

As well as the usual professional journals, the *Journal of Expert Evidence* is published quarterly and can be read in most law libraries, such as the Institute of Advanced Legal Studies at 17 Russell Square, London WC1.

Legislation

Criminal Justice Act 1987 (Dismissal of Transferred Charges) Rules 1988.
Criminal Justice Act 1987 (Preparatory Hearings) Rules 1988.
Criminal Justice Act 1987 (Preparatory Hearings) Interlocutory Appeals) Rules 1988.
Criminal Justice and Public Order Act 1994.

Case Study 1
Grape and Quince

False references

Grape is a solicitor's clerk who has still to complete his training as a solicitor. Quince is a sole practitioner, practising under the style of Quince and Co. in the London suburb of Upmarket. The practice is a general one which used to earn most of its income from residential conveyancing, some commercial work and magistrates' court advocacy.

Since the property market slump, income from domestic conveyancing has fallen badly. Grape is a promising employee who shows talent as an advocate. The salary which the firm is able to pay is limited by the practice's declining income. Grape wishes to buy a house for his own occupation. He is unable to find a house which he can afford to buy with the mortgage which he is likely to receive on the basis of his salary.

Quince writes an employer's reference for Grape which shows his earnings to be £30,000, a sum which is made up of his basic salary, inflated by a profit-related bonus. No such bonus scheme operates and the firm's income would not justify the payment of any bonus even if such a scheme existed.

Case Study 2
Drum

Drum traded as a financial services adviser and estate agent in Downmarket. Downmarket is a suburb of London with a large ethnic community, many of whom earn well below the level of income which would enable them to obtain a mortgage. Most of the housing stock in the private sector consists of Victorian and Edwardian terraced houses, with some inter-war semi-detached properties.

Drum, with assistance from others, marketed a mortgage package. For between £200 and £1500, an applicant was guaranteed a mortgage with suitable supporting references or accounts if he was self-employed. The deposit was dealt with by way of a further loan at a higher rate of interest, or by an adjustment in the purchase price, which was shown on the papers as a deposit which was paid directly to the vendor or to Drum. In fact, no deposit was paid in these instances.

There is a shortage of rented accommodation in Downmarket, both in the private sector and in the local council housing stock. Many applicants for council housing are housed in accommodation which is rented in the private sector, through a local authority scheme. Where the tenant receives housing benefit this is paid direct to the landlord.

Drum and his cronies quickly discovered that they could make more money by letting premises than by selling them. Either the tenants' names were used as purchasers but they held the property as nominees for Drum, or totally bogus applicants for finance were used. To avoid detection, Drum was careful to use a stable of solicitors.

The scam was detected when the same bogus reference was used too frequently. A local shop was shown as having more employees than could actually stand in its premises.

Case Study 3
Trumpeter and Trombone

John Trumpeter and Peter Trombone were old friends. Both were well educated to postgraduate level. On leaving university, they decided to set up shelf companies to exploit their ideas. None of the companies was a commercial successes, however. The accounts for the most successful year showed a gross profit of only £700.

The friends began to realise that exploiting bright ideas which they had had at university would not earn them enough to support the lifestyle which they wanted. Together with an old friend and undischarged bankrupt, Banjo, and an insurance broker, Flute, they decided to become property developers, particularly in the Lowlands area.

The scheme began with the remortgaging of their own houses. To support the remortgage, the companies provided references for the friends which showed earnings of £80,000 and £100,000 per annum. The proceeds of the remortgage were then used to fund the deposits in the next round of purchases and sales.

To avoid detection, two offshore companies were used, both as intervening steps in the chain of transactions and as ultimate beneficiaries of the proceeds. One company in particular, Fugue Holdings, registered in the Cayman Islands, is intended as a vehicle to avoid tax.

John Trumpeter acquired a very expensive lifestyle. At trial, analysis of his bank account showed that he seldom ate a meal other than at an expensive restaurant and the remand hearings were enhanced by the procession of expensively clad girlfriends who turned up on each occasion.

One of these ladies was a junior assistant solicitor in a well-known firm. One can only assume that her professional judgement had been overtaken by affection. She was alleged, by the defence, to have advised John Trumpeter that there was nothing illegal in the chains of rollover transactions which he and his friend were using. These transactions were further concealed by the use of a stable of solicitors. Transactions which involved offshore companies were dealt with by larger firms, while the nominee transactions were dealt with through a number of high street firms. Only one of these firms became suspicious when transactions involving a Miss Smith were dealt with by way of instructions from John Trumpeter. Two further firms of solicitors were kept in line by Flute by the promise of further work if they dealt expeditiously with a series of minor steps in the chains of transactions.

Some £45 million worth of building society money was obtained. As the property market fell, the properties were not so profitable on resale. The friends, Trumpeter and Trombone, had to enlist a corrupt valuer and also had to spend money splitting larger properties into flats. They had to resort to letting mortgaged properties to short-term tenants.

Case Study 4
Wagner, Bach and Deadlock

David Deadlock was a solicitor practising in a suburban high street. He was a sole practitioner, and employed a number of unqualified clerks. He had one office only.

Alan Wagner and his wife had been married since 1976, with two daughters, Samantha and Rose. Mr Wagner had worked in various businesses, as had his wife. These included catering, packaging and hairdressing. Both the Wagners were born abroad, but lived at Oak Cottage, Anytown, Hertfordshire. Both became unemployed because of Mr Wagner's ill health, and wished to return home. However, Mr Wagner failed to fulfil this ambition and died on 28 November 1991.

This was an extensive and calculated mortgage fraud, in which each of the main players acquired a portfolio of residential properties by fraudulent mortgage applications in respect of bottom of the market terraced houses in a generally run-down area. Only a selection of properties are included in this case study.

Pages 289–290 show a schedule of 28 transactions, all of which formed part of the Wagner portfolio. The bar chart at page 291 shows the pattern of property ownership. It was not difficult to prove at trial that both the Wagners owned more than the permitted one residential property! Deadlock's involvement in the fraud was shown from the documents supplied and from the number of files and transactions where his firm acted. On occasions there was a breach of the rule which prevents solicitors from acting for both purchaser and vendor—the schedule shows examples where both the vendor and purchaser were represented by Deadlock (transactions 20,22,23,25,26,27 and 28).

Mr and Mrs Wagner refinanced 31 Crimson Road (5) 116 Grey Road (19) 31 Crimson Road (23) 195, Chestnut Road, (27) and 131 Titanium Road (28) by dummy sales from one member of the family to another.

Addresses were recycled as reference addresses, both for employers' references and landlords' references. Applicants for mortgages also used them as correspondence addresses. Alan Wagner created various bogus businesses as well. (See false references section below.)

When the correspondence seized by the police from Deadlock's office was analysed, a schedule of addresses could be prepared showing the addresses to which Mr Deadlock wrote when corresponding with the Wagner family or their nominees. This chart appears on pages 286–288. Deadlock did not think that the Wagner failure to move was at all odd.

Many of the properties were let to local authority tenants, who are a safe source of income because they receive housing benefit which can be paid direct to the landlord—who was almost always Mrs Wagner.

Case Study 5
Salt, Peach and Kumquat

Commercial mortgage fraud

Between August 1988 and May 1989 Peach and Kumquat arranged the purchase of eight hotels for a total of £14.9m. In order to obtain sufficient finance to do so they represented that the purchase prices in fact totalled £24.3m. In the first two cases they were able thereby to obtain 90 per cent mortgages from the North Bank and South Bank respectively. The last six properties were mortgaged to the Astra Building Society, and in that case more was borrowed than was needed to buy the hotel. Between 6 March 1989 and 26 May 1989 a surplus of £2.8m was obtained from this source. Summary details of the dates and figures are set out on page 167.

The method by which the increase in price was achieved was the insertion of a bogus back-to-back purchase and sale by an offshore company controlled by Peach and Kumquat through nominees. It was only the contrived sub-sale which was put up to the lenders as a genuine arm's-length transaction.

In all the purchases Peach and Kumquat were assisted by Salt, a solicitor's clerk who did the conveyancing. In the first two cases the lenders instructed their own solicitors, and it can be seen from the correspondence that Salt was prepared to tell any lie to assist his clients. The Astra relied on Salt as the borrowers' solicitor, in the same way as a normal house mortgage, and in each case he failed to disclose anything about the original purchase price.

In the first two cases the borrowing was limited by the valuation obtained. Even by inflating the turnover figures and giving a false purchase price, they could not achieve a dramatic increase in the valuation figure. That all changed, however, when Loaf, an estate agent and valuer, became involved. With one exception his valuations accorded with the inflated bricks and mortar purchase price, even when this was over £2m more than the true price.

Two of the hotels were sold on to partners who actually ran them after the purchase. The effect of the transactions in those cases was to give them 100 per cent mortgages, with all their costs and disbursements paid, the opening stock bought and probably something for the float, at the cost of increased loans.

Individuals

Peach

Peach claimed to come from a wealthy family with interests in engineering, property and insurance. He was said to have a world-wide income in excess of £250,000 per annum. He also claimed to be a graduate of Oxford University, which was false.

Kumquat

Kumquat was an accountant apparently qualified in the USA and a partner in Kumquat Grape & Co. In fact there is no record of Mr Grape's existence, nor was he ever at the offices.

Kumquat claimed that his family owned a confirming house and a finance company in America. He was said to have a world-wide income in excess of £440,000 per annum.

Salt

Salt was an unqualified conveyancing clerk working for the firm of Widget & Co. in Southshire.

Loaf

Loaf was not a qualified surveyor. He used the initials AIBA, which might be mistaken for such a qualification, but which in fact stands for Associate of the Institute of Business Agents.

In May 1985 he joined Gold & Gold as a land buyer. In March 1988 that firm became Haematite Gold & Gold. He was not permitted by the firm to carry out mortgage valuations, nor did Haematite ever use outside surveyors. He left on 30 April 1989. Prior to his leaving, and prior to 22 March 1989, he removed about 25 Haematite files from the firm's offices.

Companies and others

Brightvale

Brightvale Services Limited was incorporated in England on 15 January 1987. Peach was appointed a director on 16 March 1987. Kumquat was appointed a director on 24 June 1987, and a Miss Gooseberry was then appointed secretary. Miss Gooseberry resigned on 31 March 1989 and Kumquat took over as secretary. The filed accounts for the period 15 January 1987 to 10 June 1990 show a net profit before tax of £10,435.

Sidepiece

Sidepiece Limited was incorporated in England on 11 May 1988. On 13 June 1988 Peach became a director and the registered office was changed. On 14 June 1988 Kumquat was appointed a director.

Sausage

Sausage Limited was registered in Jersey on 22 April 1988. It was set up as a result of a meeting in early April 1988 between Peach and Kumquat and Jane Crumb at Brightvale's offices. Jane Crumb operated Semolina Financial Services Limited and related companies in Jersey, which provided a management service for offshore companies. Nominee directors were appointed and the three shareholders were Semolina companies which executed a declaration of trust in favour of Mushy Peach, the supposed uncle of Peach, living in the USA. Correspondence and requests for payments of fees were always addressed to Peach.

On 9 May 1989 Salt gave Jane Crumb instructions to liquidate Sausage and to set up two new companies. The new companies were formed—Gisal and Teeko—but Sausage was not liquidated as Salt realised that authorisations had not been given for the various transactions in the company's name. On 8 October 1989 he sought to give Miss Crumb instructions to backdate such authorisations. However, the sample letter referred to contained a forged signature of Miss Crumb, and she wrote to Peach and Kumquat to complain about this.

The Investment Trust

When Sausage was discussed Jane Crumb also received instructions from Peach and Kumquat to set up a British Virgin Islands Trust. This was a discretionary trust in which the settlor was named as Mushy Peach and two local BVI charities were named as beneficiaries. However, the settlor could change his wishes at any time and the trustees, while in theory having absolute discretion as to the distribution of the funds, would in practice follow those wishes.

Among the papers found at Peach and Kumquat's offices, and sent to various financial institutions, were letters purporting to come from the State Ban of Utopia, stating that the net worth of The Investment Trust was in excess of £2m. The State Bank of Utopia, however, could later find no reference in any of its files to any contact with Peach, Sidepiece or The Investment Trust, nor was the typeface one used at that branch. The conclusion was that the letters were not genuine.

Alfalfa

Alfalfa Investments Limited was incorporated in the Isle of Man on 11 July 1986. It was bought by a firm of accountants acting on behalf of Loaf in

September 1986. The new directors were named as Egon Zebedee and Juan Domingo Plum, but these were in reality aliases of Loaf, who gave all the instructions. He arranged for letterheads to be printed, and it was to him that requests for payments of accounts were made.

On 25 May 1989 the accountants were told that Zebedee had moved to Panama and that no further business was to be done in the UK. The importance of this date is that it was just after the sum of £400,000 had been paid to the company in connection with the purchase of the Wonder and the Fugue hotels.

Malvern Securities

Malvern Securities Limited was incorporated in the Isle of Man. In March 1988 it was bought by Bread & Company Limited in Guernsey and new Channel Island directors were appointed. It was believed that these were nominees for one or more of the individuals involved in this case.

Gisal

Gisal Properties Limited was incorporated in the British Virgin Islands on 10 May 1989, on the instructions of Salt. The same nominee directors were appointed as for Sausage. It may simply have been intended as a replacement for Sausage, to be operated by Peach and Kumquat, but the fact that the name is made up from the first few letters of the name Giles Salt raises another possibility.

Opera

Conveyancing

The Opera was a 56-bedroom hotel in the West Country. It had been bought by Robin Pot and Steven Leg on 1 October 1986 for £600,000 including goodwill, fixtures and fittings. They ran the hotel through a company, Opera Hotel Limited. In the period to May 1988 they had carried out a number of improvements to achieve a four-star rating, and had added a hydro suite.

In July 1988, for personal reasons, the hotel was put on the market. Wheats estate agents, had advised a value of £1.2m some months previously. The asking price was set at £2m. Details were sent to Peach and Kumquat, who viewed on 4 August 1988 and again on 9 August 1988. Oddly, since he was an accountant, Kumquat showed no interest in the hotel accounts, although he was provided with a set of forecast figures. Peach and Kumquat quickly offered £1.9m, which was just as quickly accepted.

Messrs Widget & Co. were instructed to act for Peach and Kumquat, and

Salt handled the transaction. He was aware at an early stage of the possibility of a sub-sale to a subsidiary company. Contracts were exchanged on 19 September 1988 between Opera Hotel Limited and Sausage at a price of £1.9m. Completion was fixed for 10 October 1988. Salt wrote to Peach and Kumquat on 21 September 1988 to tell them of the exchange, saying that he would prepare a bundle of relevant documents relating to the sale from Sausage to Sidepiece "so that it can be presented to the solicitors acting for the bank when necessary".

In the end completion did not take place until 3 November 1988. The sub-sale to Sidepiece was incorporated in the transfer deed at a bricks and mortar price of £2.4m, together with goodwill, fixtures and fittings for a further £300,000, making a total price of £2.7m.

Finance

This was arranged through New Finance Brokers Limited. They were given information about Peach and Kumquat in the form of letters from accountants and a letter apparently from the State Bank of Utopia. This last letter was also sent to the eventual lenders, the North Bank.

The proposition was put to the North Bank as a purchase by Sidepiece from Sausage for £2.7m. Nothing was said about the original price of £1.9m, or about the relationship between Sidepiece and Sausage. An interview with Peach and Kumquat was conducted on 29 September 1988. Grand claims were made about Peach and Kumquat's experience and wealth. A number of other representations were also made:

1. The Investment Trust was a vehicle for bringing money into the UK.
2. It was Peach and Kumquat's intention to boost the share capital of Sidepiece to £500,000 within the next two months.
3. Sidepiece had agreed a purchase price of £2.7m and had exchanged contracts using its own funds for the 10 per cent deposit.
4. Peach and Kumquat would be putting £984,000 of their own resources towards the purchase. The letter from the State Bank of Utopia was produced as evidence of the existence of such funds.

It was clear from the contemporaneous records and recommendations that the size of the cash contribution was an important factor in the decision to grant a loan.

The application was accompanied by a valuation report from Biscuits, which valued the property at £1.9m, and the business as a going concern at a maximum of £2.6m, based on projected turnover figures supplied by Kumquat of £980,000 in the 12 months to 30 September 1989. Similar, though slightly lower figures were claimed as actual turnover in late 1989. These were double the turnover prior to the sale, and the projection for 1989/90 was just not possible.

The offer of advance from the North Bank was dated 5 October 1988. The sum offered was £1.716m, being 66 per cent of Biscuits' going concern value and about 90 per cent of their bricks and mortar value. It was subject to conditions, including that Sidepiece's solicitor should confirm:

1. the agreed purchase price;
2. that Sidepiece had £984,000 plus the related costs of acquisition to contribute towards the funding exercise without recourse to borrowing;
3. that Sidepiece's share capital would be increased to £500,000.

The offer was accepted by Peach and Miss Gooseberry on behalf of Sidepiece. In accordance with other conditions of the offer, Kumquat sent various Sidepiece accounts to the Bank.

Having claimed that Sidepiece were buying from Sausage for £2.7m, that transaction had to be arranged. On 7 October 1988 Salt wrote to Jane Crumb in Jersey to tell her of the purchase and sale by Sausage. He also asked for confirmation in writing that a sum in excess of £984,000 was available as a deposit on exchange of contracts between Sausage and Sidepiece. This letter was sent by fax. In order to set up the reply, Kumquat faxed a letter to Jane Crumb on the same day confirming that Brightvale would pay Sausage £1.407m if required. As a result, Jane Crumb was able to write her letter to confirm that the funds were available. The same day, 7 October 1988, Salt then wrote to the bank confirming the matters requested in the offer of advance.

Following this confirmation, the bank instructed its own solicitors, Rich & Partners. They discovered about the sub-sale and asked questions. On 18 October 1988 they asked for confirmation that the sub-sale was at arm's length (which it was not, as Salt well knew); that there was no connection in any manner, *i.e.* that none of the directors or shareholders of Sidepiece had any interest whatsoever in Sausage (which they did, as Salt well knew); and that the consideration of £800,000 would be passed to Sausage from Sidepiece at the conclusion of the transaction. Peach had apparently told the bank that Sausage was the vendor's company. Salt's reply was to confirm that none of the directors and shareholders of Sidepiece had any interest whatsoever in Sausage, and to claim that Sausage was an established client of Mr Widget, the senior partner of Widget & Co. The letter of instruction to Jane Crumb, however, came from Salt himself.

Rich had also asked for a letter of postponement of the loan from The Investment Trust to the bank's loan. Salt wrote to Mossack Fruit to ask for this, saying "Sidepiece Limited have stated that the Investment Trust is to make a capital injection of £500,000". The clear inference is that Salt knew that no such capital injection would in fact be made.

On 27 October 1988 Rich raised further queries. In reply the same day by fax, Salt again confirmed all the matters set out in condition 2 of the offer of advance, and continued:

> "Our Senior Partner has acted for the beneficial owners of Sausage Limited, who are at present resident overseas for tax purposes. We are unable to reveal their identity but can assure you that they have no connection with Sidepiece Limited, its Directors or Shareholders or Guarantors. We confirm that the consideration of £800,000 will be passed to Sausage Limited by Sidepiece Limited at completion."

On the basis of these assurances, the funds required were released for completion on 3 November 1988. If the bank had known that the assurances were untrue, the money would not have been advanced.

Valuation

Biscuits had valued the hotel, on bricks and mortar basis, at £1.9m, having been given an inflated idea of its potential turnover. On 8 March 1989 Biscuits updated their valuation, at the request of Peach, reaching a figure of £1.995m.

There is a Loaf report for the Astra dated 24 April 1989 giving a value of £2.6m. The wording makes it clear that this has been taken from the original Biscuits report. It appears to have been countersigned, but this signature is a forgery.

On 28 December 1989 Soup & Partners valued it for the Receivers of Sidepiece at £1.2m on the open market.

On 20 September 1990 the District Valuer put a figure of £1m on the hotel as a bricks and mortar valuation at 15 November 1988.

Use of funds

As a result of this transaction, Peach and Kumquat obtained a 90 per cent mortgage, but still had to find the balance of the purchase price. A sum of a little over £200,000 was required to pay the vendors, and £165,000 of this was drawn from one of Peach's accounts. The money was borrowed as a bridging loan pending the sale of Peach's house, and was secured by an undertaking from Widgets. Such borrowing was, of course, in breach of the terms of the North Bank's loan.

There is no record on Widgets' ledgers or elsewhere of any money passing from Sidepiece to Sausage. Widgets' fees amounted to £11,359.38 including VAT.

Reprise

Conveyancing

The Reprise was a 36-bedroom hotel in the west of England. It had been bought by Mr and Mrs Dun in 1986, since when substantial improvements had been carried out. They also owned Milk Lodge, an adjacent bungalow in which they lived, and a plot of building land.

They were approached by Wheats, estate agents, in August 1988. They had no professional valuation, but suggested a figure of £1.2m, which they thought was favourable to them. Peach and Kumquat inspected the hotel. They were asked whether they wished to see the accounts, but showed no interest. The price was agreed at £1.1m to include Milk Lodge and the plot of land. However, this price was reduced to £1m, with an agreement that a further £100,000 be paid in cash. The apportionment of the price was £625,000 to the bricks and mortar of the hotel, with a further £200,000 for goodwill, fixtures and fittings.

In due course the vendors' solicitors were told that the hotel was to be sub-sold by Sausage to Sidepiece. Kumquat told Mrs Dun that he was a director of Sausage and Sidepiece. The price was varied because the plot of land was withdrawn, causing a reduction of £100,000. On 15 November 1988 the vendors' solicitors handed re-engrossed transfers to "Harry Smear" and the sale and purchase was completed by contract and transfer the following day. However, Salt got his figures confused in relation to the bogus sub-sale and had to amend the transfer from £1m to £1.1m.

Finance

This was arranged through New Finance Brokers Limited, as for the Opera. This time the source of finance was South Bank Limited. The proposition was put to them as a purchase by Sidepiece at £1.3m, excluding Milk Lodge and the plot of land.

The application was supported by the Biscuits valuation, which gave figures of £975,000 for the bricks and mortar, including Milk Lodge, and £1.3m as a going concern on the basis of the projected figures. The projected turnover suggested by Kumquat was £500,000. Mrs Dun thought this was feasible, but her accountant called it "a little optimistic to say the least". Biscuits in fact assumed a turnover of £434,000.

South Bank were provided with the accountant's letter and an assurance that funds were to be injected from The Investment Trust and converted into share capital within four months of the facility being granted. They made an offer of advance of £877,000 on 22 September 1988, subject to written confirmation from Sidepiece's accountants about the loan capital from The

Investment Trust, and written confirmation from Sidepiece's solicitors that the balance of purchase moneys and expenses was coming from the company's own resources without further borrowing.

Sidepiece's solicitors were Widgets, with Salt acting. South Bank instructed Wiley. On 10 October 1988 Salt confirmed to Wiley that the purchase price was £1.3m (which was untrue) and that Sidepiece had put his firm in related expenditure without further borrowing. In fact there is no record of such funds coming into Widgets' accounts.

The accountants' confirmation was received. It was based on letters from Jane Crumb and Widgets. The Widget letter, dated 7 October 1988, states that a deposit of £493,000 had been paid on exchange by that date. Indeed, Jane Crumb wrote to Widgets on 17 October 1988 promising to deposit that sum as soon as contracts were exchanged.

Wiley, having seen a copy of the proposed contract which mentioned Sausage, asked whether it was connected with the vendor or borrower. Salt replied that it was not connected with Sidepiece, whose directors and shareholders had no interest in Sausage. A form of contract was apparently executed which did not disclose the price being paid to Mr and Mrs Dun. This may have been the form sent to Wiley.

Wiley asked again about Sausage in their letter of 24 October 1988, and also asked for further confirmation from the accountants and solicitors in accordance with the offer of advance. The accountants' letter was provided. Undertakings by Sidepiece dated 28 October 1988 and 15 November 1988 to convert the loan capital to share capital were signed by Kumquat and Miss Gooseberry.

Salt wrote to Mossack Fruit on 26 October 1988 for a deed of postponement of the "loan" from The Investment Trust. His reply to Wiley on 27 October 1988 was that Sausage had no connection with the vendor or with Sidepiece, its directors and guarantors. Wiley expressed surprise that Sausage was involved at all in that event, and Salt explained that Sausage was buying Milk Lodge and the plot of land as well, which were not being sold on to Sidepiece. He never told them that Milk Lodge was to be transferred to Peach and Kumquat.

As a result of the reduction in the original purchase price the figure for goodwill, fixtures and fittings was reduced by £35,000. In addition, the original transfer showed Sidepiece as having paid £1m for the bricks and mortar. That made a total of £1.165m instead of the £1.3m which South Bank had been told about. This caused Wiley to ask further questions. Salt had to change his explanation quickly.

Valuations

Biscuits revalued the hotel on 8 March 1989 at £990,000, little more than their original £975,000. There is a Loaf report for the Astra dated 24 April 1989 giving a value of £1.3m, based on a turnover in excess of £650,000. It appears to have been countersigned, but this is a forgery.

On 28 December 1989 Soup & Partners valued the hotel alone at £750,000 on the open market and Milk Lodge at £150,000 for the Receivers of Sidepiece.

On 9 October 1990 the District Valuer put a figure of £775,000 on the hotel as a bricks and mortar valuation at 15 November 1988.

Use of funds

Again the sum borrowed fell short of the total purchase price. The balance came into the Widgets' account from Bilges, a firm of solicitors, and almost certainly represented borrowed funds in breach of terms of the advance from Lombard.

There is no record in Widgets' ledgers or elsewhere of any money passing from Sidepiece to Sausage. Widgets' fees amounted to £5,641.99 including VAT.

Cookie

Conveyancing

The Cookie was a 59-bedroom hotel in the West Country. It had been owned by Mr and Mrs Hash for over 20 years through the Cookie Hotel Limited. Turnover in the four years prior to the sale was consistently between £600,000 and £700,000. Seven further bedrooms and a lounge extension had been completed in June 1988.

Wheats were first instructed to find a buyer discreetly in late 1987 at a price of £1.3m. By early spring 1988 the asking price was £1.5m with the new bedrooms. They introduced Peach and Kumquat in October 1988, at the time the sales of the Opera and Reprise were progressing.

On 6 October 1988 Kumquat visited the Hash home with Miss Gooseberry. He did not look at the hotel, but was interested in buying. An offer of £2.1m was made and quickly accepted. However, the sale did not progress and appeared to have been abandoned in December 1988. The reason, almost certainly, was lack of funds.

In January 1989 there is evidence of attempts by Peach and Kumquat to obtain a fresh source of finance. Offers of commission were made to Roach and Apple. Roach in turn was introduced by Pie, to whom in due course he paid a commission.

In due course the deal reopened, and contracts were exchanged on 8 February 1989 for a sale to Sausage at £2.1m. The deposit paid was £50,000. There was a sub-sale to Peach and Kumquat at £2.8m. The deposit was the

£50,000 to be paid to the original vendors. The sales were completed on 6 March 1989.

Finance

This was the first of the Astra mortgages. It was Roach who made the first contact. An application form was completed and signed on 24 January 1989. Salt signed for Peach under a power of attorney. The application form claims that Peach and Kumquat were buying for £3.3m, to include £300,000 for goodwill, fixtures and fittings. The loan requested was £2.3m, with the balance of £1m coming from Peach and Kumquat's own money.

The application was accompanied by a cashflow forecast for the next 12 months, based on the turnover of £960,000. This, the Hashes say, was unrealistic without further bedrooms.

Also with the application was a valuation report. On 24 January 1989 instructions were sent to Loaf, at his home address, to provide a mortgage valuation based on this report. The valuation, on an Astra form, was faxed from Gold Fine Art on 31 January 1989. It purported to come from Haematite and gave a valuation of £3m, based on a turnover of at least £820,000. The signatories appear to be R Square and J Loaf.

On the basis of the representations made and this report, an offer of advance was made on 3 February 1989 in the sum of £2.3m. This enabled contracts to be exchanged on 8 February 1989.

The Astra did not instruct their own solicitors, instead they relied on the borrower's solicitor as with a normal house purchase. So Salt was asked to complete a report on title, which he did on 17 February 1989. It contained a section headed "Remarks and other matters to be brought to the notice of the Society (please ensure that any significant matters are referred to the Society at the earliest moment to avoid any possible delay in cheque issue)". No mention was made of the back-to-back sale involving Sausage.

Valuations

On 28 December 1989 Soup & Partners valued the hotel at £1.5m on the open market for the Receivers of Sidepiece.

On 9 October 1990 the District Valuer put a figure of £1.4m on the hotel as a bricks and mortar valuation at 6 March 1989.

Use of funds

The net amount sent to Widgets by the Astra was £2.29m. The use of the money is shown in a completion statement. After all the disbursements there was a surplus of £145,322.37. Out of this were taken Widgets current and outstanding fees, and a loan to one of Widgets' partners was repaid with interest. That left a residue of £65,410.49.

There is no evidence of any money having been sent to Sausage, even though the conveyance acknowledges receipt of £700,000. Widgets' fees for the Cookie amounted to £14,547.50 including VAT.

Sonata House

Conveyancing

Sonata House was a 22-bedroom hotel in the West Country. It had been bought on 8 May 1987 by Mr Liver-Brown as a weak going concern. Up to the date of the sale the takings averaged about £5,000 per week. In October 1988 he instructed agents to sell it for £1.5m.

In due course Smear and Slither came to view the hotel. Smear was calling himself John Ton. They first offered £1.3m, which was rejected, and a sale was agreed at £1.45m. The property included Glebe Cottage, which adjoined the hotel. Of the total price, £850,000 was apportioned to the hotel bricks and mortar. This was later amended to £1m.

Contracts were exchanged on 21 February 1989, at which point Mr Liver-Brown first discovered that the purchaser was Sausage. A sub-sale was signed the same day to Ton and Slither for the sum of £2.5m. The only deposit paid under either contract was £50,000 to the original vendor. Completion took place on 6 March 1989.

After completion the hotel was run by Smear and Slither through a company originally called Exjazz, but then Baron Hotels and later Rosewood Hotels. Smear was known to the staff as Johny Ton. He once told the manager that Harry was another name he used in connection with his business, but on another occasion said that he was his cousin.

Finance

The first application was made to the Dolls House Building Society. The purchase price was then stated to be £2.25m plus goodwill, fixtures, fittings and stock, making a total of £2.525m. The vendor was given as Mr Liver-Brown, and the loan requested was £1.8m. In connection with this application Salt wrote a letter confirming that their respective parents had given them £700,000 to assist in the purchase.

A further application to the Astra was made on 9 February 1989. The figures were the same. The applicants' accountants were stated to be Seathe & Co., who do not exist.

Salt forwarded to the Astra a letter from the vendor's accountants, with enclosures. This had been sent to Seathe & Co. at Widgets' address. Turnover for the year to 30 April 1989 was predicted at £333,287, and for the year to

31 December 1989 in the region of £750,000. These were taken from the vendor's figures. A business proposal was also sent. The cashflow prediction for the year to 31 January 1990 was for receipts of £780,604.

On 14 February 1989 instructions were sent to Loaf, at his home address, to value the hotel. A proof copy was sent next day by fax. In relation to the trading figures he says, "the projections can be substantially improved upon and we would anticipate a higher turnover for 1989". An open-market value of £2.45m was given. The building society valuation form was also sent by fax that day, setting out the same figure and comments. The signatories appeared to be R Square and J Loaf. Thereafter the full report was amended to give a bricks and mortar price of £2.25m in addition.

As a result an offer of advance in the sum of £1.8m was made on 21 February 1989. Salt's report on title pointed out an error in the southern boundary of the plans, but failed to say that the purchase price had been inflated by over £1m.

Valuations

On 15 October 1990 the District Valuer put a figure of £800,000 on the hotel as at 6 March 1989.

Use of funds

The net amount sent to Widgets was £1,788,750. After the payment of all costs and commissions there was a surplus of £288,787.40. There is no evidence of any money having been sent to Sausage, despite an acknowledgement in the transfer.

Widgets' fees amounted to £16,905.00, Loaf received £7,000, £50,000 was paid into the account of Harry Ton trading as Duff Investments, and a further £50,000 was paid to the credit of Baron Hotels. A sum of £90,000 was placed on deposit with the Lynx Building Society and on 18 July 1989 £133,200.21 was withdrawn by Salt from this Society ("Re: J Ton").

Ripple

Conveyancing

The Ripple was a 36-bedroom hotel in the north of England. It was owned by Hodgson Hotels Limited. They marketed it in early 1989, asking for offers over £1.2m.

On 15 February 1989 Peach, Kumquat and Miss Gooseberry visited the hotel and a price of £1.2m was agreed. As in most cases, Salt asked the vendors to accept a small deposit, and £50,000 was agreed.

Contracts were exchanged on 23 March 1989. On the same day a sub-sale contract was executed between Sausage and Peach and Kumquat at a price of £2.5m, with the £50,000 deposit being paid to the original vendors. The transfer took place on 14 April 1989.

Finance

The application to the Astra was undated. The purchase price is shown as £2.3m including goodwill, with £800,000 to be provided from the borrower's own money. The application was accompanied by a business proposal. The cashflow forecast for the year to April 1990 was for an income of £836,000, more than a realistic figure.

The application was also accompanied by a valuation report from Loaf dated 15 March 1989. This gave a bricks and mortar figure of £1.87m, based on a turnover in excess of £750,000.

The offer of advance is dated 23 March 1989, and is in an amount of £1.5m. The report on title from Salt makes no mention of the original sale price.

Valuations

On 28 December 1989 Soup & Partners valued the hotel at £1.5m on the open market for the Receivers of Sidepiece.

On 12 October 1990 the District Valuer put a figure of £1.25m on the hotel as a bricks and mortar valuation at 14 April 1989.

Use of funds

The net amount sent to Widgets was £1,490,625. With a true purchase price of £1.2m, the profit to Peach and Kumquat was in excess of £200,000.

There is no evidence of any money having been sent to Sausage, despite their acknowledgement of the receipt of £800,000 in the transfer.

Widgets' fees amounted to £10,385.00 including VAT, £50,000 was used to pay the deposit on the Wonder and Fugue Hotels. £135,000 was sent by telegraphic transfer to the account of the Reprise Hotel, and £20,000 was paid into Peach's account at Boot, Clacton.

Wonder

Conveyancing

This was a 60-bedroom hotel and conference centre in north Somerset. It was bought by Boris Hake in 1985 in a derelict state from the mortgagees, Business Mortgages Trust. He operated it through two companies, Wonder Limited and Marvellous Conference Centre Limited. After £2.5m had been spent on improvements, the hotel reopened in late 1987. By that time Mr Hake was looking for a buyer, with an asking price of £4.5m. One of the agents was Mary Medlar of Square & Co.

Peach looked at the hotel and made an offer of £3.9m, which was accepted. At a later stage Mr Hake met Kumquat, who seemed to be telling Peach what to do.

In the initial stages there was some doubt as to the price. Mary Medlar reported an offer of £3.85m from Alfalfa. Loaf gave instructions to Bellows & Menders to act on behalf of Alfalfa to purchase at £3.75m or £4m with a sub-sale to Peach or his company at £4.25m. But the written instructions, purporting to come from Mr Zebedee, gave the price at £3.9m, and this was confirmed by Mr Hake's solicitors.

Mr Bellows then wrote to Salt, who was to act for Sausage in a purchase at £4.25m. The deposit agreed on each contract was only £25,000, and contracts were exchanged on 14 April 1989. The prices were £3.9m and £4.2m respectively.

A further sub-sale was arranged to Sidepiece at £5m.

Completion of the sales took place on 12 May 1989, with Salt paying the balance of £5.85m directly to Mr Hake's solicitors. The transfer deed and the assignment of goodwill are the only documents recording the second sub-sale to Sidepiece, although they were to pay £6.125m for it according to Salt's completion statement.

Finance

The Astra application was preceded by the Loaf valuation dated 16 March, sent by Roach. The figure given as the value is £5.85m, exactly one and half times the original purchase price of £3.9m, and this for bricks and mortar value only. It purports to have been countersigned by R Square, whose firm, through Mary Medlar, effected the introduction and were to receive a 2 per cent commission from Mr Hake.

The application form followed. It claims a total purchase price of £6.3m, even greater than the inflated price set out in the conveyancing documents. Of this, £5.85m is said to relate to the property, although the transfer deed gives the figure as £4.225m.

The application was supported by cashflow projections suggesting income of £2.12m and £2.47m in the years to 31 March 1990 and 1991 respectively. The manager says that these are unrealistic and that the figures should be more like £1.6m and £1.9m.

An offer of advance was made on 19 April 1989 in the sum of £5m. Salt's report on title makes no mention of the original purchase price, and does not even point out that the purchase price to Sidepiece is well below the price notified to the building society and even below the amount of the advance.

Valuations

Mr Hake had an open market valuation prepared by Honeys on 18 February 1988. The figure for the hotel when finished was £3.5m.

On 28 December 1989 Soup & Partners valued the hotel at £3.25m on the open market for the receivers of Sidepiece.

On 12 October 1990 the District Valuer put a figure of £2.5m on the hotel as a bricks and mortar valuation at 12 May 1989.

Use of funds

The net amount sent to Widgets was £4,947,116. That gave Peach and Kumquat a gross profit of over £1m.

There is no evidence of the balance of the purchase money having been sent to Sausage, despite the acknowledgement of receipt of £300,000 in the transfer deed.

The Alfalfa profit was subject to an agreement to pay two-thirds to Malvern Securities. The total amount involved on this and the Fugue sale was £400,000. Mr Bellows received instructions to send this to ABC Holdings' account at the Foreign Bank Ltd. This was required as a bond with a view to a loan being granted in the sum of US $50m to Loaf and Kevin Hook, through their company Caribbean Leisure Limited. It was later forfeited by them.

This left Malvern Securities still unpaid. Mr Bellows was promised a transfer of £266,000, but it never came. He was told that £146,000 was paid directly. He was given a cheque by Loaf for £115,000 to cover the balance, but this dishonoured. In the end the final £100,000 was sent by Mr Bellows on 12 July 1989.

Widgets' fees amounted to £31,696.38 including VAT. Two sums, of £38,500 and £12,000, were taken in cash and the remainder of the profit was transferred to Peach or Sidepiece. Bellows & Menders asked for a fee of £20,000 plus VAT from Alfalfa, but this was revised to an inclusive sum of £30,000.

Fugue

Conveyancing

The Fugue was a 52-bedroom hotel in the north of England. It had been bought by Boris Hake in similar circumstances to the Wonder. He operated it through Fugue Business Centre Limited. It reopened in November 1987 and was put on the market at the same time as the Wonder, at a price of £2.2m.

Peach and Kumquat stayed at the hotel once before their purchase, but they were never shown round by the manageress. They offered £2m for the hotel, which was accepted. As with the Wonder, the purchase was to be in the name of Alfalfa.

Thereafter the sale went hand in hand with that of the Wonder. Bellows & Menders acted for Alfalfa, ostensibly taking instructions from Mr Zehander, but when matters became urgent sending his letter to Loaf's fax number and getting a reply the same day. Salt acted for Sausage and Sidepiece.

Contracts were exchanged on 14 April 1989 for the sale to Alfalfa at £2m, the sub-sale to Sausage at £2.1m and the sub-sub-sale to Sidepiece at £3.36m. A single deposit of £25,000 was paid to the original vendor's solicitors. Completion was on 12 May 1989, with Salt paying Mr Hake's solicitors directly out of the mortgage moneys.

Finance

The Astra application is dated 13 April 1989. It claims a purchase price of £3.8m, with £1.1m coming from the borrowers' own money. The price for the bricks and mortar is put at £3.2m, although the transfer deed shows it to be £2.34m.

The application was accompanied by the Loaf valuation report dated 10 April 1989, which was countersigned. Mr Evans agreed to sign the valuation without visiting the hotel. It gives a figure of £3.2m, based on projected turnover of £1.6m.

In fact the projected turnover submitted to the building society was £1.2m, although the cashflow forecast showed £1.4m. For the period July to December 1989 the projection shows receipts of £710,000. The actual figure for this period was £371,000. A letter was sent to verify the figures from Kumquat's business, apparently signed by Mr Grape.

An offer of advance was made on 11 May 1989, just in time for the completion of the purchase. Salt's report on title makes no mention of the original purchase price, nor does it point out the difference between the bricks and mortar purchase price shown on the offer and the actual price set out in the transfer deed.

Valuations
On 28 December 1989 Soup & Partners valued the hotel at £1.3m on the open market for the receivers of Sidepiece.

Use of funds
£50,000 was transferred to Gisal and the balance of the money was used for Peach or company accounts.

Toccata

Conveyancing
The Toccata was a 37-bedroom hotel on the outskirts of Lowshire. It was operated by Breakacre Limited. In early 1989 it was put on the market at £1.5m.

Peach viewed the hotel on 15 March 1989 and made an offer of £1.2m. This was later increased to £1.3m and then £1.35m, which was accepted. At that stage the purchaser was to be Sausage, although on 17 April 1989 the name of Dire was mentioned, and a visit was arranged for him.

Contracts were exchanged on 12 May 1989, when the purchaser was shown as Gisal. A deposit of £50,000 was paid, which came from the surplus on the completion of the Wonder purchase the same day. On the same day also a sub-sale agreement was executed for Gisal to sell to Dire and Lidher at a price of £2.1m. Completion took place on 26 May 1989 when the vendors were told of the sub-sale.

Finance
The application to the Astra is in the names of Dire and Lidher and is dated 5 April 1989. The purchase price is shown as £2.1m, with £600,000 coming from their own money. The application was supported by a business proposal with projected accounts. Turnover for 1989/90 was variously forecast at £669,000, £750,000 and £700,000. For 1990/91 the figures were £769,000 and £830,000.

There is a Loaf valuation dated 27 April 1989 which gives a figure of £1.8m, referring to a projected turnover of £850,000 for the year to April 1990. It appears to have been countersigned, but this is a forgery.

An offer of advance was made on 26 May 1989 in the sum of £1.5m. Salt's report on title makes no comment on the price.

Valuations
On 4 October 1990 the District Valuer put a figure of £800,000 on the hotel as

a bricks and mortar valuation at 26 May 1989. He was denied access to the property.

Use of funds

The net amount sent to Widgets was £1,499,970, but there is no evidence of the balance of the purchase money being paid to Gisal. Widgets' fees were £11,385.00 including VAT.

Loaf received £7,000 in two equal sums, one of which was in cash. Other sums were paid to Peach and to one of the partners in Widgets. The latter sum, of £52,000, was said to be the repayment of a loan for exchange, but this money came from the Wonder surplus.

Schedule of dates and loans

Hotel	*Offer*	*Contracts*	*Completion*
Opera	15.8.88	19.9.88	3.11.88
Reprise	12.8.88	24.10.88	16.11.88
Cookie	17.10.88	8.2.89	6.3.89
Sonata House	19.1.89	21.2.89	6.3.89
Ripple	16.2.89	23.3.89	14.4.89
Wonder	3.3.89	14.4.89	12.5.89
Fugue	3.3.89	14.4.89	12.5.89
Toccata	28.3.89	12.5.89	26.5.89

Hotel	*True price* £m	*Claimed price* £m	*Loan* £m	*Surplus* £m
Opera	1.9	2.7	1.716	
Reprise	1.0	1.3	0.877	
	2.9	4.0		
Cookie	2.1	3.3	2.3	0.2
Sonata House	1.2	2.5	1.5	0.3
Ripple	1.45	2.3	1.8	0.35
Wonder	3.9	6.3	5.0	1.1
Fugue	2.0	3.8	2.7	0.7
Toccata	1.35	2.1	1.5	0.15
	12.0	20.3	14.8	2.8
Grand totals	14.9	24.3	17.393	

Sample Documents

In this section I have created a typical factory mortgage fraud, with a fictitious couple, the Wagners, at the helm.

All the documents have been created for this case study, as have the transactions on which they are based.

A table of the transactions appears on pages 289–290. These transactions are shown as a bar chart at page 291. This shows the structure of the property portfolio over the period of time analysed and also illustrates that the Wagners are *not* ordinary domestic residential borrowers, but in reality commercial landlords seeking to build up a property portfolio, as cheaply as possible.

Steps in a typical conveyancing transaction

(Bold italic type shows fraudulent activities)

1. Sale agreed subject to contract. Estate agents confirm details. ***Wagners submit false mortgage applications and false references*** (pp 172–191).
2. Solicitors for vendor and purchaser take detailed instructions from their respective clients. ***Instruction forms and letters are received from Wagners of their nominees*** (pp 192–205).
3. Vendor's solicitor applies to vendor's building society for title deeds. (When he receives them, he holds them to the order of the building society pending completion.)
4. Vendor's solicitor sends draft contract to purchaser's solicitor for approval. Its terms are then agreed between solicitors.
5. Vendor's solicitor sends "office copy entries" (*i.e.* official copies of entries of register at Land Registry) to purchaser's solicitor.
6. Purchaser's solicitor makes "local search" of local authority.
7. Purchaser's solicitor sends pre-contract enquiries (also known as preliminary enquiries) to vendor's solicitor, who replies to them.
8. Purchaser's solicitor is instructed by purchaser's building society to act for them. They send him a copy of the mortgage offer.
9. Contracts are exchanged. This may be done by telephone. ***Wagner***

correspondence shows reduced deposits, alterations in purchase price (pp 206–210).

10. Purchaser's solicitor sends requisitions on title to vendor's solicitors, who replies to them.

11. Purchaser's solicitor sends draft transfer to vendor's solicitor for approval. Its terms are agreed between solicitors. Vendor signs it in readiness for completion.

12. Purchaser's solicitors make Land Registry search.

13. Purchaser's solicitor sends report on title to purchaser's building society, and requests advance cheque (pp 211–212).

14. Advance cheque is sent by building society and paid into purchaser's solicitor's client account in readiness for completion.

15. Purchaser's solicitor obtains purchaser's signature on mortgage deed in readiness for completion.

16. Solicitors send financial statements to their respective clients, and purchaser pays to his solicitor any amount needed to make up the balance required to complete.

17. Completion takes place. This involves the following steps:

(a) Balance of purchase price is paid by purchaser's solicitor to vendor's solicitor.

(b) Transfer is passed from vendor's solicitor to purchaser's solicitor.

(c) Mortgage deed signed by purchaser becomes effective.

(d) Charge certificate in favour of vendor's building society is passed to purchaser's solicitor by vendor's solicitor who undertakes to pass on a "Form 53" when received from the vendor's building society. (Form 53 is an acknowledgement by the building society that it has been paid off in full and that its mortgage may be discharged.)

18. Vendor's solicitor, before paying any surplus to the vendor, pays to the vendor's building society the amount required to pay off the vendor's mortgage (the "redemption figure"). The building society executes Form 53 and sends it to the vendor's solicitor who passes it to the purchaser's solicitor.

19. Purchaser's solicitor lodges transfer with Inland Revenue for stamping, and pays the stamp duty. Inland Revenue returns the transfer duly stamped.

20. Purchaser's solicitor lodges the following documents with the Land Registry so that the interests of the purchaser and his building society may be registered, and the interests of the vendor and his building society cancelled:

(a) stamped transfer;

(b) vendor's building society charge certificate;

(c) Form 53 executed by the vendor's building society;
(d) mortgage deed in favour of the purchaser's building society.

21. Land Registry send to the purchaser's solicitor:
(a) Notice of completion of the registration;
(b) Charge certificate in favour of the purchaser's building society.

22. Purchaser's solicitor passes on charge certificate to the purchaser's building society.

23. ***Sample lies to building society told by the Wagners*** (pp 214-227).

24. ***Tenancy documents used by the Wagners to create illegal tenancies without lender consent*** (pp 223-233).

25. ***Arrears correspondence*** (pp 234-236).

26. ***Odd instructions which should alert prudent practitioners*** (pp 237-248).

27. ***Acting for both vendor and purchaser as well as lender*** (pp 249-285).

Section 1: False Applications and False References

Bank Reference

Bank Reference 1st December 1988

Mr A Wagner

Respectable and trustworthy, known to Bank since September 1988 and whilst appears to be fully committed, we do not believe customer would enter into a commitment he could not see his way to fulfil.

Note that this bank reference does not provide any comfort for the prospective lender, beyond confirming that the client has had a bank account for three months.

Employer's reference

London Borough of Overbridge
Directorate of Finance

Payroll Section
1 December 1988

Dear Sirs

Re: M Bach (Nursery Nurse)

In reply to your recent letter, the information required is as follows:

1. Basic salary £947.78 weekly/monthly)
2. ~~Bonus or other emoluments average/weekly/monthly)~~
3. ~~Average overtime weekly/monthly)~~
4. Details of expected increments on a scale rising to £120.36 pa in 3 increments due on 1st April each year.
5. Date of first appointment 3.6.87
6. Position is permanent/temporary
7. Position is/is not pensionable

Yours faithfully

For Principal Payroll Officer

The reference has been written quite genuinely but inspection would reveal that the job has only been held for six months. Mortgage fraudsters do still take short-term employment with large institutional employers to achieve one more or less genuine reference.

Landlord's references

Miss M Bach
12 Grey Road
London

19th July 1990

The Branch Manager
Lynx Building Society

Dear Sir/Madam

Re: Miss Sarah Tallis and Miss Adele Offenbach

I refer to your recent enquiry.

I confirm that I have known the above persons for some two and half years, in which time she has rented a room at my address. She has always been up to date with her rent and I have always found her trustworthy.

Yours truly

Miss M Bach

This and the following reference illustrate the recycling of identities. Ms Bach is both tenant and Landlady.

Mr E Smith
4 Bramble Road

14th September 1990

The Manager
Lynx Building Society

Dear Sirs

I am writing to you in relation to Mr Wagner and Ms Bach whom I rent a flat to at 3 Blue Road.

They pay £85 p.w and have been good tenants since their occupation in early 1988. I will be sorry if I have to lose them.

They pay their own gas and electricity bills.

Trusting this letter is of help to you.

Yours faithfully

E Smith

Accountant's reference

Dott and Drab Associates
Chartered Accountants

Date: 20th July 1990
Our Ref:
Your Ref:

Dear Sir
Re: Mr Alan Wagner

We thank you for your letter dated 6th July to which we reply as follows.

a) The business is as an Importer and Exporter.
b) He is a director and owns 70% of the shares in his own name with the other 30% held by his nominee.
c) He has been trading profitably for at least three years.
d) Not applicable.
e) Mr A Wagner is currently on a gross salary of £25,250.00 + 10% overtime bonus.
f) We estimate this will continue in the next twelve months.
g) There is no reason in our opinion why the level of income quoted above is likely to be lower in future.
h) We can only let you have the accounts for the year ended 31st December 1987 and 31st December 1988 as 1989 have not yet been completed.

Yours faithfully

The accounts which accompany this and the following reference show that the business will not support the staff and directors who are shown as working for it in the following letters.

Note that salaries will be tailored to fit the advance sought.

Janus (Travel Shipping and Freight) Limited
Trading and Profit and Loss Account
For The Year Ended 31st December 1988

SALES		1,055,975
Less: Purchase and Freight Costs		909,429
		146,546
Add: Bank Deposit Interest		588
		147,134
Less Expenses:		
Rent, Rates and Insurance	3,757	
Wages & NHI	29,034	
Lighting & Heating	594	
Telephone & Telex	19,613	
Book-Keeping	862	
Postage & Stationery	1,657	
Motor Expenses	8,472	
Repairs	889	
Travel	15,439	
Agents' Commissions	1,313	
Bank Interest & Charges	7,041	
Casual Labour	3,413	
H P Charges	2,397	
Promotion Advertising	4,861	
Canteen	478	
Sundries	2,572	
Bad Debt	19,500	
Lease	752	
Legal Fees for Debt Collectors	2,851	
Subscriptions	997	
Audit	1,600	
Directors' Fees	14,406	
Depreciation -		
Fixtures - 840		
Truck - 1,150		
Motor Cars - 1,478	3,468	146,236
Net Profit for the Year		898
Add: Profits brought forward		27,030
Balance carried forward		£27,928

Janus (Travel, Shipping & Freight) Limited
Dott and Drab Balance Sheet As At 31st December 1988

1987					
		FIXED ASSETS			
	2,488	Furniture & Fixtures at Cost		2,762	
	274	Additions in Year		1,440	
	2,762			4,202	
1,873	889	Less: Depreciation		1,729	2,473
	16,600	Truck at Cost		16,600	
14,800	1,800	Less: Depreciation		2,950	13,650
	13,952	Motor Cars at Cost		13,952	
12,200	1,752	Less: Depreciation		3,230	10,722
28,873				26,845	
		Investment			
	650	Lease Premium			650
29,523				27,495	
		CURRENT ASSETS			
		(Due within 1 Year)			
	109,149	Sundry Debtors & Repayments		139,783	
	13,819	Cash at Bank		4	
	122,968			139,787	
		LESS: CURRENT LIABILITIES:			
		(Due within 1 Year)			
	74,373	Sundry creditors	90,319		
	14,838	Bank Overdraft	22,953		
	7,112	Corporation Tax	7,112	120,384	
	96,323				
	26,645	Less: (Due in over 1 Year)		19,403	
(2,393)	29,038	Hire Purchase		18,870	533
£27,130		NET ASSETS			£28,028
		Represented By:			
		SHARE CAPITAL			
		Authorised Issued and Fully Paid			
100		100 Ordinary Shares of £1 each			100
27,030		Profit and Loss Account			27,928
£27,130					£28,028

STATEMENT BY DIRECTORS ON THE ATTACHED ACCOUNTS

We have relied on exemptions for individual accounts and have done so on the grounds that the Company is entitled to the benefit of those exemptions as a small Company for submitting these modified accounts.

SIGNED ....

A Wagner - Director S Liszt - Secretary

Janus (Travel, Shipping and Freight) Limited
Trading and Profit and Loss Account
For The Year Ended 31st December 1987

SALES		1,308,072
Less: Purchase and Freight Costs		1,113,342
		194,730
Add: Bank Deposit Interest		661
		195,391
Less Expenses:		
Rent, Rates and Insurance	6,767	
Wages & NHI	19,111	
Lighting & Heating	905	
Telephone & Telex	11,418	
Book-Keeping	1,933	
Postage & Stationery	3,196	
Motor Expenses	8,708	
Repairs	1,795	
Travel	9,464	
Foreign Agents' Commissions	65,748	
Bank Interest & Charges	1,834	
H P Charges	1,351	
Hire of Equipment	489	
Cleaning	840	
Sundries	616	
Bad Debt	1,279	
Legal Fees and Debt Collection	424	
Audit	1,600	
Directors' Fees	13,255	
Depreciation -		
Fixtures - 466		
Truck - 1,799		
Motor Cars - 1,753	4,018	154,751
Net Profit for the Year		40,640
Less: Corporation Tax		7,112
		33,528
Less: Losses brought forward		6,498
Balance carried forward		£27,030

Janus (Travel Shipping and Freight) Limited
Modified Balance Sheet
As At 31st December 1987

1986					
		FIXED ASSETS			
		Furniture & Fixtures at Cost		2,488	
		Additions in Year		274	
				2,762	
2,065		Less: Depreciation		889	1,873
-		Truck at Cost		16,600	
		Less: Depreciation		1,800	14,800
-		Motor Cars at Cost		13,952	
		Less: Depreciation		1,752	12,200
					28,873
		Investment			
650		Lease Premium			650
2,715					29,523
		CURRENT ASSETS			
		(Due within 1 Year)			
40,637		Sundry Debtors & Repayments		109,149	
-		Cash at Bank		13,819	
43,352				122,968	
		LESS: CURRENT LIABILITIES:			
:		(Due within 1 Year)			
	46,921	Sundry creditors	74,373		
	2,829	Bank Overdraft	14,838		
49,750	-	Corporation Tax	7,112	96,323	
				26,645	
-		Less: (Due in over 1 Year)		19,403	
		Hire Purchase			(2,393)
£(6,398)		NET ASSETS			27,130
		Represented By:			
		SHARE CAPITAL			
		Authorised Issued and Fully Paid			
100		100 Ordinary Shares of £1 each			100
6,498		Profit and Loss Account			27,030
£(6,398)					£27,130

STATEMENT BY DIRECTORS ON THE ATTACHED ACCOUNTS

We have relied on exemptions for individual accounts and have done so on the grounds that the Company is entitled to the benefit of those exemptions as a small Company for submitting these modified accounts.

SIGNED ....

A Wagner S Liszt

Employer's references

Re: A Wagner

1. How long has the applicant been employed by you? 4 years
2. Is the employment of a permanent nature? Yes/No
3. What is the applicant's occupation/position? IMP/EXP Manage
4. Basic Salary GROSS per week/month/annum? 23,200pa
5. Bonus per week/month/annum?
   Is this irregular/regular/guaranteed?
6. Overtime per week/month/annum?
   Is this irregular/regular/guaranteed?
7. Commission per week/month/annum?
   Is this irregular/regular/guaranteed?
8. If additional earnings specified in 5. to 7. are irregular can you give a useful guide by supplying either gross additional earnings for the last tax year, or earnings to date this present tax year.

Signed:
Date:
Position in Company: Executive Secretary

This is a pro forma reference like those which are still used by many lenders. They are a godsend to fraudsters, since replying to them requires so little effort and any signature will do. It is correct to query whether a reference from an executive secretary is worth having.

Re: - M Bach

1. How long has the applicant been employed by you? 3/4 years
2. Is the employment of a permanent nature? Yes/No
3. What is the applicant's occupation/position? Clerk
4. Basic Salary GROSS per week/month/annum? £6,500pa
5. Bonus per week/month/annum? £
   Is this irregular/regular/guaranteed?
6. Overtime per week/month/annum? £
   Is this irregular/regular/guaranteed?
7. Commission per week/month/annum? £
   Is this irregular/regular/guaranteed?
8. If additional earnings specified in (5) to (7) are irregular can you give a useful guide by supplying either gross additional earnings for the last tax year, or earnings to date this present tax year. £

Signed.. Date..
Position in Company: Executive Secretary

This is another reference from Janus.

Janus Freight/Shipping/Travel
20 Swordfish Road, London

26th February 1990

Astra Building Society

Dear Madam

Re: Mr Alan Wagner, 5 Barracuda Road, Anytown, Herts.

I refer to your letter of 25th February regarding the above named employee.

1. He has been employed by this company for 4½ years.
2. He is on our permanent staff.
3. He is employed as a general manager of our Import Department.
4. Basic salary and bonus total £23,000.00pa.
5. He is guaranteed in all the above.

Yours faithfully

Sylvia Liszt
Director

Janus Freight/Shipping/Travel
20 Swordfish Road, London

5th November 1989

Pisces Building Society

Dear Sir

Re: Alan Wagner

I refer to your letter of 2nd November regarding our above named employee. The information you require reads as follows:

1. Occupation - Import/Export Manager
2. He has been in this employment for four years
3. Basic salary £23,200pa
4. Overtime and Bonus is paid
5. I confirm that this employment is permanent

If you require any further information please do not hesitate to contact.

Yours faithfully

M Bach
Administrator

Janus Freight/Shipping/Travel
20 Swordfish Road, London

7th August 1990

Private & Confidential

The Manager
Mariner Building Society

Dear Sir/Madam

Re: Mr Alan Wagner - Import/Export Manager

We have today been requested to write to you in relation to our above employee verifying his employment details.

We are able to confirm the following:

1. Mr Wagner has been in our employment since 19th February 1984
2. His current salary is £23,756pa gross. There is no overtime or bonus applicable to his position
3. His position with our company is of a permanent nature
4. His salary is that of a general annual review pattern.

Finally may we mention that our Company have found Mr Wagner to be a very responsible and trustworthy person who would not enter into any financial commitment without due consideration.

Yours faithfully

S Liszt (Miss)
Company Secretary

Note that Wagner's salary fluctuates, as does Miss Liszt's position in the company.

Janus Freight/Shipping/Travel
20 Swordfish Road, London

11th April 1991

Our Ref:

Astra Building Society

Dear Sir/Madam

Re: Janet Strauss of 95 Forest Road - Stock Controller

We refer to your recent enquiry.

We confirm that Mrs Strauss is currently employed as a Stock Controller.

Current weekly salary is £134.62 gross.

There is some overtime applicable. This is not obligatory but is normally worked and varies between £14.00 per week and £27.00 per week.

No mortgage subsidy is provided. An annual bonus of approximately £100 is payable at the end of our financial year and last year we can confirm that this figure was £112.00.

Mrs Strauss has been with us since August 1987 and we would recommend her as a responsible person.

Yours sincerely

S Liszt

Janus Freight/Shipping/Travel
20 Swordfish Road, London

14th April 1991

Our Ref:

Astra Building Society

Dear Sir/Madam

Re: Janet Strauss of 95 Forest Road - Stock Controller

We refer to our letter of 11th April whereby a weekly salary of £134.62 gross was confirmed.

We regretfully have to admit to an error on our part.

The letter was supposed to read £13,462 gross per annum.

We do apologise for the error made and trust this will have no bearing on Mrs Strauss's business with your Society.

Yours faithfully

S Liszt

FACEPAINT LIMITED
20 SWORDFISH ROAD, LONDON

22nd July 1990

Our Ref -
Branch Manager
Lynx Building Society

Dear Sir

Re: Miss Sarah Tallis

Further to your recent enquiry we confirm the above named is employed by our Company as a full time Sales Representative.

She has been with our Company since 1988 and her current basic salary is £16,600pa. In addition to this, overtime at a figure between £55 and £60 per week is paid and there is a commission structure on which the sum of £1,600pa is earned.

We confirm her position with our Company is one of a permanent nature and trust that the above is of assistance to you.

Yours faithfully
S Liszt (Mrs) - Director
For and on behalf of Facepaint Cosmetics Ltd

Ms Liszt is a busy lady - the address is an accommodation address.

Inferno Restaurant
and Wine Bar

384 High Road
London

13/7/90

The Branch Manager
Lynx Building Society

Dear Sirs

Re: Miss Adele Offenbach

We have been requested to write to your Building Society with regard to Miss Offenbach, who is employed by our restaurant as an assistant manageress.

Her basic salary is £190 per week and there is normally overtime available which is obligatory, depending upon the staff situation and how busy we are. However, this normally amounts to at least £30 per week.

She has been with us since approximately January of last year and her position is permanent.

Yours truly

Eric Williams
(Restaurant Owner)

Registered Office: 384 High Road

This is a restaurant which is not in the telephone directory and does not advertise.

Community Centre
Lincoln House, 13-21 Drain Street, London

Vesta Building Society

23rd June 1990

Dear Ms Young

Employee's Name: Miss Primrose Bach

I refer to your letter of 21.6.88

The information that you require is as follows:-

1. She is employed as an Administrator
2. Basic salary £15,000
3. No overtime, commission or bonus paid
4. She has been in this employment for two and half years
5. The post is permanent
6. The post is not pensionable

Please do not hesitate to contact me if you require any further information.

Yours sincerely

L D Meade
Director

Community centres are often abused as sources of references. Because they have a large number of part-time staff and volunteers, it can be hard to check that a reference is genuine.

Community Centre
Lincoln House, 13-21 Drain Street, London

The Branch Manager
Mariner Building Society

2.8.88

Dear Sirs

We write to advise you that Ms Miranda Bach has worked for us as an administrator for some two and half years in which time she has conducted herself in a responsible and respectable fashion.

Her salary is £1112.50 per calendar month (£13,850 pa) and overtime is normally available at an average of £100-£110 per week.

Her position with "The Community Centre" is permanent in the foreseeable future.

Yours truly

J Edwards (BA)

Community Centre
Lincoln House, 13-21 Drain Street, London

17th August 1990

Private & Confidential
Mariner Building Society

Attention: Mrs M Hopkins

Dear Sir/Madam

Re: Miranda Bach of 10 Crimson Road, London

Thank you for your enquiry letter of 8th August and as requested, we enclose the information you require.

I confirm Miranda is employed by our company as an administrator and she has in fact been with us for 2 years and 6 months.

Her basic annual salary is currently £13,850. However, this is reviewable at the end of our Company's financial year, which is October.

Some over-time is compulsory and an annual figure of approximately £460.00 is paid for this.

I trust you will find the above information of assistance and I will be happy to provide you with any further details you may require.

Yours truly
Peter Wagner
(Company Secretary)

Section 2: Instruction Forms and Letters of Instruction

Solicitor's instructions

6th November 1988

Mr Peter Deadlock
Deadlocks
82 High Street
London

Dear Mr Deadlock

I have arranged to purchase the following

1. Property -	9 Cerise Street London Ground floor shop with living accommodation upstairs
2. Cost -	£75,000.00
3. Vendor-	Mr and Mrs Fink 8 Kelcross Road London
4. Solicitor -	Mark Orange & Co

Yours sincerely

Mr A Wagner
Director

This client should have been seen as a new client by the solicitor having conduct of the matter.

A Wagner Esq.
A Wagner Freight
Janus Freight Ltd
20 Swordfish Road
London

26th May 1989

Dear Mr Wagner

Re: 15 Lake Lane, London

I enclose a Purchase Instruction Form and would be grateful if you could complete this and return it to me as soon as possible.

Yours sincerely

Peter Deadlock
Deadlocks

Enc.

This solicitor does not realise the danger of sending out purchase instruction forms.

Please note new address:	Reference:..	
82 High Street London	DETAILED INSTRUCTIONS - PURCHASE	
Purchase of	15 Lake Lane, London,	Price: £....................
1. Your full name		Alan Wagner Shirley Hartley Ruth Hartley
Occupation		
Telephone Number -	Home Work	0171 333 6666
2. Do you wish to purchase jointly with another person?		as above
If so please state that person's names, address, except in the case of your wife/ husband when only Christian names are required.		
3. Amount of deposit paid (if any)		
4. Paid to whom?		
5. Please give details of any additional items included on the purchase price (carpets, electric or gas fire, wall lights etc.)		none
6. Are you dependent upon the sale of another property to enable you to proceed with this purchase?		no
7. Application for mortgage made to:		Libra Building Society
8. Amount applied for? Please advise who will be resident at the property. Please supply full names and ages (or state "Purchasers only")		£78,000.00
		Signed Dated

A Wagner Esq.
5 Barracuda Road
Anytown
Herts.

12th November 1988

Dear Mr Wagner

Re: Purchase 9 Cerise Street, London

We thank you for your letter of 6th November, 1988, and now enclose herewith our Purchase Instruction form which we would be grateful if you could complete and return to us as soon as possible in order for this matter to proceed.

Yours sincerely

Peter Deadlock
Deadlocks

enc.

Yet another instruction form is sent to the same address.

A Wagner Esq.
20 Swordfish Road
London

4th December 1988

Dear Mr Wagner

Re: Proposed Purchase of 8 Cobalt Road, London

We have today heard from the Tophole Property Services in Northshire regarding your proposed purchase of the above property.

We enclose a Purchase Instruction Form which we would be grateful if you will complete and return to us straight away.

We have written to the Vendor's Solicitors requesting a Contract for approval.

Yours sincerely

Deadlocks

Enc.

This time the letter goes to the business address but still the same addressee

Overdraft request

Janus Freight/Shipping/Travel
20 Swordfish road, London

(COPY DEADLOCKS)

20th February 1989

Mr Charles Smith
Anybank Bank plc
Anytown Branch
High Street
Anytown
Herts.

Dear Mr Smith

Further to our telephone conversation I enclose details of an 8 (eight) week plan to put some working capital into the company.

1. I wish to have an overdraft of £30,000.00 - and to be at the maximum figure for no more than 3 (three) working days.

2. I will be selling 3/4 properties which will realise £46-70,000 of which some working capital will be available.

3. We will produce '86, audited accounts.

4. We will ask Deadlocks's solicitor to give an undertaking that the first £30,000 of sales will be allocated to Anybank Bank - Anytown.

The above point will allow us to trade with the UK customers, and give me time to collect overseas funds in March and April.

Yours acceptance of the above would be greatly appreciated.

Yours sincerely

A Wagner
Director

This is a classic warning sign which no solicitor should ignore.

SALE INSTRUCTION FORM

Property Address:	10 Crimson Road London
Price Agreed:	£55,000
Owners' Full Name:	Alan Wagner & Miranda Wagner
Telephone Number:	
If property is mortgaged, please give name and address and account number of Building Society/Bank	Yes Betelgeuse Building Society
Is there a second mortgage? If so give name, address and account number.	No
Which boundary wall, fences or hedges do you think belong to the property and which do you maintain?	-
Are you aware of any disputes regarding the property?	No
Have any notices affecting the property been served by or on you?	No
Has the property the benefit of any written guarantees (i.e. NHBC or timber/damp)?	-
If so please supply copies	-
Have you made any claims under the guarantees?	No
Is the property drained into a public sewer and have water, gas and electricity from the mains?	Yes
Do you share the use of any private road, path or other facility with anyone? If so please give details.	-
Have you made any contribution towards repairs to any such shared facilities? If so how much and to whom?	No

Does anyone have permission to use your property for example to paint their own house, lay pipes or wires, or are there any rights of way over your property?	No
Has the property been extended or altered during the past 4 years? If so please supply details.	-
Are all trees, shrubs, plants, garden sheds, greenhouses, garden ornaments, aerials, fitted furniture, shelves, electric switches, points, wall and ceiling fittings included in the price?	Yes
Are there any other items included in the sale price (i.e. carpets, gas fires)?	No
Are there any fixtures and fittings that you will be removing?	-
What is the rateable value?	£-
Do you make periodic payments other than general and water rates?	No
How much are the water rates?	£-
Who is presently living at the property? Please give full names and ages	Selves
When was the property built	-
Is there a garage at the property?	No
Is there central heating at the property? If so, what kind. Has it been regularly serviced? Is it in good working order?	Yes Gas
Are you intending to buy another property to move into when your sale is complete?	No
Has an estate agent sold your property? If so, please supply name & address.	
Sold.	Miranda Bach and Rose Bach 11 Crimson Road

Solicitor.	Valerian Woundwort & Co. 2B Median Road London
Signed:	Alan Wagner
Dated:	18/2/88

Transfer of interest

Deadlocks Solicitors
Peter Deadlock LL.B

---

82 High Street
London

Our Ref: **PD.SS.Wagner**
Your Ref: **MP29**
Date: **7th November 1990**

Home Mortgages Limited
Reading

Dear Sirs

Re: A Wagner and M H Wagner
17 Orange Road, London

We are instructed by Mr A Wagner in connection with the proposed transfer of his interest into the names of himself and Mr Alphonsus Strauss.

We would advise you that we acted for you on completion of this purchase whereupon all the Title deeds and documents are presently before the Land Registry.

We would therefore request that you formally write to us with your consent to this transfer and also if you would forward to us a standard form of Deed of Covenant which Mr Strauss will need to enter into with your company concerning his observance of the mortgage.

Our client is writing to you directly also making a formal application in this connection.

Yours faithfully

Deadlocks

These are typical instructions to transfer into name of a nominee.

Memorandum

21st February 1991

To: Peter
From: Janet

Wagner to Bach
Flat 1, 11 Chestnut Road

I understand you acted for Mr Wagner when he purchased the above property and that the documentation is with HM Land Registry.

Do you have any copy documentation on your file to enable me to issue a draft Contract?

This is a transfer between husband and wife, using the wife's maiden name.

Extracts from Building Society Instructions to Solicitors and Licensed Conveyancers

These are included to illustrate typical building society and bank instructions

1. **Title**

The title should be investigated in the usual way making all appropriate searches and enquiries.

a) Please advise us if:-
   1. There is any discrepancy between the description of the Property as set out in the Offer of Loan and the deeds.
   2. Any condition of the Offer of Loan, General, Special or Mortgage Conditions or these instructions has not or cannot be complied with.
   3. There are any onerous or unusual convenants or there are any matters likely to affect the value of the Property or likely to impede the realisation of the security of which we should be aware.
   4. You become aware of a reduction in the purchase price for whatever reason: or of the existence of a sub-sale or if the purchase price includes a substantial consideration for fixtures and fittings.

b) The Property must not be affected by a repayable improvement grant.

c) The Property must enjoy full and sufficient vehicular access (including rights of way over any shared access and must also enjoy full and sufficient rights of drainage sewerage and all other services necessary for its beneficial enjoyment.

d) If appropriate the construction and adoption of the roadways servicing the Property must be supported by a satisfactory Road Making Agreement and Bond.

e) Any existing timber and damp proof course guarantees must be transferred to the Applicant.

f) The present and proposed future use of the property must be residential and in accordance with planning legislation. Any necessary permissions and consents must have been obtained.

6. **Occupation**
It is a condition of the Loan that the Property is purchased as the principal residence of the Applicant for the sole continuing occupation of the Applicant and the Applicant's family. The Company must be advised if any information suggests that this is not the case or if it is not possible to obtain full vacant possession. No tenancy or licence can be created without the Company's consent and any person 17 years of age or over who is known or believed to be occupying/sharing the Property (or will in the future do so must execute the Company's standard Deed of Consent (forming part of the Mortgage Deed and be separately advised before executing the deed).

Hebe Building Society

Account No: 123456789 Offer of Loan 22nd January 1990

The Company is prepared to grant a loan in the terms set out below, subject always to the Company's Mortgage Conditions 1987 (a copy of which accompany this Offer), and to the General conditions overleaf and Special Conditions (if any) referred to in the Offer of Loan.

1. Name & Address of Applicant(s)
Alan Wagner and Miranda Wagner
5 Barracuda Road
Anytown
Herts.

2. Address of Property to be Mortgaged
19 Red Road
London

3. Details of Property

a)	Purchase Price	b)	Tenure	c)	Ground/ Chief Rent	d)	Property Insurance
Cover							
	£71,000.00		Freehold		£0.00		£57,500.00

4. Details of Loan

a)	Amount of Loan	b)	Method of Payment	c)	Payment Period	d)	Rate of Interest (Variable)
	£66,163.88		Interest Only		25 yr. 00mth		10.300%

e) Monthly Payment (Variable)
Gross (Interest only) £567.91 Net (interest only)
£428.86

5. Company's Solicitors
Deadlocks
82 High Street

6. Your attention is drawn to the General Conditions overleaf, in addition to which the following Special Conditions apply:

See Separate Sheet

This Offer does not imply any warranty that the purchase price of the property mentioned at 2 above is reasonable.

Hebe Building Society

SPECIAL CONDITIONS

Ref: 4TX

Account No: 532526

2. The Company's Solicitor to confirm prior to completion that the applicant(s) has no existing mortgage.

This is, of course, in Mr Wagner's case, bound to involve a lie by Deadlocks.

Hebe Building Society

To: Deadlocks
82 High Street

Funds Release Date: 23rd March 19—

Dear Sirs

Re: Name of Borrower(s): Alan Wagner

Property: 19 Red Road
Forest Gate
London

Account No: 123456789 (Please quote this number in all correspondence particularly if returning moneys)

I acknowledge receipt of your Report on Title and confirm the advance moneys denoted below will be Telegraphically Transferred to your Bank account on the Funds Release Date shown above.

The loan should be completed only if the General Conditions and Special Conditions referred to in the Offer of Loan have been complied with.

Should completion not take place, or be delayed, moneys must be returned within 24 hours by Telegraphic Transfer to Anybank Bank plc, for the credit of The Hebe Building Society. Failure to return the moneys within 24 hours will result in interest being charged at gross rate applicable to the loan.

Yours faithfully

Completions Department

Note referred to:

	Amount of Loan		£66,163.88
Less:	Mortgage Guarantee Premium	£661.88	
	Amount of retention	£0.00	
	Valuation Fees/Balance/Re-inspection	£0.00	
			£661.88
		Amount of Advance	£65,502.00

Deadlocks are again reminded that they must comply with the conditions.

Section 3: Reduced Deposits and Alterations in the Purchase Price

Payment of deposit

Pinch & Pluck
Solicitors

London

Our Ref :- Date 11th July 1990
Your Ref:- PD.MC.Wagner

Messrs Deadlocks
Solicitors

Dear Sirs

RE: Ground Floor Flat 4 Gold Road

Further to our letter of the 13th June your client gave our client £1000 in cash on the 7th July as a pre-contract deposit which our client has passed to ourselves and which we are holding in readiness to exchange. Our clients are not prepared to accept such a small deposit unless there is a very prompt completion.
Can we please now hear from you.

Yours faithfully

PINCH & PLUCK

This is an example of the direct payment of deposits, which can be no more than a cash saving exercise where no actual cash changes hands.

Draft contract

Valerian Woundwort and Co.

22 March 1990

Dear Sirs,

RE: Flat 1, 11 Chestnut Road, LONDON

We now enclose the draft contract, approved.

We advise that our client is in receipt of his mortgage offer and we are now arranging for our client to immediately sign the contract and hope shortly to be able to proceed to an exchange.

We would be pleased if you would consider accepting a reduced deposit of 5% in this instance and wait to hear from you accordingly. We would be pleased if your clients have complied in all respects with the planning requirements on this property and that there are no outstanding planning matters between your client and the local authority requiring his further compliance.

Yours faithfully

Deadlocks

Enc.

Reduced deposits also sometimes equal fraud. The fraudster may not be able to finance the whole deal by borrowing and does not want to use his own resources.

Exchange of contracts

PD/JB/WAGNER

A Wagner Esq.
Oak Cottage
ANYTOWN
HERTS.

22 March 1990

Dear Alan,

Re: Flat 1, 11 Chestnut Road, London

We now enclose the contract for your immediate signature and return.

On receipt of the contract please phone us concerning the deposit cheque which becomes payable on exchange of contracts.

We would have thought that a 5% deposit in this instance would be appropriate. We wait to hear from you as quickly as possible concerning this matter.

Please be advised that we have today received your mortgage offer, but not your second mortgage which we understand is to be with the Lodestar Building Society. We would also draw your strict attention to matters raised in your mortgage offer concerning the total retention of moneys until certain works have been completed in accordance with the valuation report.

Yours sincerely

Deadlocks

Enc.

SNAGSBY & CO
Solicitors and Commissioners for Oaths

12th February 1990

Messrs Deadlocks

Dear Sirs

Re: 1A Azure Road E15

Thank you for your letter of the 8th February. We note that this transaction is now proceeding at the price of £62,700.
In view of this we confirm that our client insists that contracts in connection with both this transaction and the ground floor number 1 must be exchanged at the same time.

Yours faithfully

SNAGSBY & CO

The solicitor fails to notice that the client appears to be buying two flats at once.

If this is a re-conversion of two maisonettes into one house, this would be acceptable but there are no signs on the file of any such instructions being taken by the solicitor from the client.

A H Wagner
Oak Cottage
Anytown
Herts.

Dear Sir,

Can you please note that I have paid Kevin Batchelor £5200 direct, leaving £57,500 balance for him.

Alan Wagner

10/2/90

This deposit was never paid, this is a "for the file" letter.

Section 4: Reports on Title and Undertaking

Report on title

TO: LEGAL DEPARTMENT, JUNO BUILDING SOCIETY

REPORT ON TITLE AND UNDERTAKING
(incorporating request for Advance Cheque)

The Lender: Pallas Home Loans Limited
The Borrower: **ALAN WAGNER AND PRIMROSE BACH**
Mortgage Offer Dated **19th August 1990** Mortgage Reference **67/1/1.0385/g**
The Property **17 Brown Road, London**

The Advance	Completion Date	Purchase Price
£118,148	**6th October 1990**	**£146,950**

TITLE DETAILS

Freehold	~~Unregistered~~	Title No(s)	**NAL96999**
~~Leasehold~~	~~First Registration~~		
	Registered Absolute		
If Leasehold state term of years unexpired	N/A	Ground Rent	£ p.a.
		Monetary Burdens	£ p.a.

OFFICE USE ONLY		SOLICITOR'S BANK DETAILS	
GROSS ADVANCE	£	A/C Name	**Deadlocks Client Account**
Retention	£	A/C Number	**6720899304**
Arrangement Fee	£	Address	**Anybank PLC**
MGP	£		
Telephone Transfer Fee	£		
Net Advance	£	Sort Code	

BUILDING INSURANCE DETAILS

Will the property be insured under the Lender's block policy? YES ~~NO~~

If 'NO' name and address of insurer Amount of Cover £
Policy Number
Name of Insured Renewal Date

LIFE ASSURANCE DETAILS: (NB: All policies MUST be on risk before completion)

Life Assured	Minimum Death Benefit	Assurance Company	Policy Date	Policy Number
A WAGNER		MOON ALLIANCE		
P BACH				

Non-Owner occupant's details Name(s)(and ages if under 18)	Reasons for Occupation or Relationship to Borrower		Have they executed Deed of Consent
		N/A	YES NO

Matrimonial Homes (Family Protection) (Scotland) Act 1981 *		Have they rights in priority to/pari passu with the Lender
Entitled/Non-Entitled Persons Names	N/A	YES NO

* applies in Scotland only

The Solicitor who signs this sort of form knowing that the transaction is a refinancing exercise risks prosecution.

REPORT ON TITLE

In connection with the Advance which the Lender intends to make to the Borrower on the security of the above property, we have fully investigated the title to the Property and we have made all the usual and prudent searches and enquiries with regard thereto.

WE CERTIFY to the Lender as follows:

1. On completion:

(i) the Borrower will have a good and marketable title to the Property free from any burdens or encumbrances which are onerous or which affect the value of the Property and the Title may be safely accepted by the Lender as security for the Advance;

(ii) there are no subsisting adverse entries affecting the Property in the local Land Charges Registry and there will be no entries affecting the Borrower or the Property in the H.M. Land Charges Registry, the Companies Registry, or H.M. Land Registry (Register of Sasines, Land Register or Register of Inhibitions and Adjudication) at completion;

(iii) the Borrower will have sole and undisputed occupation of the Property (save for the occupation of per sons detailed in the Requisition for Advance), which will be free from any tenancies or rights of occupation by persons not mentioned as above and the Borrower will not have entered into any commitments to sell, lease or otherwise dispose of the Property or of any part thereof or any interest therein;

(iv) all conditions in the Offer of Advance from the Lender to the Borrower will be complied with on or before the Completion Date;

2. the use of the Property as a private dwelling house is the permitted use of the Property free from any restrictions and conditions under the Town and Country Planning Acts and conforms to the provisions of the Town and Country Planning Acts and all necessary planning permissions and bylaws consents have been obtained.

the solicitors in this firm hold current practising certificates; and

we acknowledge a duty of care to the Lender, its successors and assigns and those deriving title from them.

SOLICITORS' UNDERTAKING

We hereby undertake:

to complete the above transaction in accordance with your requirements including where appropriate the stamping and registering of the Borrower's title and registering of the Lender's charge as a "first legal charge" against the title to the Property at H.M. Land Registry within the necessary time limits;

to take all steps to perfect the Borrower's title and the Lender's security and within two days of all such steps having been completed to deliver the documents of title and all Life and other Policies required to be assigned, to the Legal Department, Juno Building Society and in the meantime hold the same strictly to your order.

Financial statement

FINANCIAL STATEMENT
MESSRS DEADLOCKS IN ACCOUNT WITH MR A. WAGNER
RE: 19 RED ROAD, LONDON

RECEIPTS		PAYMENTS	
DEPOSIT RECEIVED	£1,000.00	DEPOSIT PAID	£1,000.00
MORTGAGE ADVANCE	£65,502.00	LOCAL SEARCH	£15.30
BALANCE TRANSFERRED FROM		AMOUNT DUE ON COMPLETION	£65,492.00
1A AZURE ROAD ACCOUNT			
TOWARD COSTS	£862.88	DEADLOCKS' COSTS	£460.00
AMOUNT REQUIRED FROM YOU	£723.52	MORTGAGE ACCOUNT	£57.50
		STAMP DUTY	£690.00
		LAND REGISTRY FEE	£100.00
		TELEGRAPHIC TRANSFER FEE	£12.00
		ABORTIVE COSTS RE: LAKE LANE	£130.30
		ABORTIVE COSTS RE: COBALT ROAD	£130.30
	£68,088.40		£68,088.40

Financial adjustment of transfer from an unrelated client is in fact a transfer from a nominee.

Too many of these items can be an indication of fraud. Why is this couple looking at so many properties ?

Section 5: Lies to Building Societies

Submission of title deeds

CAPELLA SAVINGS

St Joseph's House
London

Date 07 March 1991

DEADLOCKS

(*Peter, Can you verify?*)

Dear Sirs,

Mr A Wagner
1st Floor Flat
4 Gold Road
London

Mortgage Account Number 2S 652 50029935

I refer to the above and would advise that our records indicate that we have still not received the deeds to the above mortgage which completed on 12 08 90.

I look forward to receiving your confirmation that you will be submitting the deeds and documents or advising of the reason for their retention.

I would advise that receipt of the deeds has been further deferred to 21 03 91 and trust that this gives you sufficient time to collate the deeds and documents for submission.

Yours faithfully

MORTGAGE DEEDS DEPARTMENT

PD.AB. WAGNER

29th March 1991

Capella Savings
St Joseph's House
London

Dear Sirs,

Mr A Wagner - Account number 2S 625 50029935

1st Floor Flat, 4 Gold Road, London

Thank you for your letter of the 7th March, we would inform you that the title deeds are presently at the Land Resgistry for first registration. The registration was submitted on the 20th October and the Land Registry then informed us that the application would take 40 weeks approximately to complete.

Yours faithfully

DEADLOCKS

Exchange of contracts

MEMORANDUM

To:	PETER	Date: 15th June 1991
From:	KATE	Your Ref: Wagner

Re: 17 Orange Road London

We refer to our telephone conversation of today when Contracts were exchanged with completion fixed for the 28th June.

We now enclose herewith our client's signed Contract and confirm that a deposit of £7,500 was paid direct to our clients. We look forward to receiving your client's signed Contract to complete exchange.

We also take the opportunity of enclosing herewith draft Transfer in duplicate for approval together with Requisitions on Title with a copy for your use and await hearing from you further.

Yours faithfully

DEADLOCKS

Note:

1. This solicitor is acting for both vendor and purchaser.

2. A large deposit has been paid direct to vendor.

TELEPHONE MESSAGE

From................Sue

To ....Peter

This is one of Kate's old files

You will have to sort it out

Pre-contract enquiries

SW.JB.STRAUSS

LW/JB/STRAUSS

13th August 1992

Building Society Solicitors

Dear Sirs,

17 Orange Road, Forest Gate, London E7
Re: Jupiter Building Society v Mr & Mrs Strauss

We thank you for your letter of the 9th August, the contents of which we note.

We have checked our file and unfortunately are unable to find the replies to Pre-contract Enquiries and would inform you that the person who was dealing with this matter has now left this Company.

Yours faithfully

DEADLOCKS

This is a common excuse, which is generally recognised as bogus by lenders' solicitors.

Action for misrepresentation

Building Society Solicitors

Messrs Deadlocks

Our ref.:

Your Ref:

16th August 1992

Dear Sirs,

Re: Jupiter Building Society v Strauss
17 Orange Road, London

May we advise that it appears almost certain that this property was tenanted for a period of approximately twelve months prior to the Transfer and in consequence the Society's mortgage has been granted on property which is subject to a tenancy and in consequence vacant possession was not obtained in accordance with the society's requirements.

We have dealt with your firm on a number of occasions and would not have anticipated a deliberate misrepresentation both on the part of the Vendor and of your own client as to the position regarding vacant possession. Our further enquiries appear to indicate that the Vendor was in fact the employer of your client Purchaser and it does therefore appear a fraud has been perpetrated on our client Society.

It is with regret that we note you are unable to produce Replies to Pre-contract Enquiries and Replies to Requisitions as these would have revealed the representations made to you by the Vendor's solicitors. We are therefore required by our client Society to put you on Notice of a potential claim in negligence for failing to secure vacant possession in accordance with instructions you accepted when dealing with the Jupiter Building Society mortgage.

May we suggest you let us have the name, address and reference of the Solicitors who acted for Mr Wagner on the sale to your client. They will no doubt be able to duplicate the replies they gave and their instructions as to giving vacant possession.

With your clients presently overseas there may be difficulty over an action for misrepresentation, the more so since it appears your clients were actually party and knew of the true position.

We await hearing from you.

Yours faithfully,

This needs no comment beyond a reminder that if you receive such a letter to look at the last chapter of this book again.

Letter to Building Society Solicitors

21st August 1992

Dear Sirs,

Re: Jupiter Building Society v Strauss
17 Orange Road, London

Thank you for your letter of the 16th August.

It may not surprise you to note that we ourselves have been for some time endeavouring to contact Mr Alan Wagner.

Matters are somewhat complicated in that we presently retain instructions from Mr Wagner in respect of various other general matters and until such time as we have had an opportunity to speak with our client we feel unable to assist you further.

Finally please be advised that we would wish to be as co-operative as we can in this matter but clearly until matters have been resolved directly with Mr Wagner we cannot assist you further.

Yours faithfully

DEADLOCKS

Building Society Solicitors

Messrs Deadlocks

Our ref.:

Your Ref:

24th August 1992

Dear Sirs,

Re: Jupiter Building Society v Strauss
17 Orange Road, London

Thank you for your letter dated 21st August and confirming our telephone conversation.

We will await hearing from you.

Yours faithfully

Building Society Solicitors

Building Society Solicitors

Messrs Deadlocks

Our ref.:

Your Ref:

2nd October 1992

Dear Sirs,

Re: Jupiter Building Society v Strauss
17 Orange Road, London

We refer to our earlier correspondence and write to enquire whether you have any further information regarding this matter, particularly bearing in mind the urgency of the matter.

May we hear from you by return as we are being pressed by the Society to bring this matter to a speedy and final conclusion. Have you been able to contact your client Mr Wagner?

Yours faithfully

Letter to Building Society Solicitors

4th October 1992

Dear Sirs,

Re: Jupiter Building Society v Strauss
17 Orange Road, London

Thank you for your letter of the 2nd October.

We have received no further communication from Mr Alan Wagner since our earlier letter to you.

From the enquiries which this firm has made we believe that Mr. Wagner is at the present time out of the country and has been so for some length of time. We are not anticipating that he will, in the near future, be returning.

We are still endeavouring to contact him as best we can, but clearly in the circumstances we are unable to be of any further assistance to your clients at the present time.

Should we hear from Mr. Wagner in the future we will immediately correspond with you further.

Yours faithfully

DEADLOCKS

In real life, Deadlocks should, by now, have taken legal advice and notified their insurers.

Section 6: Tenancies

Undertaking not to rent

Your Ref: PD/CMG/Wagner

6th October 1990

Peter Deadlock
Deadlocks Solicitors
82 High Street

Dear Sir,

17 Brown Road, London

I write to confirm that the above premises will not be rented out without the permission of the Juno Building Society.

Yours sincerely,

Primrose Bach
Alan Wagner

Many building society and other lenders insist on a similar letter.

Lender's consent to let

NEBULA
BUILDING
SOCIETY

Miss M Bach
c/o Deadlocks
82 High Street

15 September 1990

Dear Miss Bach

<u>Account Number 099-4-93005271-09 23D White Court London</u>

I write to confirm the Society has today consented to the letting of the above property for a period of 2 years.

Would you further note that no further tenancies are to be created on this agreement or amended without the society's prior consent.

Would you therefore please inform us of the exact term of the lease, *i.e.* the start of the lease and also the finish date.

We also require from you a copy of the signed lease for the Society's file.

I trust the above information is satisfactory to you and look forward to hearing from you as soon as possible with the above comments.

Yours sincerely

c/o addresses can be a sign that something is amiss. Solicitors should not usually agree to this without careful consideration and instructions.

TYPICAL LENDER'S CONDITIONS FOR CONSENT TO A LETTING

1. Do you have a fixed intention of returning to re-occupy the property in the foreseeable future? (Please state the length of time the property will be let.)

2. Please give the reason why you are vacating the property (e.g. temporary transfer with present employer, new employment, service posting etc.).

3. If you have not already done so, please supply a draft of the proposed Tenancy Agreement, completed in all respects, a draft of the furniture inventory and a copy of the separate notice to be served under Cases 11, 12 or 20 of Schedule 15 of the Rent Act 1977 as amended by the Housing Act 1980. (It is recommended that you consult a solicitor if you are in doubt.)

4. If not contained within the draft Tenancy, please advise of the amount of rent to be charged and whether this is inclusive or exclusive of rates. As a general rule the rent to be charged must be sufficient to cover the following outgoings:

- (a) The mortgage repayment, calculated on the balance outstanding to repay the loan within the original term.
- (b) Rates (if the rental is exclusive of rates).
- (c) Ground Rent (if applicable).
- (d) Fire Insurance renewal premium (whether paid by the Society or not).

5. The rent should be payable on a monthly basis.

6. The term of the tenancy should not, normally, exceed one year.

7. Where it is desired to let to a Company or other corporate body the agreement must contain a clause prohibiting the Company from parting with possessions otherwise than to an employee as a licensee to pay no rent or rates or as a sub-tenant paying a licence fee no greater than that contained in the Tenancy agreement.

8. Please supply an undertaking that mortgage repayments (including insurance if applicable) will be made by Bankers Order for the period of the tenancy.

9. The counterpart Lease, and a copy of the notice referred to in 3 above, must be supplied to the Society for lodgement with the Title Deeds within one month of the signing of the agreement. The copy furniture inventory and a copy of the notice must be signed by the tenant(s). A photocopy signature is not acceptable.

10. Please supply a registered postal address in the United Kingdom (e.g. C/O Bank).

11. Please supply your confirmation that you will account for any arrears balance before approval and that the Society may rearrange your account to redeem within the original term.

12. Please forward your cheque for £20.00 in respect of administrative costs.

13. Your written consent to an increased rate of 2% during the Tenancy is required.

Alan Wagner
Flat 1 11 Chestnut Road
London
28/6/90

Cires Building Society

Proposed Letting

Having received your recent correspondence I confirm as follows.

(1) I do intend to re occupy after 36 months

(2) I am being posted abroad

(3) Copy lease previously sent

(4)
a) Rent payable is £541 pcm plus £2250 as an initial payment

b) Rates are exclusive

(5) rent is payable on a 3 month basis in advance

(6) See No 1

(7) See No 3

(8) I agree to pay by Bankers order throughout the period.

(9) See No 3

(10) Deadlocks, 82 High Street

(11) This is acceptable

(12) enclosed cheque £20

(13) If this is the normal rate.

Alan Wagner

Alan Wagner
1A Azure Road
London

26/4/90

Mrs Norton
Pisces Building Society

Dear Madam,

Further to our telephone conversation of today, I enclose a copy lease agreement from the Local Borough who will rent during my absence.

Can you please confirm your terms of acceptance by return mail and I will leave the legal details to be sorted out by my solicitor.

Alan Wagner

cc Peter Deadlock Deadlocks

Rental agreement

THIS LEASE is made the *17th* day of *June* One thousand nine hundred and eighty-eight BETWEEN the Landlord of the one part and the Tenant of the other part ____

witnessed: in consideration of the premium (the receipt whereof the Landlord hereby acknowledges) and of the rent and the covenants on the part of the Tenant and the conditions hereinafter reserved and contained as follows:-

1. IN THIS Lease the following expressions shall have the following meanings and definitions

LANDLORD	Alan Wagner of 10 Crimson Road, London and including the person or persons for the time being entitled to the reversion expectant upon the determination of the term here by granted____________
TENANT	The Mayor and Burgesses of the London Borough of Elsewhere of the Town Hall, Elsewhere and their successors in title.____________
THE PREMISES	All that property known as 1 Azure Road London in the London Borough of Elsewhere.____________
TERM	Two years from the date hereof subject to prior determination as hereinafter provided ____________
PREMIUM	shall be £3,750 ____________
RENT	shall be :-
(a)	for the first year of the term the rent of £6,240 per annum with a rent free period during the first month of the year. ____________
(b)	for each succeeding year of the residue of the term a yearly rent to be calculated by increasing the rent payable during the first year or the immediately preceding year (as the case may be) by a percentage equal to the percentage increase (if any) in the rate of inflation as published by the Department of Trade (or other substituted Government Department) for the period commencing from the date hereof or each succeeding year (as the case may be) and expiring the day before the anniversary of each complete year of the term. ____________
USER	Temporary housing accommodation in accordance with the provisions of paragraph 6 of schedule 1 of the Housing Act 1987____________
INSURED RISKS	shall mean the insurance of the premises against loss or damage by fire storm tempest lightning explosion and such other risks as the parties hereto may from time to time agree in such sum as shall be the reinstatement value of the premises together with architects surveyors and other professional fees and two years loss of rent ________.
SCHEDULE OF CONDITION	is Schedule of Condition hereto or the document (including where appropriate a set of photographs) referred to as the Schedule of Condition as annexed hereto

RIGHTS are those to be granted to the Tenant as set out in the first Schedule hereto ______________

EXCEPTIONS AND RESERVATIONS those reserved unto the Landlord as set out in the second Schedule hereto ______________

INVENTORY OF FURNITURE is the furniture to be provided at the premises as set out in the third Schedule hereto ______________

2. THE Landlord hereby demises unto the Tenant the premises TOGETHER with the Rights but EXCEPT AND RESERVING TO THE Landlord the Exceptions and Reservations TO HOLD the premises unto the Tenant for the term of years from the date hereof subject nevertheless to the provisos for determination hereinafter contained PAYING THEREFORE during the term the Rent such RENT shall be paid except as hereinafter provided by equal quarterly payments in advance on the usual quarter days in every year without any deduction the first payment apportioned in respect of the period from the date hereof until the next quarter day shall be paid on or before one month from the date hereof.

3. THE Tenant hereby COVENANTS with the Landlord as follows:

(necessary for the full enjoyment of the premises by the Tenant) the gardens dustbin area and dustbins hoppers forecourts roadways and pathways in the curtilage of the building PROVIDED nevertheless that the Tenant shall not cause or authorise or permit the obstructions of any common parts of the building.

THE SECOND SCHEDULE
(Landlord's Exemptions and Reservations)

1. The right at any time during the term but (except in emergency) only after giving reasonable prior notice to the Tenant to enter upon the premises to execute any repairs or other works which should or may be executed by the Landlord under the provisions of this Lease. ______________
2. Similar rights as are contained in paragraph 1 of the First Schedule hereto. ______________

THE THIRD SCHEDULE
(Inventory of Furniture)

Cooker
Refrigerator
Three-piece Suite
Coffee Table
7 No. Dining Chairs
Double Bed
3 No. Single Beds
3 Wardrobes
3 Chests of Drawers
Lampshades, Carpets & Curtains

This is a typical local authority let.

LONDON BOROUGH
OF
ELSEWHERE

Messrs Deadlocks
Solicitors
82 High Street
London

9th May 1990

Dear Sirs,

SHORT TERM LEASING SCHEME
Re Lease of : 1&1A AZURE ROAD

LANDLORD A WAGNER to the Council

I understand from the Council's Chief Property Officer that terms have been agreed for the Council to take a Lease on the above mentioned property to provide temporary housing accommodation for homeless families under the provisions of Paragraph 6 Schedule 1 of the Housing Act 1987 and that the form of the Lease (which is in standard use with other Local Authorities, Housing Associations and Landlords) has also been agreed.

I also understand from the information supplied by the Landlord:
(a) that the Landlord has a good and sufficient title to the property to grant such a Lease;
(b) that the consent of any superior Landlord or mortgagee to the granting of the Lease has been obtained or will be obtained on or before completion; and
(c) that there is no reason why the transaction cannot proceed to an early completion.

LONDON BOROUGH
OF
ELSEWHERE

8th May 1992

Cygnus Home Loans Corporation

Dear Sirs,

General Rates
19 Red Road London

I have to advise you that the above property which is subject to your charge is being leased to tenants. The freeholder, Mr A Wagner, calls to collect the rent once a month. As he is liable for outstanding rates on the property, I shall be grateful if you will inform me whether you have a forwarding address so that I may contact him on this matter.

Your assistance is appreciated and I enclose a post paid envelope for your reply.

Yours faithfully

Director of Finance

Solicitors and potential fraudsters should note that local authorities and building societies do exchange intelligence.

Breach of mortgage conditions

25th May 1992

Director of Finance
The Recovery Section
London Borough of Elsewhere
London

Dear Sirs,

Re:- General rates - 19 Red Road London
Our Account No 123456 - Mr A Wagner & Miss M Bach

Your letter of 8th May last regarding the above matter has been passed to me for attention.

Unfortunately we were not aware that the property was being let as this is in fact a breach of our Mortgage Conditions.

We therefore do not have a forwarding address for our borrowers Mr Wagner and Miss Bach.

I will be investigating this matter further in view of the breach of the Mortgage Conditions and as soon as I find out where the borrowers are currently living I will write to you further.

Yours faithfully

SOLICITOR TO THE LENDING DIVISIONS

25th May 1992

Mr A Wagner & Miss M Bach
19 Red Road
London

Dear Mr Wagner & Miss Bach

Re: Account 123456

I have been informed by the London Borough of Elsewhere that the above property is currently being let and that you are no longer in residence.

I therefore write to point out that this is a breach of your Mortgage Conditions with this Company which state that the mortgaged property must be used as your only or main residence and cannot be let without the Company's consent.

The letting may also be a breach of the MIRAS regulations and if this is the case the Company would be under a duty to inform the Inland Revenue that you are no longer eligible for MIRAS.

In the circumstances I would be grateful if you would let me have full details of the current letting arrangements, together with a copy of any Lease or Tenancy Agreement and the reason for the letting at your earliest possible convenience.

Yours sincerely

Solicitor to the Lending Divisions

Section 7: Arrears Correspondence

**NEBULA
BUILDING
SOCIETY**

Mr A Wagner & Miss M Bach
c/o Messrs Deadlocks
Solicitors
82 High Street

16 January 1991

Dear Mr Wagner and Miss Bach

Account No 1234567890 (6 Ochre Road)

Thank you for your recent communication enclosing a cheque for £920.00 which we can confirm has recently been credited to your above numbered mortgage account, reducing the arrears to £3,140.12, with a further instalment to be debited on 11 February.

As you are no doubt aware, the Society has now obtained an Order for Possession on your property and in order to clear the arrears on your account within a reasonable period of time, we must request payments of £314.00 in addition to your instalment each month, commencing on 11 February.

Your mortgage instalment will shortly be increasing due to interest rate increases during last year and you will be advised on your year end statement of your new instalment.

We can confirm that providing the aforementioned arrangement is strictly adhered to, then no further action will be taken in this matter. However, should any one payment be late, omitted or underpaid, then the Society will not hesitate in arranging for your immediate eviction.

We trust you realise the severity of the situation and you will therefore give this matter your immediate attention.

Yours sincerely

Mortgage Administration Department

Many cash-raising mortgages run into arrears early in the term.

**NEBULA
BUILDING
SOCIETY**

Mr A Wagner & Miss M Bach
c/o Messrs Deadlocks
Solicitors
82 High Street

13 June 1990

Dear Mr Wagner & Miss Bach

6 Ochre Road, London
Account Number 1234567890

I have been instructed by our Advances Department that the above property is now being let, and consequently, the interest rate charged to the account has been increased by 1%. This increase became effective from 1 June 1990, and a revised monthly payment of £557.72 is required with effect from 11 June.

I trust this matter is in order, however should you have any further enquiries, please do not hesitate to contact me.

Yours sincerely

Mortgage Accounts Department.

29th April 1989

Mr & Mrs A Wagner
10 Crimson Road
London

Dear Mr & Mrs Wagner

Re: 10 Crimson Road

We have received a letter from the Betelgeuse Building Society in which they state that an amount of £1,235.61 is outstanding in the form of mortgage arrears.

We would be most grateful if you could arrange for this amount to be discharged to prevent any future difficulties with the Building Society when the sale of your property proceeds.

Yours sincerely

DEADLOCKS

The solicitor is now aware that this is an illegal let.

Section 8: Odd Instructions and Warning Signs

BETELGEUSE
BUILDING SOCIETY

Messrs Deadlocks
Solicitors
82 High Street
London

9th April 1989

Dear Sirs,

ACCOUNT NUMBER 12345678 - Mr A & Mrs M H Wagner
10 Crimson Road London

We note from our file that you are acting on behalf of the above named in connection with the proposed sale of the mortgage property.

We shall be pleased to receive a note of the present position: have contracts been exchanged and a date set for completion?

If little progress has been made it would be appreciated if your clients could be requested to forward a payment to the Society in settlement for the current arrears balance of £1235.61

We await hearing from you and we thank you in anticipation of your assistance in this matter.

Yours sincerely

Purchaser's instructions

TELEPHONE MESSAGE

Time .... Date 15/6 .... 19 ....
From ....
To ....

Alan Wagner Phoned

He would like to exchange on the ground floor flat and the first floor flat

at 4 Gold Road as soon as possible

Telephone messages can be very revealing - here the client is buying two flats at once.

PINCH AND PLUCK
Solicitors
479 Holloway Road

Messrs DEADLOCKS
Solicitors
82 High Street

Dear Sirs

RE : GROUND FLOOR FLAT 4 GOLD ROAD, LONDON

Further to previous correspondence we understand that your client has agreed to purchase the first floor flat at the property at a price of £65,000 and has also agreed to purchase the second floor flat at a price which has not yet been agreed. Could you please let us know whether you have instructions to that effect and if so whether your client prefers to purchase the freehold so that he can grant his own leases.

We look forward to hearing from you by return.

Yours faithfully

PINCH AND PLUCK

This is not an ordinary domestic purchase, but no further instructions are taken from the client.

Financial statement

DEADLOCKS IN ACCOUNT WITH MR A. WAGNER
RE: 23D WHITE COURT, LONDON

RECEIPTS		PAYMENTS	
DEPOSIT RECEIVED	£1,000.00	DEPOSIT PAID	£1,000.00
MORTGAGE ADVANCE	£57,000.00	LOCAL SEARCH	£72.45
		AMOUNT DUE ON COMPLETION	£56,500.00
		DEADLOCK COSTS	£460.00
AMOUNT REQUIRED FROM YOU	£267.95	MORTGAGE ACCOUNT	£57.50
		STAMP DUTY	£575.00
		LAND REGISTRY FEES	£90.00
		TELEGRAPHIC TRANSFER FEE	£12.00
		BANKRUPTCY SEARCH	£1.00
	£58,767.95		£58,767.95

DEADLOCKS

To: Mr A Wagner

Re: Purchase of 23D White Court

	To Professional Charges in connection with your Mortgage Advance by the Society on the security on the above property. Taking your instructions; reporting on title to the Building Society and attending completion; to include all correspondence, attendance and advising throughout.	£50	00
	Plus VAT at 15% THEREON	£ 7	50
	TOTAL	£57	50
	This Account is discharged by deduction in our statement of Account of this date		

DEADLOCKS

To: Mr A Wagner

Re: Purchase of 23D White Court

	To Professional Charges in connection with your purchase of the above property. Taking your instructions; making all necessary searches and to Preliminary enquiries; approving the draft Contract; reporting to you on the results of our searches and enquiries and obtaining your signature to the Contract; arranging for exchange of Contracts; investigating title and raising Requisitions ; preparing the draft Conveyance/Transfer/Assignment and submitting it to the Vendor's Solicitors for approval; engrossing it (and obtaining your execution thereof); attending completion and stamping the Conveyance/Transfer/Assignment.	£400	00
	Plus VAT at 15% THEREON	£ 60	00
	TOTAL	£460	00
	This Account is discharged by deduction in our statement of Account of this date		

Suspect correspondence

JANUS FREIGHT/SHIPPING/TRAVEL
4 Gold Road London

01-08-1991

To:

From: M Bach

REF: 23D White Court

FAX Message

Thanks for your fax of today.
Please note the following.

I do not know the date that the house was purchased, so please contact the solicitor at the following address.

DEADLOCKS SOLICITORS
82 HIGH STREET
LONDON

Yours sincerely

M Bach

Considering the purchase would, if this client were genuine, be her major investment and her own home into which she has just moved, this letter gives the game away, when read in conjunction with the previous three documents.

23 WHITE COURT FREEHOLD LTD
23 WHITE COURT
LONDON

1 August 1991

DEADLOCKS Solicitors
82 High Street

Dear Sirs,

M Bach
Purchase of 23D White Court
From Mr S Shaw

Ms Bach has suggested that we contact you with reference to her purchase of the above property from Mr S Shaw.

In order that I can complete the Annual Return to Companies House, I need to know the following:

The date the flat was purchased by Ms Bach.

The name and address of Mr Shaw's solicitors in order that we can either retrieve the share certificate that was issued to him or get him to sign a letter of indemnity.

Thank you in advance for your assistance and we would be grateful if you could reply by fax or telephone.

Yours faithfully

Director & Company Secretary

See previous letter—a single ordinary residence does not need a management company.

NEBULA BUILDING SOCIETY

APPLICANT	Ms Miranda BACH	ADV. CHQ	£57,500	DATE	11 May 1990
ADDRESS	23DWhite Court, London				
CHEQUE NUMBER	983493	REF NO.	099-4-93005271		

Thank you for your Report on Title.
I have pleasure in enclosing the Society's advance cheque.

If completion or settlement cannot be effected within seven days of the date of this letter please return the cheque to this office. In Scotland, do not place the cheque on Deposit Receipt.
Interest will be charged from two working days after the date of the advance cheque.

Please complete and return the completion advice attached ON THE DAY OF COMPLETION

Yours faithfully

for Branch Manager

NEBULA BUILDING SOCIETY

ANYBANK PLC

No. 983493

DATE	PAY TO THE ORDER OF	AMOUNT	
11/05/90	DEADLOCKS (RE: BACH)	£ 57500	00

MORTGAGE ADVANCE 099-4-93005271

FOR AND ON BEHALF OF NEBULA BUILDING SOCIETY

HUNDRED THOUSANDS	TEN THOUSANDS	THOUSANDS	HUNDREDS	TENS	UNITS
***	FIVE	SEVEN	FIVE	ZERO	ZERO

AUTHORISED OFFICERS

The cheque is directly placed to the credit of Bach's vendor.

12 May 1990

Mr A Wagner
Oak Cottage
ANYTOWN
Herts.

Dear Alan,

Re: Purchase of 23D White Court London

We are pleased to confirm that the purchase of the above property has today been formally completed.

We will now attend to the stamping of the Transfer document and registration of the title in the name of Miranda Bach.

If you have any queries do not hesitate to contact us.

Yours sincerely

DEADLOCKS

Why report a genuine purchase to the vendor of the property?

6th September 1990

Miss M Bach
Oak Cottage
ANYTOWN
Herts.

Dear Miss Bach,

Re: Purchase of 23D White Court London

We now enclose copies of the inside of the Charge Certificate for your information.

Yours sincerely

DEADLOCKS

Correspondence is again sent to the pre-purchase address.

RIGEL
BUILDING SOCIETY

17 August 1991

DEADLOCKS
82 HIGH STREET
LONDON

Dear Sirs

Account Number:	94-135-15669
Name & Property Address:	Mr Alan Wagner Ms Miranda Bach Ground Floor Flat 4 Gold Road London

Thank you for your letter enclosing the Title Deeds. A receipted copy of the schedule is returned herewith. Also returned is the Charge Certificate/Legal Charge which requires further attention. Will you please therefore attend to the following amendment/s bearing in mind Note 2 on the front cover of the Charge Certificate:

M Bach is not entered on the Charge Certificate or Mortgage deed.

I would also point out that the policy document is still outstanding.

Yours faithfully

Supervisor

Deeds Department

These are serious errors which indicate culpable negligence.

DEADLOCKS

---

82 High Street
LONDON

16th August 1990

Miss S Tallis and Miss A Offenbach
c/o Mr A Wagner
Oak Cottage
Herts.

Dear Miss Tallis and Miss Offenbach

Re: 21 Silver Road, London

With reference to your above purchase, we enclose herewith Transfer Deed which should be signed by both of you and by Mr Wagner. This document should be signed in the presence of a witness, who should add his name address and occupation also where marked by pencil crosses.

Please return the deed when all three parties have signed it without delay.

Yours faithfully

DEADLOCKS

Why write to these ladies at Mr Wagner's address unless they are only nominees?

SARAH TALLIS
12 Grey Road
London

21 Silver Road, London

19/7/90

I hereby agree to purchase the above property from my family Alan Wagner.

Sarah Tallis

An example of a bogus letter written to square the solicitor's file.

Section 9: Acting for Vendor and Purchaser

A. Transfer from husband in wife (in married name) to husband and wife (in maiden name) 10 Crimson Road

MEMO

To : Sue

From: Peter

Date: 28th September 1990

Re: 10 Crimson Road, London

We act for Mr & Mrs A. H. Wagner in connection with their proposed sale of the above property to your client.

We accordingly enclose herewith draft Contract together with replies to preliminary enquiries. We also enclose a copy of the Charge Certificate. We have applied for up to date Office Copy Entries and as soon as these are received we will forward them to you.

P. D.

26th September 1990

Mr & Mrs A. H. Wagner
Oak Cottage
Herts.

Dear Alan,

Re:- Sale of 10 Crimson Road, London

We refer to your sale of the above property and now enclose the Contract. We would be pleased if you and your wife could both sign this where indicated by the pencil crosses and then immediately return it to us.

Yours sincerely

DEADLOCKS

Why write to Oak Cottage again?

Contract of sale

CONTRACT OF SALE

Vendor ALAN HAROLD WAGNER and MIRANDA HOPE WAGNER both of Oak Cottage, Herts.

Purchaser

Registered Land				
District Land Registry: Stevenage	Purchase Price	£	80,000	00
Title Number:	Deposit	£		
Agreed rate of interest: 4% above the base rate of Any Bank for the time being	Balance payable	£		
	Price fixed for chattels or valuation money(if any)	£		
	Total	£		

Property and interest therein sold ALL THAT freehold property situated at and known as 10 Crimson Road, London as the same is registered at H. M. Land Registry with Title Absolute under the above Title Number

Vendor sells as	Beneficial Owner	Completion Date	Do not date

AGREED that the Vendor sells and the Purchaser buys as above, subject to the Special Conditions endorsed hereon and to the National Conditions of Sale, Twentieth edition so far as the latter Conditions are not inconsistent with the Special Conditions.

* Signed Alan Wagner

M Wagner

Date DO NOT DATE

This is an example of sloppy paperwork, as mentioned on page 30.

MEMO

To : Sue

From: Peter Date: 3rd October 1990

Message:

We now enclose herewith Office Copy entries.

We look forward to hearing from you, in due course.

Peter

MEMORANDUM

To : Peter From: Sue

Re 10 Crimson Road, London Date: 4th October 1990

Thank you for your memorandum of the 28th September with enclosures for which I am obliged.

The Contract is approved subject to one small amendment in Condition D, the time of completion should be amended to 2.15 p.m. Please confirm that this is agreed.

As you are aware I am still awaiting the local search.

Sue

4th October 1990

A Wagner Esq. and Ms M Bach
Oak Cottage
Herts.

Dear Mr Wagner and Ms Bach

10 Crimson Road, London

With reference to the above property I enclose herewith the Contract for your purchase and would be grateful if you could both please sign this where your initials appear in pencil and then return it to me.

I would mention that I am still waiting for the return of the local search.

Yours sincerely

DEADLOCKS

A letter to Oak Cottage again!

CONTRACT OF SALE

Vendor ALAN WAGNER and MIRANDA WAGNER both of Oak Cottage, Herts.

Purchaser ALAN WAGNER and PRIMROSE BACH both of Oak Cottage, Herts.

Registered Land				
District Land Registry: Stevenage	Purchase Price	£	80,000	00
Title Number:	Deposit	£		
Agreed rate of interest: 4% above the base rate of Any Bank for the time being	Balance payable	£		
	Price fixed for chattels or valuation money(if any)	£		
	Total	£		

Property and interest therein sold ALL THAT freehold property situate at and known as 10 Crimson Road, London as the same is registered at H. M. Land Registry with Title Absolute under the above Title Number

Vendor sells as Beneficial Owner Completion Date Do not date

AGREED that the Vendor sells and the Purchaser buys as above, subject to the Special Conditions endorsed hereon and to the National Conditions of Sale, Twentieth edition so far as the latter Conditions are not inconsistent with the Special Conditions.

* Signed Alan Wagner

M Wagner

Date DO NOT DATE

This is an incomplete contract and no other correspondence or other instructions are with it to suggest a genuine redistribution of assets on divorce; the addresses should be a warning bell.

Report on title

4th October 1990

Area Manager
Lynx Building Society

Dear Sir,

Re: Application No. 01T3560749
Alan Wagner and Primrose Bach
10 Crimson Road, London

With reference to the above property we enclose our Report on Title duly completed and look forward to receiving the mortgage advance in time for completion on the 10th October 1990.

Yours faithfully

DEADLOCKS

The building societies are not told that the solicitors are acting for both vendor and purchaser and the respective lenders.

Completion of purchase

MEMORANDUM

To :	Peter	From:	Sue
Re	10 Crimson Road, London	Date:	13th October 1990

I formally confirm that I duly transferred to your client's account yesterday the sum of £73,538.04 representing the completion moneys.

I look forward to receiving the Title Deeds and your undertaking to discharge the mortgage of Betelgeuse Building Society, Any Bank and the caution in favour of the Feet Company PLC.

Sue

13th October 1990

A Wagner Esq. and Ms M Bach
Oak Cottage
Herts.

Dear Mr Wagner and Ms Bach

Re: 10 Crimson Road, London

I formally confirm that I duly completed your purchase of the above property yesterday.

I enclose herewith the completion statement from the Lynx Building Society for your retention.

I am now dealing with the stamping and registration of the property and on completion of these your Title Deeds will be sent to the Building Society for safekeeping.

I would like to take this opportunity of thanking you for kindly entrusting me with your business.

Yours sincerely

DEADLOCKS

Why write to Oak Cottage again ?

13th October 1990

Area Manager
Lynx Building Society

Dear Sir,

Re: Application No. 01 B11111111
Alan Wagner and Miss Miranda Bach
10 Crimson Road, London

We formally confirm that we duly received the mortgage advance cheque on the 12th October and the purchase was completed on that date.

We also confirm that the mortgage documents have been dated the 12th October 1990.

We would like to thank you for your assistance in this matter.

Yours faithfully

DEADLOCKS

MEMORANDUM

To : Sue

From: Peter Date: 18th October 1990

Further to completion of the above matter we enclose herewith Deeds and documents. Kindly accept this memo as our undertaking to discharge all mortgages and send you Form 53 duly sealed. With regard to the Caution relating to the Feet Company PLC we enclose two letters which are self-explanatory.

Peter

18th October 1990

Betelgeuse Building Society

Dear Sirs,

Re 10 Crimson Road, London

Further to completion of the above matter we now enclose herewith cheque for £41,328.77 in redemption of our Client's mortgage with the society, together with Form 53 for sealing by the Society and return as soon as possible.

Yours faithfully

DEADLOCKS

MEMORANDUM

To : Sue

From: Peter | Date: 12th December 1990

Wagner

Enclosed herewith Form 53.

Peter

MEMORANDUM

To : Peter | From: Sue

Re 10 Crimson Road, London | Date: 4th January 1991

I acknowledge safe receipt of Form 53 duly sealed by the Betelgeuse Building Society.

Sue

Mortgage arrears

Lynx Building Society

Messrs Deadlocks
82 High Street
London

Dear Sirs

ACCOUNT NUMBER: 01 E9999999
NAME: Mr Alan Harold Wagner and Miss Miranda Bach
SECURITY: 10 Crimson Road, London

We note from our records that you acted in the purchase of our security.

In view of arrears which have accrued on this account we intend to instruct the Society's Legal Proceedings Section. Would you please forward the Title Deeds by return. If they are lodged at the Land Registry please arrange for registration to be expedited.

Your co-operation in this matter is appreciated.

Yours faithfully

Assistant Manager
Arrears Department

Again there are early arrears. The building society of course, have not been told this is not a genuine transaction.

Arrangement to let

29th June 1991

A Wagner Esq.
Oak Cottage
Herts.

Dear Alan,

10 Crimson Road, London

We enclose herewith the Lease which we should be glad if you and Miranda would sign where your initials have been pencilled, having your signatures witnessed by an independent witness who should add his or her name, address and occupation. Please return the Lease to us as soon as possible.

Yours sincerely

DEADLOCKS

The solicitor is aware that the property is being let without building society consent.

B. Mr Wagner and Mrs Wagner (using maiden name) to nominees

Draft contract

Memo

To: Peter

From : Diana Date 28th November 1990

Wagner to Tallis
19 Red Road, London

We write to confirm that we act on behalf of Mrs S Tallis in connection with her proposed purchase of the above property from your client Mr A Wagner at the price of £87,000, subject to Contract.

We look forward to receiving a draft Contract for approval in due course.

Diana

Acting for both purchaser and vendor—see page 37.

Memo

To: Diana

From : Peter Date 1st December 1990

Wagner and Bach to Tallis
19 Red Road, London

Thank you for your memo of 28th November and confirm that we act for Mr Alan Wagner and Miranda Bach in connection with the sale of the above property to your client Mrs S Tallis at the price of £87,000 subject to Contract.

We enclose draft Contract for approval (in duplicate) together with office copy entries.

Exchange of contracts

Memo

To: Peter

From : Kate

Date 27th February 1991

19 Red Road, London
Bauhin & Amphora to Bach & Wagner

I write to confirm our telephone conversation of today when Contracts were exchanged, with completion fixed for the 9th March next.

I now enclose herewith my clients' signed Contract and confirm that a deposit of £4,000 has been paid direct to your client.

We look forward to receiving your clients' signed Contract to complete exchange.

In the meantime we enclose draft Transfer for approval together with Requisitions on Title with a copy for your use and await hearing from you further.

There is no way that this file can be anything other than a breach of the Guide to Professional Ethics

4th April 1991

Ganymede & Co.

Dear Sirs,

Cygnus Home Loans Corporation
Miranda Bach and Alan Wagner
19 Red Road, London

Thank you for your letter of the 31st March.

We would advise you that exchange of Contracts took place on the 23rd February 1991 with a completion date of the 9th March 1991.

Unfortunately the purchasers have lost their Mortgage Offer and have not been ready to complete as a result.

We understand that they have found alternative Mortgage finance and they are however merely awaiting the new Mortgage instructions from the building society and once this is to hand matters can be completed.

We hope to write to you again shortly.

Yours faithfully

DEADLOCKS

C. Fictitious purchaser—12 Grey Road

HYDRA PAVAN
Solicitor

Messrs Deadlocks
82 High Street
London

14th September 1990
By Fax and Post

Dear Sirs,

Re 12 Grey Road, London

I understand that you have instructions to act for Ms M Bach and Ms S Weeks in their proposed sale of the above freehold property to my clients Ms P D Bach at a price of £79,950.00 subject to Contract.

Will you be kind enough to confirm your instructions and let me have the draft Contract and supporting documents as quickly as possible.

Yours faithfully

Hydra Pavan

Borrower's references

Creon & Co. Estate Agents

2nd December 1990

Ajax Building Society

Dear Sirs

Re: Amadeus & Over purchasing 12 Grey Road, London

Further to the mortgage application that our company submitted to the Leytonstone office which was forwarded to yourselves, we have taken the opportunity of enclosing a photocopy of the applicant's local authority rent card, which may be of assistance to you as we are not aware of whether the local authority actually give out answers to such enquiry references.

Yours faithfully

F. K. Kraken & Co.
Accountants

December 1st 1990

Ajax Building Society

Dear Sirs

Re Mr Charles Amadeus (Mini Cab Driver)

Thank you for your letter of 29th, regarding our above client.

According to the books, documents and accounting records of Mr Amadeus, the Net Profit for the year ending 4/4/90 was £22,563.

Based on current drawings and the records above, it is anticipated that the Net Profit for the current year will be in the region of £23,100.

Yours faithfully

F. K. Kraken & Co.

A false reference.

The Manager
Ajax Building Society

Miss T. Over
Flat 123 Sycamore Court
London

Dear Sirs,

12 Grey Road, London

Creon Estate Agents have told me to forward to you a copy of my last P60 and I enclose this for you here.

The tenancy, where I am leaving, is with me and my brother in our original family names. However my brother has moved on and my name has been shortened. My fiancé moved in approximately two years ago and we have been living as man and wife since then.

Yours sincerely

T Over

Teresa Over

False details for a nominee.

Purchase by nominee

Memo

To: Peter

From : Kate Date 25th November 1990

12 Grey Road
Wagner to Amadeus and Over

We write to confirm that we act on behalf of Mr C Amadeus and Miss T Over in connection with their proposed purchase of the above property from your client Mr A Wagner at the price of £85,500, subject to Contract.

We look forward to receiving a draft Contract for approval as soon as possible.

Again Deadlocks are acting for both vendor and purchaser in a nominee's purchase which is a simple refinancing exercise.

MEMO

To: Kate Date: 29 November 1990

From: Peter

Re: 12 Grey Road, London, E11 - BACH & WAGNER to AMADEUS & OVER

We now enclose herewith draft Contract for approval in duplicate. We also enclose Office Copies.

We look forward to hearing from you with the Contract approved in due course.

PETER

MEMO

To: Peter　　　　Date: 30th November 1990

From: Diana

---

12 Grey Road, London
Bach & Wagner to Amadeus & Over

Thank you for your memo of the 29th November with enclosures. We now enclose herewith some pre-Contract Enquiries together with a copy for your use.

1st December 1990

Mr A H Wagner,
Oak Cottage,
Herts.

Dear Alan

Re: Sale of 12 Grey Road, London

We now enclose herewith pre-contract Enquiries and would be grateful if you could answer these as far as possible and then return them to us, in due course.

We await hearing from you.

Yours sincerely,

DEADLOCKS

Draft contract

1st December 1990

Miranda Bach and Samantha Wagner,
12 Grey Road,
London

Dear Ms Bach and Ms Wagner

Re: Sale of 12 Grey Road, London,

We now enclose herewith the Contract. If you wish to proceed with the sale then we would be grateful if you could sign this where indicated by the pencil crosses and return it to us.

If this is not the case then please advise us.

Yours sincerely,

DEADLOCKS

Enc.

MEMO

To: Peter   Date: 16 December 1990

From: Kate

12 Grey Road, London
Bach & Wagner to Amadeus & Over

Further to previous correspondence I now return herewith one copy of the Contract approved as drawn subject to satisfactory replies to my Enquiries which I raised with you on the 30th November and am still awaiting replies.

MEMO

To: Kate

Date: 6th January 1991

From: Peter

Amadeus & Over
12 Grey Road

Further to your memo of the 16th December 1990 I now enclose herewith one copy of the Enquiries together with replies. We look forward to hearing from you once you are in a position to exchange Contracts.

PD

2nd February 1991

Lynx Building Society
DX ....

Dear Sirs

Re: Alan Wagner & Miranda Bach - 12 Grey Road, Account No. 1234

We now enclose herewith the Title Deeds and Documents relating to the above matter.

We would be grateful if you could acknowledge safe receipt of the same by signing and returning one copy of the enclosed schedule.

Yours faithfully,

DEADLOCKS

Enc.

Exchange of contracts

Lynx Building Society
DX ....

13th March 1991

Dear Sirs

Mr A Wagner and Miss M Bach
12 Grey Road - Account No: 1234

We write to confirm that we act on behalf of Mr A Wagner and Miss M Bach in connection with the sale of the above property. We would be obliged if you could forward to us the Title Deeds, which were forwarded to you on the 2nd February 1991.

We would inform you that Contracts have now been exchanged with completion fixed for the 31st March and we would be grateful if you could supply us with a redemption figure made up to that date.

Yours faithfully,

DEADLOCKS

13th March 1991

Mr A H Wagner,
Oak Cottage,
Herts.

Dear Alan

Re: Sale of 12 Grey Road, London.

We write to confirm that Contracts in respect of the above property have now been exchanged with completion fixed for the 31st March. We would be grateful if you could confirm to us in writing that the property will be vacant on completion.

We shall be writing to you again shortly with a Transfer for signature together with our financial statement and accounts.

Yours sincerely,

DEADLOCKS

MEMO

To: Kate

Date: 13th March 1991

From: Peter

Wagner to Amadeus & Over
12 Grey Road

We write to confirm that Contracts in respect of the above property were exchanged today with completion fixed for the 31st March. We enclose herewith our clients' signed part of the Contract and look forward to receiving your clients' signed part to complete exchange.

PD

MEMO

To: Peter

Date: 14th March 1991

From: Kate

Wagner to Amadeus & Over
12 Grey Road

Further to our telephone conversation of today when Contracts were exchanged on the above matter with completion fixed for the 31st March.

I now enclose herewith my clients' signed contract by way of exchange and look forward to receiving your clients' signed Contract to complete exchange. I confirm that I have transferred to your ledger account the sum of £2,000.00, in respect of the deposit. I would mention that the purchase price of this property is £81,750.

I now enclose herewith draft Transfer in duplicate for approval together with the requisitions on Title with a copy for your use and await hearing from you further.

Yours faithfully,

KATE

P.S. I now have your Memo dated the 13th March 1991.

Sale contract

CONTRACT OF SALE

Vendor
MIRANDA BACH and SAMANTHA WAGNER both of 12 Grey Road, London,

Purchaser
C Amadeus and T Over of

Registered Land		
District Land Registry: Peterborough	Purchase price	£81,750.00
		81,750.00
Title Number: ***	Deposit	£ 5,000.00
		2,000.00
	Balance payable	79,950.00
	Price fixed for chattels or valuation money (if any)	£
	Total	£79,950.00
Agreed rate of interest: 4% above the base rate of Any Bank Plc for the time being		

Property and interest therein sold ALL THAT freehold property known as 12 Grey Road, London as the same is registered at H.M. Land Registry with Title absolute under Title Number ***

Vendor sells as Beneficial Owner	Completion date: 31st March 1991

AGREED that the Vendor sells and the Purchaser buys as above, subject to the Special Conditions endorsed hereon and to the National Conditions of Sale Twentieth Edition so far as the latter Conditions are not inconsistent with the Special Conditions.

Signed

Date 13th March 1991

15th March 1991

Mr A H Wagner,
Oak Cottage,
Herts.

Dear Alan

Re: Sale of 12 Grey Road

Further to previous correspondence we now enclose the Transfer for signature by Miranda Bach and Samantha Wagner. We would be obliged if you could obtain their signatures on the back where indicated. Their signatures should be witnessed in the presence of an independent person who should also sign adding his or her name, address and occupation also where indicated. Once signed please return to us immediately.

Yours sincerely,

DEADLOCKS

MEMO

To: Kate

Date: 15th March 1991

From: Peter

12 Grey Road
Wagner & Bach to Amadeus & Over

Thank you for your memo of the 14th March. We return one copy of the Transfer approved as drawn together with one copy of the Requisitions together with replies.

PD

Title deeds

LYNX BUILDING SOCIETY

Messrs Deadlocks

Your ref: PD.AB.WAGNER
Our ref: SECURITIES/***/AC

15 March 1991

Dear Sirs

ACCOUNT NO. *** - BACH
116 GREY ROAD

I enclose the title deeds subject to the following:

- You act for the borrower(s)
- The deeds will be held by you on behalf of the society.
- You will repay the mortgage or return the deeds on demand.
- You will advise the society if you are aware of anything which might affect its security.
- The deeds agree with the accompanying schedule.

The legal charge in favour of the society is held by the society's principal solicitors Messrs *** of *** (ref: ME), who will supply a photocopy on request.

The property is registered under Title Number ***.

If the above mentioned property is sold then you are hereby appointed to act as the society's agents in respect of the redemption moneys for the purpose of the Law Society's code for completion by post (1984 Edition) subject to the redemption money being received by us within 3 days of completion.

We will claim from you any shortfall due to what we consider to be an unacceptable delay in receipt of the money at either this office or one of our branch offices.

If you do not wish to accept the instructions under the above terms as our agents, please return the deeds.

Please quote the reference MORTGAGE SERVICES/*** on any request for redemption figures.

Yours faithfully

For ***
Securities Manager

Redemption

Note of telephone message

Building Society

Bach & Wagner

Redemption Figure

£52,978.84 (31/3/91)

16 Grey Road

LYNX BUILDING SOCIETY

Messrs Deadlocks
DX ***

Your ref: PD.AB.WAGNER
Our ref: SECURITIES/***/CB

17 March 1991

Dear Sirs

REDEMPTION STATEMENT

ACCOUNT NO. *** - WAGNER & BACH
116 GREY ROAD

This redemption statement is valid until 31 March 1991.

The amount required to redeem the loan to the above date is £52,978.84.

The last payment shown in the records was received on 3 October 1990.

(Any payments made after the last payment shown should be deducted from the redemption figure quoted above.)

Redemption administration charge

- The redemption figure includes a charge of £50 to meet administration expenses where redemption takes place within 3 to 5 year(s) of completion of the loan and where a new loan with the society has not been arranged.

Banker's order

- If monthly payments have been made by banker's order, it should be cancelled after the last payment in the month of redemption.

Insurance

- It is important that insurance cover of the property is continued until the property is sold or alternative arrangements are made. The existing cover will therefore be maintained until the next renewal date unless contrary instructions are received.

If the court hearing (date not yet known) proceeds, additional costs will be charged.

For ***
Redemptions Section Head

Sale completion

21st March 1991

Mr A H Wagner,
Oak Cottage,
Herts.

Dear Alan

Re: 12 Grey Road, London

Further to previous correspondence we now enclose herewith your Financial Statements together with our accounts.

You will see that on completion there is a balance due to you of £28,311.16.

If there are any queries regarding this statement then please do not hesitate to contact us.

Yours sincerely,

DEADLOCKS

Enc.

MEMO

To: Kate Date: 31st March 1991

From: Peter Ref: Amadeus & Over

We write to confirm that we have today exchanged Contracts on the sale of the above property as arranged.

We now enclose herewith the Title Deeds and Documents relating to the same. Please kindly acknowledge safe receipt.

We are awaiting the Charge Certificate from the Mortgagees and as soon as this is received we will forward it to you.

PETER

MEMORANDUM

To: Peter

From: Kate 3rd April 1991

Re: 12 Grey Road, E11
Amadeus & Over to Bach & Wagner

Thank you for your memo of the 31st March confirming that completion took place on the 31st March.

We acknowledge receipt of the Title deeds and documents and await receipt of the Charge Certificate in due course.

31st March 1991

Mr A H Wagner,
Oak Cottage,
Herts.

Dear Alan

Re: 12 Grey Road, London,

We write to confirm that completion of the sale of the above property took place today as arranged.

We now enclose our cheque in the sum of £24,637.66, which you will note is £3,673.50 less, as this sum was the amount due from Mr Amadeus and Miss Over.

We thank you for your instructions in this matter and if we can be of any further assistance to you in the future please do not hesitate to contact us.

Yours sincerely,

DEADLOCKS

DEADLOCKS **SOLICITORS**

To - Mr Wagner & Miss Bach

Re - Sale of 12 Grey Road, London

	To Professional charges in connection with the sale of the above property; taking your instructions, perusing the title deeds and documents; preparing the draft Contract and submitting it to the Purchasers Solicitors for approval; replying to Preliminary Enquiries obtaining your signature to the Contract and arranging for exchange of Contracts; deducing title and replying to Requisitions; approving the draft Conveyance/Transfer, arranging for your execution of the engrossment and completing the matter; accounting to you for the net proceeds of sale, and to our professional charges in connection with the repayment of your Mortgage and to include all correspondence attendances and advice throughout	£400	00
	VAT thereon at 15%	£60	00
	This account has been discharged by deduction in our statement of account	£460	00

DEADLOCKS **SOLICITORS**

To - Mr Amadeus & Miss Over

Re - Purchase of 12 Grey Road, London E11 1/3/91

	To Professional charges in connection with your purchase of the above property; taking your instructions; making all necessary searches and raising Preliminary Enquiries; approving the draft Contract; reporting to you on the results of our searches and enquiries and arranging for exchange of Contracts; investigating title and raising Requisitions preparing the draft Conveyance/ Transfer and submitting it to the Vendor's Solicitors for approval; engrossing the same and obtaining your execution; attending to completion and stamping of the Conveyance/ Transfer	£400	00
	VAT thereon at 15%	£ 60	00
	This account has been discharged by deduction in our statement of account		
		£460	00

DEADLOCKS **SOLICITORS**

To - Mr Amadeus & Miss Over

Re - Purchase of 12 Grey Road, London E11 1/3/91

	To Professional charges in connection with your Mortgage Advance by the Society/Bank on the security of the above property; taking your instructions reporting on title to the Building Society/Bank and attending to completion, to include all correspondence, attendances and advice throughout	£ 50	00
	VAT thereon at 15%	£ 7	50
	This account has been discharged by deduction in our statement of account		
		£ 57	50

Tables and Bar Chart

Exercise 1: Schedule of Wagner addresses in correspondence

Date	Addressee	How Addressed	Address	Ref	Tran No	Property
1988						
November						
12-11-88	A H Wagner	Dear Mr Wagner	5 Barracuda Road	PD	2	9 Cerise Street
December						
04-12-88	A Wagner Esq.	Dear Mr Wagner	20 Swordfish Road	PD	3	8 Cobalt Road
18-12-88	A Wagner Esq.	Dear Mr Wagner	20 Swordfish Road	PD	3	8 Cobalt Road
1989						
January						
07-01-89	A H Wagner Esq.	Dear Mr Wagner	12 Grey Road		10	1 Azure Road
14-01-89	A Wagner Esq.	Dear Mr Wagner	20 Swordfish Road	PD	3	8 Cobalt Road
February						
2-89	Mr A Wagner	Dear Mr Wagner	20 Swordfish Road	PD	3	8 Cobalt Road
March						
April						
24-04-89	A Wagner Esq.	Dear Mr Wagner	20 Swordfish Road	PD	6	15/16 Lake Lane
29-04-89	Mr & Mrs A H Wagner	Dear Mr & Mrs Wagner	10 Crimson Road	PD	5	10 Crimson Road
May						
26-05-89	A Wagner Esq.	Dear Mr Wagner	20 Swordfish Road	PD	6	15 Lake Lane
June						
July						
August						
September						
October						
November						
December						

Note: this exercise consists of listing addresses used in correspondence.

Date	Addressee	How Addressed	Address	Ref	Tran No	Property
1990						
January						
08-01-90	Mr Wagner & Miss M Bach	Dear Mr Wagner & Miss Bach	Oak Cottage	PD	9	6 Ochre Road
22-01-90	Miss Bach, Mr A Wagner	Dear Mr Wagner & Miss Bach	Oak Cottage	PD	9	6 Ochre Road
26-01-90	Miss Bach, Mr A Wagner	Dear Mr Wagner & Miss Bach	Oak Cottage	PD	9	6 Ochre Road
26-01-90	A Wagner Esq.	Dear Alan	Oak Cottage	PD	12	17 Orange Road
February						
01-02-90	Mr Wagner & Miss Bach	Dear Mr Wagner & Miss Bach	Oak Cottage	PD	9	6 Ochre Road
05-02-90	Mr Wagner & Miss Bach	Dear Mr Wagner & Miss Bach	Oak Cottage	PD	9	6 Ochre Road
08-02-90	A H Wagner Esq.	Dear Mr Wagner	Oak Cottage		11	1A Azure Road
10-02-90	Mr A Wagner & Miss Bach	Dear Mr Wagner & Miss Bach	Oak Cottage	PD	9	6 Ochre Road
15-02-90	A H Wagner	Dear Alan	Oak Cottage	PD	12	17 Orange Road
16-02-90	Mr A Wagner	Dear Alan	Oak Cottage	PD	13	23D White Court
18-02-90	A Wagner Esq.	Dear Alan	Oak Cottage	PD	13	Flat 1 11 Chestnut Road
22-02-90	A H Wagner Esq.	Dear Mr Wagner	Oak Cottage		11	1A Azure Road
24-02-90	Mr A Wagner	Dear Alan	Oak Cottage	PD	12	17 Orange Road
25-02-90	A Wagner Esq.	Dear Alan	Oak Cottage	PD	13	23D White Court
March						
07-03-90	A Wagner & Miss M Bach	Dear Mr Wagner & Miss Bach	Oak Cottage	PD	9	6 Ochre Road
11-03-90	A Wagner & Miss M Bach	Dear Mr Wagner & Miss Bach	Oak Cottage	PD	9	–
22-03-90	A Wagner Esq.	Dear Alan	Oak Cottage	PD	14	Flat 1 11 Chestnut Road
24-03-90	A H Wagner Esq.	Dear Mr Wagner	Oak Cottage	PD	11	1A Azure Road
30-03-90	A H Wagner Esq.	Dear Mr Wagner	Oak Cottage		11	1A Azure Road

Date	Addressee	How Addressed	Address	Ref	Tran No	Property
April						
06-04-90	A H Wagner	Dear Mr Wagner	Oak Cottage		11	1A Azure Road
11-04-90	A H Wagner	Dear Mr Wagner	Oak Cottage		11	1A Azure Road
13-04-90	A Wagner Esq.	Dear Alan	Oak Cottage	PD	13	47S White Court
14-04-90	A H Wagner	Dear Mr Wagner	12 Grey Road		10	1 Azure Road
15-04-90	A H Wagner	Dear Mr Wagner	Oak Cottage		10	1 Azure Road
15-04-90	A Wagner Esq.	Dear Alan	c/o 10 Crimson Road	PD	15	GFF Gold Road
25-04-90	A H Wagner Esq.	Dear Mr Wagner	Oak Cottage		10	1 Azure Road
25-04-90	A H Wagner Esq.	Dear Mr Wagner	Oak Cottage		11	1A Azure Road
25-04-90	A H Wagner Esq.	Dear Mr Wagner	Oak Cottage		11	1A Azure Road
25-04-90	A Wagner Esq.	Dear Alan	Oak Cottage	PD	13	23D White Court
25-04-90	A Wagner Esq.	Dear Alan	Oak Cottage	PD	14	Flat 1 11 Chestnut Road
26-04-90	A Wagner Esq.	Dear Alan	Oak Cottage	PD	14	Flat 1 11 Chestnut Road
26-04-90	A Wagner Esq.	Dear Alan	Oak Cottage	PD	13	23D White Court
27-04-90	A Wagner Esq.	Dear Alan	Oak Cottage	PD	14	Flat 1 11 Chestnut Road
28-04-90	A Wagner Esq.	Dear Alan	Oak Cottage	PD	13	23D White Court
28-04-90	A Wagner Esq.	Dear Alan	Oak Cottage	PD	14	Flat 1 11 Chestnut Road
May						
04-05-90	A Wagner	Dear Alan	5 Barracuda Drive	PD	14	Flat 1 11 Chestnut Road
06-05-90	A H Wagner Esq.	Dear Mr Wagner	Oak Cottage		10	1 Azure Road
12-05-90	A H Wagner Esq.	Dear Mr Wagner	Oak Cottage		10	1 Azure Road
13-05-90	Mr A Wagner	Dear Alan	Oak Cottage	PD	13	23D White Court
23-05-90	A H Wagner Esq.	Dear Mr Wagner	Oak Cottage		10	1 Azure Road
23-05-90	A Wagner Esq.	Dear Alan	10 Crimson Road	PD	15	GFF Gold Road
24-05-90	A H Wagner Esq.	Dear Mr Wagner	Oak Cottage		10	1 Azure Road

Schedule of transactions

No.	Property	Vendor(s)	Purchaser(s)	Building Society	Vendor's Solicitors	Solicitors for Purchasers and Building Society	Date Instructed	Completion (or last document)
1	12 Grey Rd		Miranda Bach Samantha Wagner	Lynx			c Sep '88	Dec '88
2	9 Cerise Street	Mr & Mrs Fink	Alan Wagner		Orange & Co	Deadlocks (PD)	06-11-88	(12-11-88)
3	8 Cobalt Road	John Kern	Alan Wagner	Gemini	Weller Budger	Deadlocks (PD)	02-12-88	(25-02-89)
4	12 Grey Rd	Miranda Bach Samantha Wagner	Alex Alcott Claudette King		Deadlocks (PD)	Valerian Woundwort & Co	17-02-89	(23-07-89)
5	10 Crimson Road	Alan Wagner Miranda Wagner	Miranda Bach Rose Bach		Deadlocks (PD)	Valerian Woundwort & Co	18-02-89	(13-08-89)
6	(A) 15 Lake Lane	Amersia Piston	Alan Wagner	Libra	Tulkinghorn & Co	Deadlocks (PD)	22-04-89	(30-07-89)
	(B) 16 Lake Lane	George Piston Andras Piston	Alan Wagner	Titan	Tulkinghorn & Co	Deadlocks (PD)		
7	18 Pink Court	Mr Liszt	Alan Wagner			Deadlocks	27-10-89	(04-11-89)
8	19 Red Road		Alan Wagner Miranda Bach	Hebe Corporation		Deadlocks (PD)		
9	6 Ochre Rd	River Properties	Ralph Wagner Miranda Bach	Nebula	Valerian Woundwort & Co	Deadlocks (PD)	22-12-89	11-03-90
10	1 Azure Rd	Kevin Bliss	Alan Wagner	Astra	Snagsby & Co	Deadlocks	22-12-89	29-04-90
11	1A Azure Rd	Kevin Bliss	Alan Wagner	Pisces	Snagsby & Co	Deadlocks	22-12-89	08-04-90
12	17 Orange Rd	Alice Falla	Alan Wagner	Vesta Ltd Home Mortgages	Snagsby & Co	Deadlocks (PD)	26-01-90	08-07-90
13	23D White Court	Stephen Smyth	Miranda Bach	Nebula	Bells & Co	Deadlocks (PD)	16-02-90	12-05-90
14	Flat 1 11 Chestnut Rd	Rollover Ltd	Alan Wagner Miranda Wagner	Ceres Lodestar	Valerian Woundwort & Co	Deadlocks (PD)	16-02-90	05-07-90

Note: this exercise will reveal patterns where none should exist, **e.g.** ***where Deadlocks repeatedly act for vendor and purchaser.***

No.	Property	Vendor(s)	Purchaser(s)	Building Society	Vendor's Solicitors	Solicitors for Purchasers and Building Society	Date Instructed	Completion (or last document)
15	GFF 4 Gold Road	Patrick Marks Eugene Weber	Alan Wagner	Mariner	Pinch & Pluck	Deadlocks (PD)	05-04-90	02-09-90
16	17 Brown Road	Samuel Hyden Denise Hyden	Alan Wagner Primrose Bach	Pallas	Sikes Wosky	Deadlocks (PD)	08-06-90	11-11-90
17	21 Silver Road	Joan Avon	Alan Wagner	Mariner	Guster & Son	Deadlocks (PD)	08-06-90	08-08-90
18	FFF 4 Gold Road	Patrick Marks Eugene Weber	Alan Wagner	Capella Savings	Pinch & Pluck	Deadlocks (PD)	15-06-90	12-08-90
19	12 Grey Rd	Miranda Bach Samantha Wagner	Miss P D Bach		Deadlocks (PD)	Hydra Pavan	26-07-90	(16-11-90)
20	12 Grey Rd	Miranda Bach Samantha Wagner	Charles Amadeus Teresa Osei	Astra	Deadlocks (PD)	Deadlocks	25-11-90	31-03-91
21	SFF 4 Gold Rd	Patrick Marks Eugene Weber	Miranda Bach	Astra	Pinch & Pluck	Deadlocks (PD)	14-06-90	27-09-90
22	21 Silver Rd	Alan Wagner	Sarah Tallis Adele Offenbach	Lynx	Deadlocks (PD)	Deadlocks (PD)	25-06-90	18-08-90
23	10 Crimson Rd	Alan Wagner Miranda Wagner	Alan Wagner Miranda Bach	Lynx	Deadlocks (PD)	Deadlocks	11-09-90	20-10-90
24	7 Copper Rd	Mr & Mrs Holst	Miss M Bach Mr R Wagner		Merdles	Deadlocks (PD)	Sep '88	(22-09-90)
25	19 Red Road	Alan Wagner Miranda Bach	Sarah Tallis		Deadlocks (PD)	Deadlocks (Diana)	23-11-90	(10-08-91)
26	17 Orange Rd	Alan Wagner	Alphonsus Strauss Janet Strauss	Jupiter	Deadlocks (PD)	Deadlocks	24-01-91	21-07-91
27	Flat 1 11 Chestnut Rd	Alan Wagner Miranda Wagner	Primrose Bach Miranda Bach	Europa	Deadlocks	Deadlocks	27-01-91	04-04-91
28	The Bungalow 22 Titanium Road	Alan Wagner Miranda Wagner Samantha Wagner	Alan Wagner Miranda Wagner	Nebula	Deadlocks	Deadlocks	27-01-91	(15-01-92)

Mr & Mrs Wagner's property ownership over three years

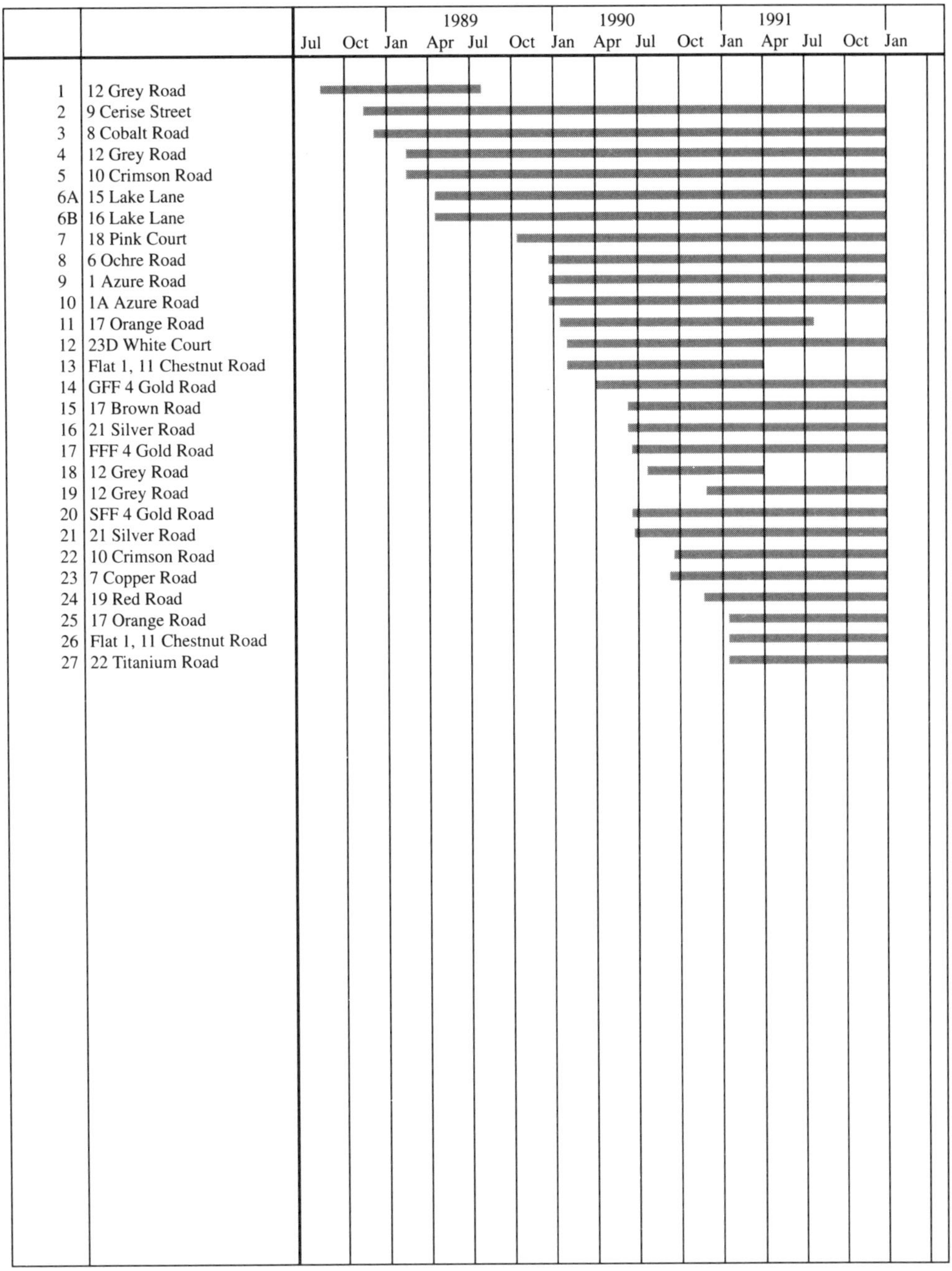

Note: it will be obvious from this chart that the Wagners owned more than one property at once.

Index

Abuse of process,
fraud cases, in, 115
Accounts,
checking, 33
Anton Piller injunctions,
effect of, 64

Bankers' books,
duty of confidentiality, material subject to, 81, 82
evidence, as, 80, 81
Bibliography, 141
Broker,
dishonest, arrangements by, 5
rollover fraud, assisting, 7
track records, 78
Building society,
audit department, 79
instructions, 202-205
investigations, 78, 79
irregularities, dealing with, 42, 43
lies to, 35
requirements of acting for, 42
special security unit, 79
Business property,
improvement in value, yielding, 2
Buyers,
fictitious, 30

Charge,
equitable, 69
Civil litigation,
Anton Piller injunctions, 64
emergency remedies, 60-64
expense of, 59
information, obtaining, 66, 67
Mareva injunctions, see also **Mareva injunctions**
place of, 59
purpose of, 59
recovery, maximising, 75, 76
remedy,
categories of, 67-74
compensation claims, 69-74
salvage claims, 67-69
selecting, 65-67
solicitor, role of, 59
Client,
established, meaning, 38
identification of, 48
identity and bona fides, checking, 31
papers, handing over, 83
requirement to meet, 46, 47
Client account,
moneys held in, 44, 45
Commercial mortgage fraud,
case study, 149-167
risks, 8
valuation, variation in, 8
Company search,
importance of, 32
Compensation claims,
fraud actions, in, 69-71
professional negligence actions, in, 71-74
Compensation Fund,
breach of undertaking, applications following, 15
conspiracy cases, 16
dishonesty of solicitors,
compensation for, 13
establishment of, 13
financial burden on solicitors,
reducing, 16, 17
funding, 14
hardship by failure to account,

compensation for, 13
last resort, as, 14
lending institutions, treatment of, 15, 16
operation of, 14, 15
Solicitors' Indemnity Fund, merger with, 19
Completion,
documentation, 255-259, 280-285
exchange, simultaneous with, 49
Computer,
evidence, see **Evidence**
fraud trials, use in, 112-114
Confidentiality,
bankers' books, of, 81, 82
duty of, 32
extent of, 85, 86
informal or quasi clients, extending to, 86
overriding, 86
statute, effect of, 86
exceptions,
criminal conduct, retention of benefits of, 87, 88
drug trafficking, in case of, 86
money laundering offences, 87
terrorist funds, in case of, 86, 87
fraud or crime, in case of, 66, 67
legal professional privilege, and, 84, 85
obligation of professional confidence, 83, 84
Conflicts of interest,
avoiding, 40, 41
ceasing to act on, 72
Conspiracy,
Code for Crown Prosecutors, 128
Compensation Fund, applications to, 16
defraud, to, 120
execution of valuable security, to procure, 120
Contract,
draft, letter accompanying, 207, 262, 271-272
example of, 251
exchange, 208, 210, 216, 263-265, 272-274
sale, 275, 276
Conveyancing,
mortgage advance, operation of, 42
Correspondence,
checking, 34
suspect, 243-250
Council of Mortgage Lenders, 2
CRANS system, 114
Criminal conduct,
concealing or transferring proceeds of, 88
retention of benefits of, 87, 88
Crown Prosecution Service,
cases reported to, 125, 126
Code for Crown Prosecutors, 127, 128
creation of, 123
fraud cases, prosecuting, 123
Fraud Investigation Group, see **Fraud Investigation Group**
Serious Fraud Office, and, 126

Damages,
contributory negligence, 74
mitigation of loss, 73
professional negligence action, in, 73
Deception,
obtaining property by, 117-119
obtaining services by, 117
Deposit,
direct payment of, 206
reduced, 207
solicitor, to be placed with, 46, 49
unpaid, letter as to, 210
Detection,
methods of, 7

Dishonesty,
proof of, 120, 121
Documentation,
accounts, 33
addresses, schedule of, 286-288
arrangement to let, 261
borrower's reference, 265-267
breach of mortgage condition, 232-233
building societies, lies to, 35
building society instructions, 202-205
buyer and seller, acting for, 37, 38, 262
completion of purchase, 255-259, 280-285
consent to let, 224-227
contract of sale, 251-254, 275, 276
correspondence, 44
deposit, payment of, 206
draft contract letter, 207, 262, 312-313
exchange of contracts, 208, 210, 216, 263-265, 272-274
false, 4
financial statement, 213, 240-242
husband and wife, transfer
between, 201
incomplete, 30, 31
ledger card entries, 35
misrepresentation, action for, 218-222
mortgage arrears, 234-237, 260
nominee, purchase by, 268-270
odd instructions, 36, 37
overdraft request, 197
pre-contract enquiries, 217
purchaser's instructions, 238, 239
redemption, 278, 279
references, 33, 34, 172-191
rental agreement, 228-231
report on title, 211, 212, 255
sale instruction form, 198-200
solicitor's instructions, 192-196
specimen, 32
suspect correspondence, 243-250
tenancy arrangements, 35, 36
title deeds,
letter accompanying, 277
submission of, 214, 215
transactions, schedule of, 289-291
transfer of interest into name of nominee, 200
undertaking not to rent, 223
Drug trafficking,
benefits, retention of, 86

Ethic minorities,
frauds by, 5
Evidence,
bankers' books, 80, 81
civil cases, in, 92, 93
computer,
admissibility, conditions for, 101-102
hearsay, 101
witness, expertise of, 102
copies of documents in, 94
discretion to admit, 98
documentary,
business documents, admission of, 97
first-hand hearsay, admission of, 96
hearsay, discretion to exclude, 99, 100
maker of statement in document, meaning, 99
not admissible, where, 94
statements prepared for pending proceedings, admission of, 98, 99
duplicate documents, legal status of, 115

expert, 95
advance notice of, 108
counsel, role of, 102, 103
examples of use, 106
foreign law, as to, 107
nature and content of, 107, 108
preparation and use of, 102, 103
primary and secondary facts, 107, 108
status of, 107
witnesses, see **Expert witness**
foreign, 94, 95
fraud cases, problems in, 92-96
graphics, use of, 113
hearsay, 93, 94
initial handling, 111-116
opinion, statutory provisions, 109
oral testimony, 92
poor quality, warning as to, 100
presentation,
technology, use of, 110, 111
visual aids, 110, 111
reforms, effect of, 109, 110
rules, creation and application of, 92
statutory reforms, 96-99
Exchange,
completion, simultaneous with, 49
documentation, 208-210, 216, 263-265, 272-274
Expert witness,
legal advisers, consultation with, 102, 103
person being, 106, 107
report,
admissibility, 109
contents of, 104, 105
form of, 104
leave for, 109
need for, 106
prosecution based on, 103
requirements of, 103, 104
solicitor as, 77
status of evidence, 107

Factories,
frauds involving, 6, 169
Financial statement, 213, 240-242
Fraud Investigation Group,
cases handled by, 123
cases referred to, 124-126
creation of, 123
fraud cases, handling, 115
investigations, role in, 114
objectives of, 123
structure, 123
Fraud prosecution,
investigations, 77-83, see also **Investigations**
solicitors, role of, 77
Fraud trials,
abuse of process, 115
charges, 116
computers, use of, 112-114
documents at, 121, 122
evidence, see **Evidence**
existing system, need for change in, 91
expert's report, prosecution based on, 103
information technology in, 114-116
length of, 93
sentencing, 121
testimony, 92
views of, 91, 92

Green card, 30, 32, 45, 46
Guide to the Professional Conduct of Solicitors, 39, 40

Hotels,
fraud involving, 149-167
Housing benefit,
income from, 6

Information,
analysis of, 55, 56
Inland Revenue,
investigations, 77, 78, 129, 130
proceedings by, 129
production of documents to, 130
professional privilege, and, 131
search, powers of, 130, 131
Instructions,
odd, being alert to, 30, 36, 37
sample, 192-196
Investigations,
building society, 78, 79
clients' papers, handing over, 83
documents, 80-82
Fraud Investigation Group, role of, 124
Inland Revenue, by, 77, 78, 129, 130
legal privilege, items subject to, 82, 83
lender, by, 77
police,
defendants, dealing with, 79
fraud squad, 79

Law Society,
communications, 53
ethical guidance, 52
interests of members, representing, 51
mortgage fraud working party, 53, 54
practice and procedure, information on, 52, 53
property and commercial services strategy, 51
role of, 51
solicitors in private practice,
supporting, 52
subcommittee on mortgage fraud, 51, 52
Ledger card entries,
specimen, 35
Legal Information Network, 137, 138
Legal professional privilege,
criminal purpose, intention of furthering, 83, 85
definition, 84
effect of, 83, 84
fraud or crime, in case of, 66, 67
Inland Revenue, documents required by, 131
items subject to,
definition, 82
use as evidence, 82, 83
obligation of professional confidence, and, 83, 85-86
statutory provisions, 84
Lender,
discovering fraud, 57
investigations, 77
mortgage fraud, role in fighting, 55
recovery by, 57
systems, use of, 55, 56
validation by, 56
Lending institutions,
Compensation Fund, applications to, 15, 16
contributory fault, 17
mortgage fraud, victims of, 2
Lucas, Guy, 2, 31

Mareva injunctions,
ancillary orders, 61, 62
application for, 62, 63
assets and accounts, identification of, 63
assets, freezing, 64
breach of terms of, 61
court procedures, 62, 63
effect of, 60
expiry of, 64
form of, 60

full and frank disclosure, duty of, 62
living and legal expenses, figure for, 63
notice of grant, 61
self-incrimination evidence, 62
set-off, right of, 63
undertakings, 63
Misrepresentation,
action for, 218-222
Money judgment,
borrower, against, 68
Money laundering,
offences, 86, 87, 88
reporting procedures, 138
tipping off offences, 89
transactions involving, 26
Mortgage,
several, discharge of, 47
Mortgage advance,
deception, obtaining by, 117-119
meaning, 117
offer, origin of, 48
operation of, 42
procuring execution of valuable security, 119
conspiracy, 120
tracing and recovering, 67, 68
Mortgage applicants,
circumstances, misrepresenting, 3
different names, applications in, 4
false identities, using, 6
fundamentally dishonest, 4
restrictions on borrowers, overcoming, 3
undiscovered fraudsters, 3, 4
Mortgage arrears,
documentation, 234-237, 260
Mortgage condition,
breach of, 232, 233
Mortgage fraud,
avoiding, 23
commercial, see **Commercial mortgage fraud**
compensation claims, 69, 70
deceptions involved, 3
detection, 7
disadvantage to fraudster, 2
education on, 137, 138
false documentation, 4
financial pressure, factor of, 24
green card, 30-32
indications of, 46-48
most likely, where, 23-25
motivation, 27
occurrence of, 1
precautions against, 48, 49
prevention and recognition, check-list for, 135-137
prosecution, see **Fraud prosecution**
recovery, maximising, 75, 76
scale of, 2, 3
sentencing, 121
signs of, 30-32
solicitors, position of, 1
sources of assistance, 139, 140
technique, change in, 2
trials, see **Fraud trials**
types of, 116

Nationwide Anglia Building Society, 2, 55, 56
Nominee,
purchase by, 268-270
transfer of interest into name of, 200

Offences,
conspiracy to defraud, 120
dishonesty, proof of, 120, 121
money laundering, 86, 88
obtaining property by deception, 117-119
obtaining services by deception,

117-119
procuring execution of valuable security, 119
conspiracy, 126
Offshore companies,
efficient use of, 24
unusual use of, 29, 145
Overdraft,
request, 197

Pre-contract enquiries,
replies, failure to find, 217
Premiums,
income from, 28, 145
Professional indemnity insurance,
provision of, 17
Professional negligence,
breach of duty, 71-73
claim in, 9
damages, measure of, 73, 74
duty of care, 71
proceedings, grounds for, 69, 70
retainer, terms of, 71
valuation, in, 72
Property development,
attraction of, 28, 145
Purchase price,
allowances, 47, 48
changes in, 31
initial instructions, differing from, 48
misrepresentation of, 30, 149
true, showing in documentation, 31

Redemption,
documentation, 278, 279
References,
accountant's, 175-179
bank, 33, 172
borrower's, 265-267
character and financial standing, as to, 28
employer's, 172, 180-191
false, 33, 34, 143
improving, 3
landlord's, 173, 174
Rental income,
using properties for, 29, 147
Repossession,
fraud, in case of, 4
Resale of property,
simultaneous transactions, 47
warning signs, 49
Residential property,
improvement in value, yielding, 2, 3
rental income, bringing in, 3
Rollover fraud,
example of, 8
method of, 7

Sale instruction form, 198-200
Salvage claims,
charge, declaration of, 69
money judgment, obtaining, 68
possession and sale of property, 68
purpose of, 67
Security,
requirement of, 42
Self-incrimination,
provision against, 61, 62
Sentencing,
mortgage fraud, for, 121
Serious Fraud Office,
acceptance of case, criteria for, 132, 133
accountability, 132
Case Controller, 133
case, definition, 124
caseload, 132
Crown Prosecution Service, and, 126
decision to prosecute and charge, 133, 134
internal organisation, 133

objectives, 132
origins of, 131-132
prosecution by, 77
setting up, 124
small proportion of fraud cases, dealing with, 115
technology, funding, 114
Solicitor's clerk,
competence and honesty, checking, 29
Solicitors,
buyer and seller, acting for, 37, 38, 41, 249
caution, need for, 45, 46
complacency, danger of, 46
conduct, guide to, 39, 40
confidentiality, see **Confidentiality**
conflicts of interest, 40, 41
dishonesty, compensation for, 13, see also **Compensation Fund**
expert witness, as, 77
irregularities, dealing with, 42, 43
moneys held by, 44, 45
mortgage fraud,
avoiding, 23
concern about, reasons for, 13
duty in context of, 71
losses caused by personal liability for, 21
mortgage fraudster, as target for, 1
obligation of professional confidence, 83, 84
prosecution, role in, 77
public respect and confidence, loss of, 20
staff supervision, 25, 26
tenants, duty as to, 43, 44
Solicitors Complaints Bureau,
guidance from, 53
Solicitors' fraud,
guilty knowledge, proof of, 9, 10
involvement in, 9, 10
media interest in, 10
portfolio of properties, acquisition of, 29, 147
professional negligence, claim in, 9
Solicitors' Indemnity Fund,
Compensation Fund, merger with, 19
legal liability, fund of, 18
policy exclusions, 18
professional indemnity cover, provision of, 17, 18
reorganisation of funds, 19
role of, 18
Staff,
supervision of, 25, 26
Status,
abuse, 5-7

Tenancies,
arrangements for, 35, 36, 261
consent to, 224-227
reasons for, 36
rental agreement, 228-231
solicitor, duty of, 43, 44
undertaking not to rent, 302
Tenants,
protection of, 43
Terrorism,
funds, retention or control of, 86, 87
Title,
deeds,
letter accompanying, 277
submission of, 214, 215
report on, 211, 212
report on, 255

Validation,
areas to be examined, 60

Witness,
court, compelled to attend, 80
expert, see **Expert witness**